A Tune For Bears

A Childh

Linda McCullough-Thew

Bridge Studios
Northumberland
1992

First published in Great Britain in 1992
by Bridge Studios,
    Kirklands,
    The Old Vicarage,
    Scremerston,
    Berwick-upon-Tweed,
    Northumberland.
    TD15 2RB

    Tel. 0289 302658/330274

ISBN 1 872010 75 X

By the same author:
The Pit Village and the Store
From Store to War

Typeset by EMS Phototypesetting, Berwick upon Tweed

Printed by CP Printing & Publishing Ltd, Darlington

Front cover
Painting by the author

Photographs
Aunt Bella and Uncle Andrew with George, Eliza
and Archie Hyslop.
Billy and Linda Summers. Archibald Summers.

*La parole humaine est comme un chaudron fêlé où nous battons
des mélodies à faire danser les ours, quand on voudrait attendrir
les étoiles.*

Gustave Flaubert *(Madame Bovary)*

——————— ———————

Human language is like a cracked tin kettle on which we beat out
tunes for bears to dance to when our heart's yearning is to touch
the stars that they feel compassion.

Flaubert.

To Malcolm
with love

Contents

Acknowledgements

I am grateful to Les and Evelyn Hallowell for their kind generosity in offering me the use of any of the photographs in their private collection. The photograph of the Ashington Hospital Ambulance is theirs.

Chapter 1

The Beginning

My earliest memory is a happy one. I was lying in what was probably a cot in front of the fire in the kitchen-cum-living room of our flat in Ashington, Northumberland and my father was making a clumsy attempt to change my nappy. My mother arrived in outdoor clothes bringing with her the cold air from outside. There were smiles and words of glad welcome from each of them, and my mother, with expert hands took over the job of making me comfortable.

I felt my father's ineptitude in the matter of the nappy, his joy and relief in seeing my mother come in, and their shared laughter at what he had done that was wrong. My understanding of the situation was as complete then as it would be now. Perhaps more so, for at that time my mind was uncluttered by confusions.

I lay back, happy, comfortable and secure. As far as I was concerned, in that moment, the universe was created exactly as things then were. It was many years before I really recognised that there had been a time before I existed; that things had been other than they were then. This room, as far as I was concerned, was the centre of the universe; this kitchen where it all began. The big black warm fireplace with its dancing flames – the fire that never went out – the world of wonder captured in the glinting bookcase with its browns and greens and golds and below it the chest of drawers full of mystery and delight. And opposite the fireplace the kitchen table, its scrubbed boards covered in a wealth of red plush. In the corner, the cupboard of gleaming cups and glowing tins and on the floor the new fireside mat bright with colours and stories too, 'That was grandad's trousers. That was my dress. It was a lovely dress......'

There were three doors from this kitchen. One led into the front room which opened straight onto Station Road. It wasn't really a sitting room; neither was it a bedroom but a bit of both. Near the window was a brass bedstead. The adjacent wall had a fireplace, never used, and the wall next

Linda with mother.

to it had the dark, upright, aloof piano as little used as the fireplace. It was waiting (in vain as it turned out) for me to grow up and play it. In the corner on an occasional table stood the ancient gramophone with its square base and huge fluted green horn. Two easy chairs, a set of dining chairs and a sofa completed the room. The various bits of furniture always tended to look sulky as if they would be happier elsewhere, but, however little they liked it, they had to get on together.

The second door from the kitchen led to a bedroom which was a proper bedroom, darker and more sombre than the kitchen. It had a big bed, its nether regions covered in a white bed valance that the chamber pot residing under-neath might keep its modesty. There was a dressing table which obliterated most of the light from the window. Displayed on the runner that covered the surface of the dressing table were two japanned glove boxes (one of which held handkerchiefs), my mother's silver backed hair brush and my father's china stud box full of hair pins, trouser buttons, safety pins, some bits of tangled thread and a fragment of broken comb, but no studs. Studs led wayward, secret, adventurous lives. They were never where they should have been. Next to the dressing table was the huge wardrobe with, up top, its burden of paper parcels and hat bags. The wash-stand, basin, ewer and lidded slop pail completed the bedroom suite. Usually, my brother Billy and I slept in this room. My father also slept here when he was on night shift.

The third door led to the scullery, which interested me hardly at all, and a walk-in pantry. In this last, on the stone floor stood the huge bread bin and an equally large flour bin and baking dish. Also the jar containing eggs that had been 'put down'. As we had a cold tap in the scullery we did not need water pails. The scullery had a cupboard, bench, mangle, poss tub and poss barrel. The door in the scullery led to the yard. Against the scullery wall was a tap and under it a sink. Hanging between the scullery window and the door was a zinc bath. At the far end of the yard was the coal-house and next to it the privy, or nettie as it was most often called but, not, I must say, in our house. With us it was dignified by the name, lavatory. But, privy, nettie or lavvy it was a frightening place to go to and it was a long way from the house. When the door was closed it was terrifying because the only light there came from three small holes at the top of the door. Also when I sat on the extreme edge of the wooden box (in case I fell down the hole) my feet were still left dangling, and, alas, I didn't always sit on the hole where it mattered.

The rent for this flat was eight shillings per week (40p). I learned very early on that money didn't grow on trees, a fact which I took at face value then and later learned was true. My mother was thrifty, sometimes tediously so. Everything had to be counted, kept or used to the last drop or shred as the case might be. Paper and string were saved, butter paper scraped and used to line cake tins, fruit tins (rare) cleaned out and used in the garden to encourage growth, as were superannuated coal pails whose bottoms were so frail and worn they could not support a cardboard substitute. Her meticulous account books, kept since the day she married, bear testimony to her strenuous attempts to make every penny do the work of two at the very least.

The flat was big enough to house four people, my parents, my brother Billy and me. In addition, we were the unwilling hosts to an army of black beetles, the big, broad, well-fed and well-cared for kind. They were there, my mother said, because we lived next door to a fish and chip shop. Every night a large round grey tin rimmed with smooth sloping sides, the hole at the top partially filled in by four curved blades, was placed at the bottom of the cupboard where, it appeared, the cockroaches came to take part in their nocturnal revels. Whether or not bait was put into the tin I cannot say but each morning when we got up this tin was brought out and we gazed at the haul below, always sizeable. Either my mother or my father took the tin away to kill the occupants and dispose of the carcasses. One morning, when my brother was about eighteen months old they were awakened to hear him shouting with glee and clapping his hands. It was light enough to see and he had got out of bed, gone to the cupboard, pulled out the beetle tin and turned it upside down. The beetles thus liberated scuttled away as fast as their lumbering bodies would allow to live another day and Billy clapped his hands at their antics and those of the beetles who had, unfortunately for them, fallen on their backs and were kicking frantically in an effort to right themselves.

Visitors frequently came to the flat, mostly men, relatives or friends of my father. The hour at which they came depended upon the shifts they and my father were on. Among the most frequent were my grandfather, my father's uncles Tommy and Andrew and my father's brothers, Uncles Will, George, Lance, Jack and Kit, the latter my father's brother-in-law.

To me, my grandfather was a huge awe-inspiring man who seemed almost as broad as he was tall. And when he 'op'd his lips, no dog barked.' He was a pom-pom man at the pit – as my father had been before he went away to the war and was wounded. A pom-pom was an early form of coal cutter, arc shaped. It was heavy to operate and while it was working it made a noise like a pom-pom. The men who worked it had to be strong. When the machine had to be moved they simply lifted it up bodily and carried it to where it had to go. Incidentally, my brother tells me that one day, when he was a student, he was on the coal-face and the man in whose charge he was (Billy Allison) said to him,

'You see that pom-pom. Well, your grandfather worked the first that ever came into this pit. Now see what you can do.' Billy did as he was told. 'As far as I know,' he said, 'that was the last time a pom-pom was used in Ashington pit.'

Uncle Tommy was an onsetter, that is, he worked at the shaft bottom putting the full tubs into the cages which took them to the surface. He lived with Aunt Martha and Lady, their dog, in a spick and span plush house in Council Terrace, their only child, Hilda, having died of diphtheria when she was six years old.

They were comfortably off, possessing one or two houses other than the one they lived in – or so I gathered from the scraps of conversation I heard from the adults when I was supposed to be asleep or convalescent, the only way children *could* learn things they were not supposed to hear, which was just about everything concerned with the adult world.

Apart from Lady and a double allotment, Uncle Tommy

11

was interested in gadgets and making things. Well, not actually making them – thinking of making them and getting the component parts together. They rarely ate tinned food except the almost obligatory tin of fruit with Sunday tea. Aunt Martha wasn't allowed to throw out these empty tins. She had to wash them out and keep them against the day when Uncle Tommy would invent some sort of clip-on handle arrangement that would transform these empty tins into mugs. Who would drink out of these mugs I do not know because they only used bone china, even on week-days. Not for Uncle Tommy the pint pots and extra saucer from which blown-on tea (to cool it) was noisily 'sooked' up. Similarly with thermos flasks. When the inside of one was broken it couldn't be thrown away because Uncle Tommy was thinking about perfecting an inside that wouldn't break and he would need empty thermos flasks to practice on when his thinking actually came to fruition.

Uncle Andrew was a tall man with a slow gait and a slight stoop. He had the strong features of a Duke of Wellington without the curve to his nose and he spoke with a soft, deliberate Scottish accent. He stooped slightly because he had a beat (bad) back. He was a filler, one of the worst jobs he could have had considering his affliction. He filled the tubs with the coal hewed by the hewers and cutter men.

Uncle Will and Uncle George both worked at the coal-face but I cannot recall what they did. I think Uncle Will was the only one of my relatives not taken on after the 1926 strike and eventually he emigrated to Canada. We really didn't see quite as much of Uncle George who lived at 'the Horst' at this time and suffered a protracted illness which kept him in bed for many months.

Uncle Lance was the only one who did not work at the pit. He worked in the Store (Co-op) grocery. He and my father were the most studious members of the family. Uncle Jack was a blacksmith and master ferrier. He also worked as a shaftsman repairing and inspecting the shafts down (and up) which the cages went. He did this work standing on top of the cage. Later, he became head engineer at Burnopfield Colliery.

Uncle Kit Wanless was Auntie Anna's, (my father's only sister's) husband. He was a very kind and generous man (within the limits of his income) and I felt slightly more at ease with him than I did most of my male relatives. He, like Uncle Andrew, was a coal-filler.

Visitors to see my mother were less frequent and, I am afraid, not always very warmly received. Most of the time she was wholly concerned with the keeping of my brother and me and our flat spotlessly clean. She was not, she often repeated, going to have it said she had a dirty house or not well-looked-after children. Thus we were constantly inured to keep clean and not to make a mess and the house was either being prepared for a domestic onslaught, or in the process of such an attack, or the shining end product of the two former states when nothing had to be touched or disturbed. And not only had the flat to be done, the yard had to be swilled and scrubbed with the yard brush, the step scrubbed and stoned and the pavement outside the front door swept, not to mention a token sweeping of the dirt road outside the backdoor.

We soon learned that when my mother said 'No' (or 'Yes') that was what she meant. Like most adults she never felt she had to explain but sometimes she did. 'Because I say so' or, less frequently, 'Because you are a boy/girl/the eldest/the youngest/a child'. No amount of tears, pleading or endless lists of people you knew who had what you wanted made any difference. My parents knew the straight-forward rules by which children were brought up. Parents knew best, children should be seen and not heard and spare the rod (or quick, hard, stinging hand slap) and spoil the child still held sway. We were trained in obedience because there was nothing worse than a disobedient child. The bounds of parental responsibility had not yet been blurred by child psychology (words they had never heard of) and the Welfare State and what few guidelines there were concerning the upbringing of children had been based on experience and were handed down by word of mouth. In this fairly enclosed community we were, to a large extent, isolated from world events.

There was a great deal of laughter too, mostly instigated by the men as they talked about some incident that had happened in the pit which the passage of time had made funny or, more often, an incident from their younger days. All my uncles and most of my aunts had an ear for the funny or ridiculous.

I listened to their stories as I did to the stories my mother read out of our story books; they meant the same to me. I could not conceive of the adults ever being young.

Similarly, when my mother told me stories about things that had happened to me which I couldn't remember I couldn't regard them as real either.

'You know that scratch on Grannie Summers' chest of drawers?' Mum said to me one day when she was trying to keep me amused as I lay in bed, 'Well. It happened when you were in the pram. It was standing beside the chest of drawers and your grandfather came in and he had been to the club and he was a little bit – well – not very steady and he fell against the pram and tipped it up and the handle scratched the drawers as it came down and you were thrown forward. What a fright we all got. Everybody shouted out .."The bairn." I think you were more frightened at the shout than the fall. Your Grandad got his Sunday name that night I can tell you.'

I couldn't imagine it happening to me not even when I saw the scratch nor could I imagine anyone telling my grandfather off. I was completely in awe of him although it appeared I hadn't always been.

'It was just after Christmas. They were talking about what they would get in for New Year and your grandfather would keep on insisting that the only thing they need concern themselves with was whisky. The next time he came you pulled yourself up at the cot side and pointed at him saying "Bo' wicky, bo' wicky." He was very annoyed. He thought we had put you up to it. It was cheek on your part he said. As if your Dad or I would do a thing like that.'

I couldn't imagine that I would do a thing like that either. It didn't seem to be about me at all and I couldn't have been more than eight and a half months old at the time. How on earth had I learned to be cheeky in that time and to my grandfather of all people.

One thing she did tell me about and which I couldn't think had happened but which I very much hoped would be repeated, was my first Christmas when 'You got so much you didn't know where to look first. Every kind of toy imaginable. You were thoroughly spoiled. When we went round to Granny Summers' they had hung Arthur's (my father's youngest brother's) stocking up at one end of the mantlepiece and filled it full of cinders and old potatoes and wrapped up the fire irons in a parcel and put a big notice up saying FOR ARTHUR – FROM SANTA and on the other side they had put his stocking proper and his presents with a big notice saying FOR LINDA.' I liked that story. I liked the idea of being thoroughly spoiled. I didn't think I was being spoiled then, thoroughly or otherwise, not by any stretch of the imagination. And what had happened to all those toys? Every Christmas Billy and I shouted up the chimney, after being cautioned not to ask for too much in case we didn't get anything and not to be cheeky in ordering what we wanted in case Santa didn't like it, when once again we wouldn't get anything. We told Santa how good we had been and what we would like. It was better, my mother said, to leave it to his discretion. Well, whatever discretion meant, the end product was that Santa wasn't given to flights of imagination.

The chimney, by the way, had been previously prepared for this event by being 'set fire to' i.e. a number of burning sheets of paper had been bunged up the chimney to set fire to it and to bring the soot down, thus cleaning it out. We went outside to see if the chimney had 'tekken haad', that is, had taken fire. Evidence was found in the smoke and sparks belching therefrom. We never got the sweep in those days.

Most of the toys we did have were much played with. My favourite toys were a teddy bear, an ABC book, Billy's tricycle, a blackboard and a shared box of building bricks. The teddy bear was my constant companion. He was talked to, played with, fed, nursed to sleep, hugged, cuddled and kissed. When I was taken out and he didn't go with me, the first thing I did was to rush in and take him in my arms and say 'Oh my teddy.'

Alas, he had a sad end. We had gone to Wooler and he had stayed behind to 'look after the house'. When we returned it was to find a mouse had made a nest in teddy's

15

accommodating tummy and was now rearing a large healthy family. The affect on poor teddy was mortal and he was laid to rest in the midden. My doll, newly kitted out in knitted garments the previous Christmas was less than no consolation. I regarded her so lightly I hadn't even given her a name. I felt the same about the pram I had. You could dress the doll, put her in the pram, walk it up and down in front of the fire in the kitchen or round the yard, take the doll out undress her and that was that. Her china face and hard body did not have the understanding and cuddle-ability of teddy.

Fortunately, I still had my ABC book. I never tired of turning the pages over. A for Apple. B for Bat and Ball. C for Cat. I knew them all by heart and the picture of the girl on the swing was etched into my heart for ever.

The blackboard was worth its weight in gold and so, to a lesser extent, were the building bricks. There were all shapes and sizes in those bricks and marvellous things could be built with them – as long as most of the bricks were there. Building bricks are like teaspoons and ludo counters. They can cloak themselves in invisibility and disappear to some secret paradise that no one ever discovers.

After the bricks our joint favourite plaything was the cracket. After my first funeral it did sterling work as a coffin (Billy and I underbearers), a hearse (me the body in the upturned cracket, Billy the horse), a cab (me wiping my eyes sitting crying inside – Billy the horse), where this particular game usually ended 'Why have I always to be the horse? It's not fair ....' It could be a train, a store counter, or anything we cared to make it. Of course, where we played and what we played at, or, indeed whether or not we played at all but sat still, depended on the day with its burden of housework and the point at which the housework had reached and whether it was ahead of schedule or, more often, behind. When we did play we usually had to keep moving our venue to keep 'out of the way'. Indeed, you could almost tell what day it was and what shift the man-of-the-house was in by state of the housework.

As far as the cracket was concerned, as everybody had a cracket, it was possible to play these games at Grannie

Summers' and at other houses we visited but not at Aunt Martha and Uncle Tommy's in Council Terrace. There we were sometimes given the cherished toys once played with by Hilda but as we had been warned by my mother before hand to be very, very careful we hardly dared to touch them.

My mother had other talents beyond those required by day to day house cleaning. She could knit socks and stockings and 'turn a heel' and all without a pattern. This achievement, was greatly appreciated and she knitted stockings for other members of the family. She also did the decorating and became adept at graining doors and was soon recognised in the family as a decorator of no mean repute.

In those days when it was decided that a room would be papered at either the Spring or Christmas cleaning, it was customary to show the paper to neighbours and relatives before it was edged. To prevent damaging the pattern there was a small strip of extra paper down each side of the wallpaper which had to be cut off (edged) when the paper was required.

Edging had to be done with the cutter sitting down. She grasped the top of the paper in her left hand while the remainder was allowed to run down her stiffened, out-stretched legs where it rested against her rigid, upturned feet. The right hand edging was then cut off the paper. As this was being done, with her left hand the cutter used a smooth downward motion to roll the paper, using the upper part of her leg as a base. When all the right hand edge had been removed, the task was completed and the paper had to be re-rolled.

My mother's tools for the actual job of papering were a battering brush, a piece of clean rag and an old dinner knife worn down to just the right shape by constantly cleaning with bath brick. She did her measuring with discarded bits of battered paper torn off at the right measurement.

When she went to paper at Grannie Summers' we went with her. It was done the week that Grandfather Summers' was 'in back' so that the kitchen was upside down while he was at the pit. The goal was to get the papering finished before he came home and the reward was great. When it was over and they were clearing up Grannie sent us to the chip shop for fish and chips. This, to us, was a rare treat. We never had bought fish and chips.

My mother wasn't so enthusiastic about mending and darning. Things tended to be left till after the last minute.

We left Station Road when I was about six. Before we left an incident, one of many, stands out in my mind. It took place when I was suffering the aftereffects of small pox and was bedridden.

'Borrow a spinal chair,' said Dr Bruce, 'and take her out for some fresh air.'

A spinal chair was a long wicker basket arrangement with handles and four wheels. In fairness I should say it would have been very difficult to manoeuvre in the house and it would have taken up a great deal of room.

Among the characteristic Northern traits two were, not to be beholden to others and not to pay for anything which could be contrived for nothing out of something else.

'You don't want one of those things,' said Uncle Tommy when he paid his daily visit to 'see how the bairn was and what the doctor said'. 'She's only got one bad leg. I'll tell you what it is, I've got a champion bit of wood there up at the 'lotment. I can fetch it and we'll ask Andrew for the loan of their pushchair. They'll not be needing it any more. All we have to do, look you, is nail that bit of wood onto the pushchair.'

Whether or not Uncle Andrew and Aunt Bella had finished with the pushchair is doubtful but they offered it with a good heart and the pushchair and wood being assembled together with an assortment of nails and a hammer, my father, Uncle Tommy and Uncle Andrew were ready to start. My mother, being sensible, went out taking Billy with her so that my father also had charge of me, which duty he fulfilled by telling me to be good and chalk on my blackboard. I was propped up in bed in the front room where the pushchair was to be modified.

It would be difficult to find three men less adept with a hammer and nails than the three who now took off their jackets to complete the job in hand. They were all three good living men so they didn't swear. However, even good living men are apt to get tetchy and overwrought in this frustrating life. In these circumstances my father (Church of England) said, 'Gorr sink.' Uncle Tommy (Methodist) said, 'By the hokey pokey,' and Uncle Andrew (Brethren) said 'Ye buckets of hen's feathers', so that as they worked, and one nail bent itself, another refused to go in, the piece of wood moved, the upside down chair toppled over, and other setbacks presented themselves, the 'hokey pokies', 'sinks' and 'hen's feather's' flew round the room tingeing the air a very, very delicate blue. Also the wood having sojourned for sometime in the allotment was danker and somewhat dirtier than had first been thought so that the idea occurred to them to cover it. Uncle Tommy thought a bit of the mangle cover would be the very dab and wouldn't be missed, a fact which my father viewed with no great certainty but felt he couldn't say anything.

Finally, they stood back and surveyed the finished article. It was more than a little unbalanced and tended to tip forward at the slightest provocation but they were satisfied and my mother had to be too. Naturally, I wasn't consulted.

By the time we left 180, the rigid domestic pattern had been set. Things were done in the same order on the same day.

We were, it seemed, often at the mercy of the house. Each week the place was made steamy and uncomfortable when all clothes were washed. All food had to be prepared and cooked. At the end of these two operations the house had to be given a mini-spring clean after which we had to be given out mini-spring clean inside and out. Water from the rain barrel (and oatmeal soap) for the outside, Gregory powder and liquorice (UGH!) for the inside.

Chapter 2

Ashington

Ashington. Valley of the ash trees. In fact, Ashington is part of the coastal plain. If the area was once covered in ash trees, they had gone long before my time. It is not difficult to visualise what the land on which Ashington was built was like a hundred and fifty or so years ago. All one has to do is drive out to one of the quiet country roads. There, around one, are fields, hedges, stone walls, grazing land, trees, streams, gorse bushes and, here and there, lone farms. In such surroundings stood Ashington farm. It still stands overlooking the banks of the river Wansbeck. It was from this farm that Ashington took its name. In the mid eighteen forties, when it was discovered that there were rich deposits of coal in the area, miners came with their families and rows of houses were built round the pit head to accommodate them. Whatever else they might not have, they certainly had plenty of room. The miners' houses were built in long rows, each house being well endowed as far as gardens were concerned. All roads were of a generous width. This was especially true of the main street which is among the widest I have ever seen in any town or village.

The rows themselves were of fairly uniform, unimaginative construction. Some houses were bigger than others, the largest, the double rows, having a kitchen and sitting room downstairs with three bedrooms upstairs. Across the road, not only did they have the usual open midden with an earth closet (nettie) at each corner, this to serve four families, they also had a wash-house. The smaller houses had a kitchen and two rooms upstairs, a share of the midden, their own nettie, but, generally speaking, no wash-house.

They were quite well constructed houses most of which are still being lived in today.

During my early childhood the roads separating each house from the remainder of its messuage were dirt roads.

Joyce and Linda in front of the Tenth Row coal-houses, wash-houses and netties.

Although each house was provided with a front and back door, the foot scraper embedded in the ground was only supplied for the back door. This was because the front door was used solely when any member of the family wished to go into the garden. It was at the bottom of these gardens that the idiosyncracies of the man of the house were manifest. Here there was an agglomeration of pigeon duckets, hen crees, pig sties and huts, no two exactly the same except for one particular practice. Each construction was made out of bits and pieces that had already seen service elsewhere. Almost anything did. Scraps of corrugated iron, old doors or odd bits of wood lying there in some neglected spot doing nothing were seen by the man of the house as treasure trove, just the 'very dab' for his garden. Somehow these oddments were jigsawed into a serviceable unit as economical of design as it had been of cost. The multicoloured paints used were the obvious left-overs from a variety of other jobs.

A very uneven dirt access, too wide to be called a path, too narrow to be called a road, ran the length of the gardens. This thoroughfare was never used except by children who sometimes played there, the girls who did so having to wait for a passing miner to lift them over the wall because the first and second blocks of each row were sealed.

The houses themselves were functional. Not an inch of space was wasted. The house I knew best was my grandmother's, Grannie Summers'. I have described their house, one in a double row, in some detail elsewhere. It is sufficient to say here that it sheltered, at its peak, my grandparents, their eight children and a lodger, the latter an uncle who would be treated as a slightly superior member of the family.

Where a large family had to be catered for as far as sleeping accommodation was concerned, it was quite common for children to sleep top to bottom four, or even five, to a bed. Even some adults slept three to a bed. As far as my grandparents' home went, the uncle does not seem to have been a permanent fixture and sadly, Eliza, the second youngest child, died in infancy of diphtheria.

I was lucky in that, being an only girl, I not only had my own bed for the greater part of my childhood, I had my own room. On one occasion, however, I was invited to stay overnight at a house and I slept in a room where there were six adults in two beds, the men sleeping in one bed, the women in another, a situation which they considered normal.

Bedrooms were very cold places except in a heat wave. In winter they were refrigerators. Beds apart, there was really only space for necessary bedroom furniture, the chamber pots, the slop pail and somewhere to put clothes. Those clothes that did not make the wardrobe were hung on the backs of the doors or on the sides of the wardrobe. If they were best clothes they were covered in old sheeting to keep off the dust.

The added refinements of a washbasin and ewer were for decoration only. Who would want to go to the trouble of carrying water upstairs when everything was to hand in the kitchen? One necessary appurtenance was the candle, the tin candle holder and a box of matches. There was no electric light upstairs, though there was downstairs. The wash-house across the road, though small, was a very useful place. It housed the poss barrel, poss stick and mangle. The set pot and bench were built in. It was also the place to put pensioned-off mats. Here they could lie unmolested from Monday night to Sunday night content in the knowledge that their useful life was not yet over. Here also, a candle was a necessity in winter. Washing days began as early as five o'clock when the housewife was up long before the sun.

Almost every house had a rain barrel either in the yard or in the front garden. Rain water was considered ideal for hair washing and for blanket washing. I believe that, at one time, urine was collected and, in this, the blankets were washed. I never saw this happen.

All houses at that time, as far as I knew, were draughty. We just never thought about it. Wind whistled through gaps in windows and doors so that nowhere was absolutely draught-free. Sitting in front of these roaring fires in winter, one was red hot at the front and icy cold at the back. As nearly all back doors opened into the kitchen, anyone arriving at the house in the middle of winter let in an icy blast straight from the North Pole. We had no idea that there were other sorts of houses to live in where there were no draughts. In spite of this I loved coal fires, especially on a winter's evening. I loved sitting in front of the fire when the light was fading and seeing pictures therein.

'Tell me, were you ever nearer to the land of Heart's
Desire
Than when you sat dreaming with your feet before
the fire?'

One doesn't see pictures in a gas fire, nor yet an electric one, not even those which burn with a real flame or those that have coloured glass coals and a fan underneath.

Throughout my childhood the Rows always looked the same. When a house was vacated and new people moved in there would be no noticeable change in the appearance of the house, nothing to indicate that the Smiths used to live here and now the Robinsons do. However, if Mr Smith had been a non-gardener and a pigeon-fancier and Mr Robinson was a non-pigeon-fancier and a gardener, then those who frequented the fronts (a rare thing) would undoubtedly see a difference.

Thus there was a basic uniformity about all the rows, outside as well as in. One kitchen looked very like another. This led to a feeling of security and belonging. There was something very constant, permanent and durable about the colliery and its houses. We did not take exception to the fact that, while our Rows were simply numbered First, Second, Third and so on, the colliery houses at Hirst had been dignified by names from Shakespeare, Rosalind Street, Ariel Street, Portia Street etc. or that others had been called after trees, Sycamore Street, Poplar Street, Acacia Terrace, Laburnum Terrace etc. They even had a road called after Queen Alexandra.

We knew our neighbours and we spoke to them daily as we went about our business. We did not doubt that, if things went wrong, they would be there to give what help they could. They came when there was sickness in the house and they gave what they could to those who were worse off than themselves.

My father called to see his mother (Grannie Summers) every day without fail, either going to or coming back from work. Sometimes, if he was in back shift, he visited both going and coming. Thus, Grannie was kept informed of our goings and comings, although possibly not as fully as she or my father would have wished because frequently my mother instructed my father not to go telling them such and

Linda and Billy playing at 29 Ninth Row.

such. It wasn't that she wanted to be secretive, it was just that she, herself, liked to be the harbinger of news.

Just going to Grannie's was exciting. We ran the last part of the way eager to say 'hello'. She always stopped what she was doing when we went in and she always had a smile. She had the gift of life which, of itself, always made us feel welcome. The same sort of work went on in her house as went on in ours, but there was not the same veto on our activities. Often we were given something to eat from the pantry, a scone or a piece of bread and jam. We were as much at home there as we were in our own house, and the neighbours treated us as if we, too, were neighbours. We ran in and out of their houses almost at will, the Ledgerwoods, the Millicans, the Thompsons, the Algars. Here, as at our house, scrubbing brushes, donkey stones, bath brick and washing soda were much evidence. Uncle Lance once attempted to bring a labour saving device into the house. He bought Grannie an Acme wringer which was fixed on the end of the poss tub, but she and Auntie Anna continued to wring the clothes out by hand, to save the wringer!

There was a great deal of laughter in their house and a fair amount of singing. They were all good singers. On one occasion while I was there Grannie was busy with some chore and she sang as she worked. Two of my uncles were at home and they joined in. She stopped what she was doing and the three of them sang a song in harmony. It seemed to me a wonderful thing for them to do in the middle of a weekday.

Throughout the day there were many itinerant travellers in the Rows among which were the rag and bone men. They came round with their flat carts never entirely denuded of cast-offs of all descriptions. It seemed to be a mark of their calling that they wore tattered clothing and that they looked as if neither they nor their clothing ever saw soap and water. No doubt, they wished to be in keeping with their stock. If the men epitomised the rags, then the horses epitomised the bones.

Virtually, they took everything. Their carts were enlivened with a few large, colourful balloons and one or two birds attached to sticks by pieces of string. The idea was to swing the stick round above one's head when the bird flew whistling as it went round. As these were the only things on view a small child might well surmise, as he or she was meant to do, that these were the rewards for bringing the rags or cast-offs the man wanted. Some rag and bone men had tin trumpets which they blew tunelessly. Others relied on their considerable voices calling, 'Ra' a' bo' ' adding for the benefit of the children gathering around, 'Go and get some rags from your mam,' the rags being interpreted as old woollens, clothes, jam jars, broken grates or anything else no longer serviceable.

The rag and bone men had capacious pockets. It was from these pockets that the child got his or her reward for bringing offerings to the cart. These rewards were, most often, a paper squeaker or a small balloon. For those who brought jam jars, the rate was one Billy Stamper (transfer) per jar.

The large balloons and singing birds were strictly for bait.

Some rag and bone men catered for housewives only. Their currency was scrubby stones used to decorate steps after they had been washed. 'Rags and bones for scrubby stones', they called, the stones in question being pieces of sandstone that could be found freely at Sheepwash. They were no more than adequate. Twopenny donkey stones were far more efficient.

Apart from the Rows, there was the High Market, the original hub of Ashington now somewhat faded and neglected because Station Road had taken pride of place as the Main Street and principal shopping area.

At the point where High Market ended and Station Road began was the Church of the Holy Sepulchre. It still stands there, tidied up, manicured and modernised but with enough of its original features still in being so that one can remember it as it once was.

From the church, Station Road ran in a more or less direct line, up and over the Station Bridge to the Grand Hotel.

The Council Chambers were on the bridge itself. Next to it was the Fire Station. Also on the bridge were one or two shops, the Sale Rooms and the Penny Bazaar. Near the top of the bridge was an opening from which a flight of steps led to a path which in turn led to the tankey stop. The tankey was a small engine used for taking men to and from the pits at Lynemouth and Linton where they were employed. The carriages were plain wooden ones. I believe they did take other passengers but those who travelled as such were advised to take a newspaper to sit on.

I am not sure at what point Ashington ended and Hirst began. Some thought the Station Bridge marked the dividing line, others that the Grand Corner did. In fact there should have been no dividing line. Originally the station had been called Hirst Station. At that time Ashington was considered to be part of Bothal. However, when the community was large enough to be considered a village in its own right, the name Ashington was adopted in preference to Hirst. This was because those whose responsibility this was, thought there were too many Hirsts in the vicinity. In fact, of the two, Hirst was probably the larger place. All the larger shops were on the Hirst side of the Station Bridge. On both sides of this part of the street shops of all descriptions stood adajacent each other.

But for some, Ashington was the centre of the Universe. At least two people I knew couldn't bear to cross the Station Bridge because they felt they were away from home, almost in a foreign country.

Wherever one walked in Ashington and Hirst there were signs of life. The streets, roads and back lanes always had people in them. There were children playing, older children minding young ones, elders calling for this child or that one to come in, a group of Salvationists giving an open air meeting in the Rows, women going to the shops, miners going to work or returning therefrom, retired miner sitting on the seats smoking clay pipes and having a crack, younger miners sitting on their hunkers outside their doorways or at corner ends, women standing in the doorway knitting. Only on Sundays were the streets relatively quiet, though never abandoned.

Among the plethora of shops there was always at least one shop open, even on a Sunday, whatever the hour. Here, I'm speaking as a child when there was a curfew on the time I was allowed outside. Nevertheless, on certain occasions, Billy and I did walk home at a late hour with our parents after a visit. It seemed to me then that ice-cream shops and fish and chip shops never closed, the chip shops where potatoes that had been peeled by hand were stood on end and the chip chopper brought down smartly so that the chips fell into a waiting pail and where the fish were battered before one's very eyes.

The shops on the Main Street were an attraction at any time, whether one had money to spend or not. Some still had ornate signs stating their wares, Gowns and Mantles, Millinery, Tea and Coffee Merchants, Ironmongery, Boot and Shoe Makers, Tin Smith, Provision Merchant (not grocer). Some of the names conjured up visions of a world beyond the pit heaps, the Meadow Dairy, the Maypole, the Home and Colonial, the Parisienne Mantle.

It was almost impossible to 'go down the street' without meeting someone one knew. At no time did Ashington suddenly close down leaving us bereft in a deserted street. Even though we had only gone to look at the shops, not to spend money, we'd have thought it wrong not to find at least a few shops open.

I recall a friend, Alice Ramsay, an only child, telling me that one Christmas Eve she went 'up the street' with her parents to look at the shops. There in the front of Arrowsmith's window was a most beautiful doll which captivated Alice's parents as much as it did Alice. However, they'd already done all their Christmas shopping. They went home and had supper. Alice went to bed. Her parents put out her presents from Santa Claus and they, too, went to bed but they could not sleep for thinking of the doll they had seen in Arrowsmith's window. They knew how much it would please Alice to see it among her gifts. They got up, dressed and went back up the street. As they passed the Council clock, it struck twelve. When they got to Arrowsmith's, the shop was still open.

Incidentally, among the shops were those who put a ceiling on the price of goods they had to offer, Woolworth's 'Nothing over sixpence', the Penny Bazaar 'Nothing over a penny', Marks and Spencer's 'Nothing over five shillings' and The Guinea Shop where no dress cost more than a guinea (£1.05p).

For so young a community there was a very great deal happening in Ashington. There was, too, a sizeable amount of interaction between people. Most lived near enough to work to walk or cycle there. In the Rows, lavatories, middens and stand taps were situated across the road from the houses they serviced. Women kept themselves abreast of family news by 'popping along' to see how this or that relative or friend was getting along. Men paid frequent visits to the allotments where they met up with other men to discuss matters of interest to them. For some, the Working Men's Clubs were a substitute for family life. Others went only at week-ends.

For women, mat making and embroidery were agreeable ways of spending winter evenings. To the committed embroiderer the list of things which could be so adorned was endless, table cloths, tray cloths, doyleys, nightdress cases, handkerchiefs, chair-back covers, teapot cosies, dressing table sets, sideboard runners, serviettes, seat covers, egg cosies, a plain blouse (better left plain), a ditto dress.

When young, unmarried girls did embroidery, it was for their bottom drawers. All girls started collecting for their bottom drawers when they left school. At first, they did this in a general way, but after Mr Right entered their lives it took a more positive turn. Brides were still supposed to provide the future nest with all table linen, towels and bed linen, and, of course, they had to have trousseaux which included at least three sets of underwear, best, second best and ordinary. We had a best of everything. Some children even had best toys, toys they were only allowed to play with when they were clean and being supervised so that the toy in question might not get damaged or broken. This was particularly true of dolls when a girl might have a 'Sunday' doll.

There were a number of societies and groups that flourished in the village. Among these was a group of men dedicated to the playing of Pitch and Toss, an illegal gambling game. To throw those in authority off the scent, they cleverly called themselves the Colliery Runners, or some such name, and, on Pitch and Toss nights they dressed as for running practice, that is, they tucked their trousers and linings inside their socks and wore sandshoes. I think their venue was Piggy Moor Lonnen. One evening,

One of Ashington's many football teams of the day (uncle George 2nd left, back row, Father, goal-keeper, centre 2nd back row)

while they were deep in their game, one man chanced to look up and saw the bobby bearing down on them from the horizon. In less time than it takes to tell, they had pocketed the evidence and were off, running, the policeman, lumbered as he was in his thick uniform, heavy boots and helmet, after them. He caught up with them and, running alongside, said, 'It's all right, lads. I've got all your names. I know what you were up to. You'll be hearing from us. Tarra well. Enjoy your run.'

Another person who often collected a small group round him was the night watchman. The one I have in mind was the man who sat in a sort of upturned coffin, next to a coke burning brazier. People came to see him, not so much for the pleasure of his company, but more to enjoy the red hot fire on a cold night. The fires were cheerful, but they gave off coke fumes which tended to clutch at one's throat and lungs. Also, it was lovely to feel the heat for the first few seconds, but soon the side facing the blaze became too hot, while the rest of one's anatomy remained icy cold.

Whatever it was that was being guarded, those in authority thought that one elderly retired man was all that was needed. Perhaps it was. No-one would think of knocking an old man down.

After the 1926 strike, for some years, the pits worked short time. This meant that, many miners did not work a full week. Those miners who were employed were guaranteed three shifts a week which was barely enough to make ends meet. For those people who were not employed the situation was very, very much worse. Even for those who worked a full week, wages were not high. My father was a safety man which meant that he worked seven days a week, but even that made for financial belt-tightening when his shift rate was reduced. My parents were buying a house in the Colliery Scheme where we were then living. Some years later, when Dad was on an upstanding wage (i.e. he was paid on a fixed seven days a week basis at a higher rate) my mother told me that after the mortgage and other off-takes had been deducted from my father's pay, she was left with only nineteen and sixpence (less than a pound) on which to keep house.

To help over this period, my parents did what many did in those days, they took in a lodger. Lodgers, generally, lived as members of the family. The first was a member of a Music Hall act 'doing' a week at the Miners' Theatre. His name was W. E. Scerme Peach. He was lively and pleasant company and we all went to see him on stage. The next was a very avant-garden young man, a Mr Tucker whose home was somewhere in the south so that he was able to tell us all about what really up-to-date living was like. He always carried a cane. He would also have carried his ukulele with him wherever he went had it been possible. As it was, he had to be content with playing it from the moment he got in till he went out again. His repertoire was not large. 'By a babbling brook' is the song I most remember. He stayed only a few weeks before he went on to pastures new. A Miss Doughty stayed rather longer. She was also abreast of the times. Her wardrobe was limited but it was up-to-the-minute. She wore a magnificent (to me) pair of blue Russian boots, zipped up the side. For the rest, she washed and ironed her blouse and underwear every night, brushed her clothes and pressed them.

For those who could not, or would not, pay their rent, there was only one sad outcome, they were put out onto the street, literally. Their furniture was taken out, stacked on the street and the house was locked against them. I did not know any to whom this happened. I heard of some who were threatened and the family rallied round to stave off this disgrace and hardship.

There were several whom we knew who struggled hard to make ends meet and appear decent during this time. Whatever privations they suffered at home, they kept up appearances and saw to it that they and their family were clean and decent. Of those I knew, almost all went to church devoutly thanking God for their blessings.

As a family we felt misfortune to one was the concern of all and there were others much worse off than we. We had also developed certain sayings which could defuse potentially explosive situations in family relationships. These arose from incidents, if not apocryphal, then, at the very least, slightly embroidered in the telling.

One of these was the result of an old uncle who had never in his life been to the shows, or Hoppings. He was taken there by some young blade trying to acquaint him with Life before it was too late. The thing that attracted Uncle was the shooting range where a number of clay pipes were strung across the back of the range. He watched an unsuccessful young man waste his money before he decided to have a try, or rather, three tries. The first time he put paid to a doll on the first shelf, the second to a jug on the next shelf and the third to a half tea-set on the top shelf. He handed the gun back and smiling with satisfaction said,

'I'll take one of them clay pipes.'

When anybody smashed anything after that, they said, 'I'll take one of them clay pipes.' We still say this, but perhaps the most moving occasion on which it was said was on a Sunday just before the War. This particular branch of the family was about to sit down to Sunday dinner. One member had been sent to bring down the Sunday plates. As she lifted them she overbalanced and the plates slipped from her hands and crashed onto the stone floor. At such a time it was a minor tragedy. They all looked at the floor, aghast. It was the father who helped the situation most. He put his hand on the shoulder of his weeping daughter. 'You'll get a clay pipe for that,' he said.

This, then, was the warm, close community of which I was part. However, this closeness was also inhibiting. There was a constant vigilance on the part of members of the community to see that the individual did not get above himself or herself. That one remembered 'who you are and what you are', a requirement which was often very deflating to the ego. It was useless to try to adopt any grandiose feelings. One was soon cut down to size. Everyone knew too much about everyone else.

But, having lived in a community like Ashington one misses, for the rest of one's life, the unexpected visitor, the relative who has just 'popped in', the walk up the street when one was assured of meeting an acquaintance and have a 'bit crack'. All the Summers and Barnfather families lived within a short radius. I had cousins, uncles and aunts in abundance.

The pit yard Linda crossed to take Dad's bait

Chapter 3

Wooler

The name 'Wooler' means 'a hill over-looking a stream'. Wooler is part of the Glendale Valley. Long years ago, way back in the mist of Time, this valley was a huge lake.

I have known Wooler for as long as I can remember. It was the home of my mother and her family. Here I have known happiness, the exhilaration of feeling well, the heady enjoyment of running over springy turf, of walking gingerly on sharp stones in the middle of ice-cold streams, of following the hay bogies. A thousand delights tumble for recognition.

At the time of my birth, little over eighty years had passed since the first shaft was sunk in the midst of a gorse-covered area that was to become Ashington. Wooler, on the other hand, has a long, dignified history. It is a market town of solid grey stone buildings and red pantile roofs, although there seem to be fewer red roofs now than there were. On its door-step are the Cheviot Hills, gentle hills, covered for the most part in turf cropped by many sheep, heather and bracken.

In a county where, because of its 'Claggy Times' – the constant raiding between the Scots and the English, the marauding of the Moss Troopers (freebooters who took their name from the type of border country in which they operated) and the Reivers who plundered, spoiled, stole and snatched – numerous castles were builts, yet there is none at Wooler. There are the ruins of a Tower but this was devastated at some time before 1254. Perhaps there is no castle because, although so near the border, Wooler itself seems to have escaped much of the strife.

There are however battlefields at Homildon Hill, Flodden, Hedgeley Moor, Piperden and Geteringe.

Because of two devastating fires, exacerbated, perhaps, by the thatched roofs of the cottages, few really old buildings have survived in Wooler. The first fire took place in 1722, the second in 1862. This last event was chronicled by a T. Fordyce who wrote thus;

'A fire broke out in the Half Moon Inn, Wooler, and before its destructive rage could be arrested a great number of dwelling houses were laid in ruins. It appeared that a chimney in the Half Moon had taken fire and communicated the devouring element to the roof, which was of thatch, many of the adjoining buildings being covered with the same inflammable material. The greatest consternation prevailed in the town, as house after house was destroyed by the fire, which was fanned by the hurricane of wind that prevailed at the time. The fire at last was got under, but not until sixteen houses and shops were destroyed. Many families were rendered both houseless and homeless by the calamity.'

Apparently there was no fire engine in Wooler. It took seven hours for the Belford fire engine to get there.

Our early journeys to Wooler, thirty miles away, were by train which we caught at Longhirst station having walked the intervening three miles across the fields.

Outside Wooler station a musty cab, perhaps a Growler, at any rate a survivor of a bygone age, stood waiting for our custom.

As we got into the cab and waited for the driver to activate the horse, there was time to look around and take in the familiar sights, among them the painted wooden café opposite, the café which, as far as I could see, never had a customer. There was something uninviting about its façade; it didn't appear to want custom.

The driver cracked his whip, said 'Gee up, there' to the horse which, after consideration, ambled up the hill with its burden.

The first shop we passed on the right as we veered round the first bend was Mitchell's bright little sweet shop. Almost opposite was Tully's garage and, a little further up on the same side, the ruins of the Tower with, next to it, the Archbold Hall. Originally this building had been the Tower Hill Presbyterian Church. When it was deemed no longer suitable for that purpose, in April, 1904, Jane and Mary Archbold acquired it and gave it to the people of Wooler in memory of their parents and their uncle, Peter Whyte, who had been a minister at Tower Hill. A little further on was (and is) the Church of St Mary. Almost opposite this was Padley's, the chemist, while, on the same side as the church was Renton's wet fish shop, another shop, and, on the corner, the Wheatsheaf Hotel. In fact, at this point we had reached a staggered cross-roads which was, in effect, the Market Square.

HIGH STREET, WOOLER

In the centre of the Market Square stood the drinking fountain with its chained iron cup. This had been erected in 1879 to the memory of William Wightman. Throughout its history it was a great meeting place, not only for the young of Wooler, but also, at harvest times, for the Irish labourers who came to help. They congregated round the fountain, many sitting on the steps. Mrs Hetherington, from the Black Bull Hotel, used to give the men soup and bread.

Opposite the drinking fountain was a terrace of shops fronted by black iron railings which survived the War, probably because they were necessary. There is quite a steep drop from the terrace to the road. At one corner of the terrace was Martin's the photographer, at the other, the British Linen Bank. From here the road turned left where it branched to Church Street or to the Peth. In this area were McCaskie's butcher's, the Cheviot cafe and a taxidermist who displayed samples of his art in a small window on his premises.

To the right of the Market Square was the wide High

36

Street with Archbold's on the corner and, on both sides a wealth of shops, buildings and hotels, among them Mary McEwan's. Both Miss McEwan and her shop were noted in Wooler. The shop itself was crammed to more than capacity with goods of every description. This necessitated taking up, not only the floor space and the wall space, but the ceiling space as well. Several stories are extant regarding the proprietress. Apparently on one occasion a gentleman came in for cartridges for his gun, 'Ye'd be better buying a rope,' she is reported to have said, adding, 'It's cheaper.' On another occasion a man came in in a hurry and asked for a mousetrap, quick, he had a bus to catch. 'My mousetraps,' she is said to have replied, 'only catch mice.'

Having negotiated the Market Place, we turned left into Ramsay Lane where two shops stand out in my memory, Laing's, the grocer's (later Strangeway's) and Hope's. What a misnomer this last was, as far as I could see. It was a small shop which seemed to operate from what had been a room in a cottage. There were quite a number of this type of shop at that time. The goods on display in the shop window were mostly sweets in their cardboard boxes minus their lids. A long, undisturbed sojourn basking in the sun when it came, had robbed the sweets of their original colour and, thereby, had given them all a certain uniformity. This was further emphasised by the fine, very fine, film of dust in which they were coated. It was a restful place to be because, sometimes, a large cat also basked there on a shelf above the display.

Mrs Hope appeared overburdened with this world's cares, and perhaps she was. She was most often at the seat of custom enveloped in a very large overall tied at the back. I cannot tell what else they sold (or did not sell, but kept) because the interior of the shop was dark, dingy even. Little light seemed to penetrate beyond the doorway. I saw more of Mr Hope, a large shambling man who often came and just stood there, leaning against the wall outside the shop, his trousers concertina-ed over his untied boots with their trailing laces. That shop drew me like a magnet. I was much more interested in Hope's shop than I was in Mitchell's. Not that this did the Hopes any good. I had no money to spend in either, and thus my ultimate allegiance was never put to the test. How the shop existed I do not know. Perhaps it was an indication of how little it took to supply the bare necessities of life. On the other hand, my view was, naturally, limited and their trade might have been a great deal better than I thought because, although I never heard Mr Hope's name mentioned, Mrs Hope was highly thought of, at least in the circle I knew.

The various stages of the journey, not the least of which was the sedate finale, gradually brought us to the different level of life to be found here in Wooler. There was no wild rush to get out of the cab and dash into the house shouting, 'Grannie, Grannie, I'm here.' However great the joy was in our actually being there, the cab and the clear, ordered air had modified it so that it was two suitably docile children who were welcomed by my grandmother and those of my aunts who happened to be at home. Any last vestiges of excitable joy in danger of exploding when at last we were in the kitchen, were quelled by the heavy, authoratitive, stern ticking of the indifferent grandfather clock which had marked the passage of time for many, many years and knew what it was about.

At that time Grannie Gallon lived in the end house of Woodbine Terrace, a group of five or six that climbed up Ramsay Lane towards Common Road. Between her house and that of Mr John Rule were the huge wooden gates of an adjoining farm (now Oliver Road).

Mr Rule was one of Wooler's most respected citizens although, in fact, he was born in Belford. He must have been about ninety years of age when I first remember seeing him take his daily walk up the Common Road, a tall gentleman hardly stooping at all. He always returned carrying a handful of dried sticks for the fire.

He was an elder and Sunday School teacher of the Presbyterian Church, offices which he had filled for more than forty years. On his nintieth birthday the church presented him with a silver topped walking stick.

All the family held Mr Rule in high regard, even Auntie Isa, the second youngest and the only one to be actually born in Wooler, a circumstance in which she took great pride. As far as Auntie Isa was concerned, someone not born in Wooler, while not actually being beyond the Pale, was yet deficient in this one important element and excuses had to be made for the poor unfortunate. 'Ah, but you see, she is NOT a Wooler person', said with sorrow and forbearing.

My two grandmothers were totally different. Grannie Summers was small and plump while Grannie Gallon was tall and slim. She was, unfortunately, very deaf, her disability the aftermath of an attack of measles. She could not easily take part in a general conversation, but she could converse on a one to one basis, especially with someone whom she knew.

She was widowed after only eight years and nine months of married life yet she managed to keep alive the memory and the person of my grandfather, John Gallon. I've often heard one of my aunts say, 'Father would have been pleased', or 'Father would not have approved of that', etc. when, in fact, the only member of the family who would remember Grandfather with any clarity would be Auntie Nan. She was the eldest child, almost eight years old when her father died.

When Grandfather died, part of Grannie probably died too. She kept the hair style she wore at the time of his death and from then on, never wore anything but black. When, after reading the paper, she had reason to disagree with what the Government was doing, she usually assumed the Queen would agree with her, the Queen in question being Queen Victoria.

However, both grandmothers did have something in common; both suffered from stomach complaints. In Grannie Summers' case, she simply said, 'My stomach's bad the day,' as if she were talking of a recalcitrant child who was causing her pain and discomfort and who should know better. When this happened, she just got on with her work as normal, and, I'm afraid, it was normal for everyone else to expect her to. To counteract her malady she took a Seidlitz Powder and confined her food for that day to dry Crumpsall Cream Crackers. If it was her Guild night, she went just the same saying it would take her mind off her stomach. She had great faith in Crumpsall Cream Crackers in that, to give her stomach nothing to complain about, she finished every supper with three or four Cream Crackers well buttered. These were easily digested, she said, and they would ward off further upsets. That they never did didn't seem to matter.

Grannie Gallon, on the other hand, put her faith in Benger's Food, milk warmed in front of the fire before bedtime and a daily afternoon rest. As far as Grannie Summers was concerned, she ate what she fancied. No member of the family ever said, 'Mother, you should not be eating pork crackling. It is NOT good for you. You'll upset your stomach.' Grannie Gallon would never have got away with it. Either Auntie Isa or Auntie Ethel would intervene. 'Mother. You are NOT to eat that. You know it doesn't agree with you. You'll be up all night if you eat that.' Her reply to this was, 'Howt'. It could mean whatever she wanted it to mean; it had an all-purpose utility. It was her answer to the little day to day annoyances that tend to upset us all at some time. It served for when she was angry or put out or just couldn't understand something.

Grannie Gallon never lived on her own. Usually either Auntie Ethel or Auntie Isa was at home. Throughout my childhood Uncle Lin also lived with them.

Uncle Lin was a shadowy figure in my life. He was a man and, therefore, he went about his own pursuits about which one would never have dreamed of asking. When I first knew him, he worked at the quarry then operating at the top of Common Road. I never found out exactly what he did after it closed, but he seems to have been a very good fisherman and a fair shot. Whenever he went off for a day's fishing or shooting, he always came back with either fish, rabbits or game.

All adults felt it was their duty to instruct the young members of their family on how to behave. It was a duty some were only too anxious to fulfil. (For children there were a great many more than ten Commandments.) Both Auntie Ethel and Auntie Isa had been children's nurses (nannies) and thus they had specialist knowledge. Both had probably been robbed of their right to a husband and children by the First World War. Auntie Isa certainly was. Now, they cared for Grannie with complete devotion. To them she was the epitome of perfection. They thought she was wonderful and, in a way, this was true. She was widowed in 1898 when there were no such things as pensions, yet she gave her six children a loving and settled family life.

Being at Wooler so impressed me that I thought I spent all my summer holidays there, but this was not so. However, in my later childhood, I spent enough time there with my brother and my Edinburgh cousins, Charles, Greta and Jack Tocher and my cousin, John Ellacott, for it to be memorable. Largely, it was Aunties Ethel, Isa and Amy who looked after us and for this I, personally, am very grateful. We must often have been nuisances.

The household in Woodbine Terrace was very ordered. We rose early. The windows were opened as wide as possible and the bed-clothes turned back. We washed in the bedroom using the china wash-basin and ewer that stood on the wash-hand stand. Meanwhile, my aunts had already been up and cleaned out the fire which, unlike ours, had been allowed to die overnight. The table was set for breakfast with the tablecloth and china reserved for that meal. For breakfast we had something cooked with

On holiday at Wooler with Mother and Father. Left to right, Charles, Linda, John, Greta, Billy.

41

absolutely delicious freshly baked morning rolls from Bryson's the baker's, to follow. After this the housework was done methodically, the special work for the day first, then the routine work of dusting, sweeping, doing the bedrooms and preparing the midday dinner. On one occasion I watched Auntie Isa as she made the beds in one of the bedrooms. There were two double beds in this room, one which it was possible to walk around and one which was jammed up against the wall. This bed was much too heavy to be moved for regular bed making so, as an aid, Auntie Isa used a stick to smooth that part of the bed she could not reach and to tuck the sheets down the wall side of the bed. The mattresses were feather ticks which took an awful lot of shaking and thumping to even out. The next morning I thought I would do her a good turn and make the beds for her. Accordingly, after breakfast I went upstairs and, using the stick, I gave each tick a little whack here and there to straighten in out a bit and I carefully pulled the blankets and sheets back into place, being particularly careful to smooth the top cover. It hadn't taken me nearly as long as it took her. Filled with virtue at the good deed I had performed, I went down stairs and said,

'Auntie Isa, you won't have to make the beds in our room. I've already done them.'

'Thank you,' she said. 'I'll go up and look at them in a moment.' Pleased at what I'd done, I went out to play. I wasn't out very long before I was called in.

'It was kind of you to think of making the beds, Linda,' she said, 'but as you've said you made the beds, you're going to make them properly. Now come upstairs with me.'

In the bedroom she stood while she instructed me on how to make a bed properly. I had to take all the clothes off again including the undersheet and blanket, shake them as best I could, plump up the pillows and the almost impossible feather ticks, and put each blanket and sheet back individually instead of dragging them all up together as I had done. My arms ached with the effort and I was near to tears (I was about eight at the time) and I wasn't allowed to crawl about the bed pressed up against the wall as I had done when I made the beds originally.

'Now,' she said, when I'd finished, 'they are not as good

as they would have been if I had made them, but they will do. The next time you feel you want to help somebody, if you cannot do the job properly, don't offer. It is no help to anyone if the work you do has to be done again. That makes more work. Now off you go to play.'

My earlier effort and her giving instructions must have interfered with her morning's work considerably, but she saw what she did as necessary. It would have been a great deal quicker for her to have remade the bed and said nothing other than if she needed help in the future she would ask for it, but that wasn't her way.

Once the midday meal was over and the dishes washed and put away, Grannie lay down for her afternoon's rest and my aunts went upstairs to wash and change. If we children were not going out, then we had to sit quietly while Grannie was having her rest. If we went out, then we hadn't to come back till tea-time. Dinner was always at twelve o'clock when the table was set with the full complement of vegetable dishes, gravy boats and the like. Tea was at four. For this last meal again there was a special cloth and the tea service. After tea Auntie Amy usually came to visit and there was general conversation while my aunts knitted, sewed or did embroidery. Sometimes we went for a walk.

We children went to bed early. When we were very young, Auntie Isa came upstairs to see that we said our prayers properly. At Ashington, my mother was perfectly satisfied with the Lord's Prayer and the list of 'God blesses' leading to the final 'and please make me a good girl'. Auntie Isa thought it fitting that I should also learn a verse to be included in this nightly ritual and I learned two:–

> Gentle Jesus, meek and mild,
> Look upon a little child.
> Pity my simplicity.
> Suffer me to come to Thee.

and

> Now I lay me down to sleep,
> I pray the Lord my soul to keep.
> If I should die before I wake,
> I pray the Lord my soul to take.

This last verse frightened me. I used to lie awake terrified in case I died in my sleep. Sometimes I tried to prop my eyes open thinking that if I fell asleep that way I couldn't die.

I found going to sleep a difficult thing to do sometimes anyway. I usually shared a bed with Auntie Ethel. This was as awkward for her as it was for me. We were both used to sleeping alone. If I had fallen asleep, I usually wakened when they came to bed and I watched them undress in the flickering candle-light, fascinated by the heavy abundance of underwear my grandmother, who slept in the other bed, wore. Waist petticoats, bust bodice, camisole, knitted stockings, combinations, knee-length knickers, stays and chemise all discarded and replaced by a voluminous white wyncyette night-dress. After her hair had been let down, Grannie brushed it then plaited it, licking her fingers to make it easier.

By this time I was wide awake. Once the candle had been blown out, the room was dark and warm for the windows were not opened at night because the night air was harmful. I dared not move in case I disturbed Auntie Ethel. Rigid, I dared not cough. Even breathing was a risk. As for turning over! 'Stop fidgeting, lassie,' she would say. 'Go to sleep.' This was one command I could never understand. One cannot go to sleep to order. I wanted to go to sleep, but the more I wanted to, the less I was able to and I lay, listening for my heartbeats, convinced that they had stopped.

Sunday meant Church and Sunday School at the Presbyterian Church. I loved it all. Sunday School was held in the morning after which we went to the eleven o'clock service. We took our Bibles with us turning to the scriptures and following the text as the elder read it. When the time came for the Minister to preach, he was escorted to the pulpit by an elder and locked in. I never knew whether this was because he'd forgotten the way, or because they wanted to make sure they got their money's worth sermon-wise. They certainly did the latter.

When he was sure the congregation was paying attention, the Minister spoke slowly and emphatically, lengthening his vowels and using a strong 'r'.

'My text is taken from the sixteenth chapter of St Jorn,

the thirrty-thirrd verrse. "These things I have spoken unto you that in me ye might have peace".' There was a rustling of Bibles being opened. Again, the Minister. 'These things....' For those who had opened their Bibles there wasn't that much to read and I began to worry in case they were checking up on the text and the Minister had made a mistake in which case somebody was going to correct him. Actually, this might have created an interesting little diversion, except that I was afraid that I knew who might do the correcting. Fortunately, the Minister knew what he was about. When compared with Mr Davidson, it could be said that he thundered through his sermon. When Mr Davidson preached, one knew the sermon had started when he climbed into the pulpit and that it was over when the congregation started quietly shuffling and coughing and he said, 'Now to God, the Father....'. What he had said in between was not at all clear, especially as one was busy with one's own thoughts. With the Minister, however, everyone sat up smartly, paying attention. I was never any wiser at the end, but that didn't matter. I felt I had grown in righteousness by the mere fact that I had listened.

There were other differences between Wooler and Ashington apart from going to Church and the fact that life was so much more ordered in Grannie's house. At home, we did not have gas. The houses were lit by electricity and cooking was done on the kitchen range. All one had to do when the daylight was fading was depress a switch and there was light. If it suddenly went out, the penny had run out in the meter and there was sufficient light from the fire to allow us to feed in another penny.

At Wooler, they did not throw buckets of coal on to the kitchen fire. Their coal had to be bought at the door and it was delivered in bags and had to be used sparingly. In addition, the house was lit by gas, the two downstairs rooms that is, and cooking was done in the scullery on a gas stove. As we were not used to it, to us, the gas had a heavy all-pervading smell.

The gas was not lit till the daylight had almost gone and the furniture had lost all individuality and become darkened shadows. No-one commented upon this state of affairs. When Grannie said, 'I think we'd better light the gas', one of my aunts performed the ceremony with great care. The gas mantle was delicate and fragile and precious. Then, suddenly, with a plop the light came on. It was a warm light, far more personal than the cold electricity. As it burned it hissed gently and tunelessly to itself. It never quite dispersed the shadows from the corners.

The house doors were always kept closed so that any callers had to knock and wait to be admitted. Only on the coldest weather were house doors in the Rows at Ashington closed. Usually callers jiggled the sneck on the way in. However, there were small differences in the jiggles and those sitting in the kitchen could identify the caller and forecast their mission before they'd completed the few steps that took them over the threshold and into the room.

'That's our Betty's man. He's been to pay his dues and he's on the way back.'

At Wooler I never saw children playing along the gutter or sitting on the kerb stones as I sometimes did at Ashington. Nor did they stand at the door and call one's name when they wanted a play-mate.

Christian names were used very sparingly at Wooler, whereas at Ashington, few people were given their titles, Christian names and nicknames being much more common. In Wooler it was Mrs Charles Smith, in Ashington, Annie Binks, her that married Sticky Smith.

In Wooler, ordinary day to day encounters, however brief, made news. Even if they were no more than an exchange of greetings, they were important and the telling of them often took longer than the incident itself. It was an indication of how much more *time* there was.

All our contacts with Grannie Gallon were gentle and considerate. These were born of respect. Although Aunties Ethel and Isa were the ones who told us how we should behave and what we should do, it was Grannie who was head of the house. It was her wishes that were paramount.

Generally speaking, my aunts had a very positive view on life and ethics. Everything was right or wrong, black or white, and doing one's duty was all-important. There were no intermediate shades of grey or off-white. It did not seem to occur to them that others who did not share their view might have a point.

'That is wrong.'

'But why is it wrong?'

'Because it is not right.'

'There was no need for thanks. She was only doing her duty.'

There were no blurred edges. They considered their standards and ideals were of the highest and could not be called to question. Newfangled ideas were not really acceptable. The old ways were the best: they had stood the test of time. And for those who did their duty faithfully, there was an ultimate reward.

It seemed to me, as I was growing older and becoming more aware, that, just as they starched some laundry so that it deflected the dirt, thereby staying spotless and stiffly immaculate longer, so they starched their minds so that any other view-point was easily discarded and ended up in some mental oubliette. It was one of the thoughts I'd rather not have thought, conjuring up, as it did, the fact that I should be pure in thought, word and deed. To think thus of those who were looking after me was wicked indeed.

We divided our time in Wooler between staying with Grannie and staying with Auntie Amy, Uncle Will and John who lived successively at Akeld, Humbleton and Walker Wall before they moved into Wooler proper.

Akeld, three miles distant from Wooler, was once a sizeable village. The church has completely disappeared but the few dwellings that remain are indications of the fact that, once, this area was well fortified. Akeld Bastel guarded one of the principal passes to the Border.

The house in which Auntie Amy, Uncle Will and my cousin John lived (which still stands) was in the left hand corner of a solidly built square of linked houses entered by an archway. The inside area was cobbled. Each house had a wood pile and a contraption for sawing logs. There was a central block of earth closets, one for each family. It was here I saw my first dragonfly droning through the summer air. I only saw its delicate beauty: I did not realise I should be afraid of it, it might sting.

Living in that stronghold, even for a short time, it was possible to see how people and livestock could be herded into the square and the entrance barred against marauders.

My aunt and uncle lived there till I was about five. My earliest memory is not of Wooler itself, but of returning here late at night from what was probably Wooler show. A fine, insistent rain fell and the dark glistened blackly on the unlit road leading from Wooler. Auntie Amy pushed the pram in which John lay and, dropping at the edge, his legs dangling, his hands gripping the handles to steady himself was my brother, Billy. I alternately was carried and walked hanging on to my mother's hand. We were a silent group bunched on that quiet road, tired and intent only on getting back to the house. We children had each been bought a fairly sturdy balloon in orange and black tiger stripes. When we got back we realised that John's balloon was missing. Early next morning, Uncle Will, who arrived home later than we did, went back along the road and returned with the deflated balloon, much battered after its encounter with a thorn bush. Patiently he patched it all over and blew it up again.

Next to Auntie Amy's house was a field of corn due to be cut by the reaper with its huge flailing arms. We children were forbidden to go near the field. We were told that a boy had done so. He had got in the way of the reaper and both his legs were cut off. This was probably a piece of fiction concocted to keep us out of the field. It certainly kept us away when the reaper was there. I was always apprehensive of large farm machinery thereafter.

I was more aware of the countryside when we went to stay with Auntie Amy at her next house, a cottage at Humbleton. It was quite spacious with low-beamed ceilings, stone floors, a front room and a large area upstairs which had been partitioned off to make two or three rooms. Behind the cottage was a hayfield, the hay of which was cut with a scythe. Every day we walked from here into Wooler at least once.

It was probably about this time that we stopped travelling by train and came to Wooler by bus. What miserable affairs those bus journeys were! The buses smelt of petrol and the road to Wooler was much narrower and much more winding than it is now. Indeed, over the years I have seen workmen operating at every widening of the road, every bend that has been taken out, every new piece put in. I have seen houses built, gardens and trees planted that have grown to maturity and cottages enlarged and modernised so that it is difficult to see what they once were.

In the early days of our travelling by bus, no sooner had we lurched round one corner than we had another to contend with. We had the sympathy of the driver and conductor and the medical lore of the passengers, but none of these abated the travel sickness one iota. The driver obligingly stopped the bus from time to time that either Mother or I might be sick, a humiliating experience.

With what relief I can hardly describe, we got off at the terrace of shops near the British Linen Bank in Wooler. We were always allowed off first. On our climb up the hill, hardly had we passed Strangeway's and Hope's when I began to feel better and, by the time we reached Woodbine Terrace, I felt as I always feel at Wooler, fit and well.

Travel-wise, things improved when Billy got his bicycle for passing the scholarship (as the eleven plus was then called). As Mother and I both had bicycles it was decided all three of us would cycle to Wooler. Naturally, this was of interest to the family generally and Uncle Tommy, in particular, gave much thought to the expedition. He arrived one night with a route which, he said, would be the easiest and quickest way to get there. The details indicating which way to go plus the diagrams for greater clarity covered three pages. Mother had had some idea of going to Pegswood and picking up the Wooler road just out of Morpeth.

'You don't want to do that,' Uncle Tommy told her. 'It's miles out of your way. This'll be far quicker,' and he took us through his instructions and diagrams of left turns, right turns, forks, T junctions, villages and farms with injunctions to go that way, not this way and, at the next turn to go this way not that way, to all of which we listened respectfully. It never occurred to us not to use his itinerary after all the trouble he'd gone to.

Unfortunately, on the day in question, Mother woke with a terrible migraine. She took what she could to lessen the attack and, suitcases strapped to the carriers of our bicycles and food for the journey tied to the fronts, we were waved off by a small group of neighbours and relatives. My mother felt too ill to do anything but just keep going and it was left to Billy and me to make what we could of Uncle Tommy's directions. Every road junction in that maze of winding country roads necessitated our dismounting and deciding which way to go. On and on we pedalled, this way and that, till finally, after about two and a half hours when we reckoned we must have covered at least half of our thirty-mile journey, we sat down to eat and Mother, white and drawn, lay on the grass looking as if she would never get on her bike again.

We recommenced our journey and finally hit the Wooler road at Fenrother. Before long we came to a sign-post which informed us we still had twenty-four miles to go. Thereafter till we got a car, we cycled to Wooler. By this time Auntie Amy had moved to Walker Wall.

In Walker Wall, contrary to the regulations imposed of necessity in Wooler, our playground was limitless and the house rules were more relaxed. The cottage we stayed in was the middle one of three and there were no other houses or cottages in sight. All around were fields, trees and hills. At the bottom of the garden was a well, but my cousin Greta was so emphatic that it was a stream, I thought I was wrong. However on a recent trip to Scotland my cousin Jack was there and we talked of Walker Wall. 'I went back for the first time for forty years,' he said, 'and went down the garden to look for the well but it had gone.'

'Then there WAS a well,' I said.

'Oh yes,' he replied. 'I drew too much water from it to forget.'

The drinking water had to stand all day to allow the 'screws' to settle to the bottom. The kitchen was lit by an oil lamp which cast a cosy, warm glow. It could be carried from room to room where it cast dark shadows beyond the circle of light. Most often, however, the lamp stayed put and candles were used, not merely because they were cheaper, but because they were easier to use. All one needed was a candlestick and a box of matches.

Lamps, on the other hand, took looking after. When they were carried, they had to be held steadily. Lighting a lamp was a delicate business which required a sure hand. The wick had to be lit evenly and turned up slowly so that the glass chimney was not blackened by smoke or cracked through careless use. On no account had the lamp to stand in a draught. It had to be cleaned thoroughly every day, the wick trimmed and the chimney carefully washed and dried. And, of course, the level of paraffin had to be monitored.

Outside there were no street lights and, as we were so far from a sizeable town, it was so dark. The stars shone clear and high above us, brighter than ever before. Pin-point lights from distant windows could be seen clear and distinct. When the moon came up we were all, the houses, the fields, the sleeping animals, the hills, enveloped in its mellow balmy glow.

Noises carried in the daytime. The silence allowed us to hear the singing telegraph wires, the bleating sheep, near and distant, the lowing cattle and the clanking of milk churns.

Ordinary things went almost unnoticed in Ashington and even on Wooler High Street, but here the solitary walker and the rare visitor were events. There was still the occasional pedlar with his large wicker pack in which were threads, buttons, tapes, pins and needles. His sales from the cottages could not have been more than meagre. Perhaps of greater value were the cups of tea, pieces of bread, scones or cake he got. How far he travelled to make a living and how little, it seemed, he needed to survive.

Then there was the oil-man. As he came at regular times, we ran to the bend in the road to meet him when he made room for two or three of us to ride beside him to the cottage. He didn't only sell paraffin, he sold black lead, soap, washing soda and other such commodities. He even sold sweets, toffee, gob-stoppers and liquorice which he kept in a small separate compartment. Before he served this part of his stock, he wiped his hands on a piece of waste and lifted out the item to be purchased with the tips of his fingers.

Any traffic that passed was of the utmost interest. Who was it? Where were they going? There was time to ponder these things because all traffic was sparse and slow-moving. We stopped what we were doing and stood silently watching till the cart, man on horse-back or hill walker had passed us and was gone from sight. We were always wished 'Good-day' at least.

However, the thing we were most anxious to take part in was the leading of the hay. We were not the only children in the hay fields. Like them, we took our midday meal wrapped up in newspaper.

When it came to actually leading the hay, the flat cart, or bogie, was backed onto the pike. The man in charge walked round the pike, kicking it to release it from the grass into which it had settled. He then passed two ropes from the windlass round the base of the pike and told the horse to 'gee up' when the animal moved forward dragging the pike with it. This loosened the pike sufficiently to allow it to be drawn onto the now tilted cart when it was led away to the barn. One child was usually allowed to get onto the cart beside the driver, the rest followed on foot.

At the barn two men dug their hay-forks into the pike, the horse moved forward and the pike slid off the cart when it was fork lifted into the barn. On the way back all we children got onto the bogie. The surface was very slippery and, minus its load of hay, the cart dipped at the back so that our feet almost touched the ground.

The hay harvest over, we could turn our attention to other things, notably making bows and arrows with suitable twigs and branches and saved-up bits of string. We walked, played in the streams nearby and, occasionally went on picnics when we were always reminded of the country code, shut all gates behind you, keep to the paths, be careful not to disturb the sheep or cows, clear your picnic site, do not trespass and leave no rubbish.

The high-water-mark of our Wooler holiday was the Agricultural Show then held in the Cottage field. My grandmother and my aunts prepared busily for this event for sometime beforehand. First of all, there were the exhibits for the sections in which they were entering and then there was the food, for on that day Grannie kept open house. Relatives who lived in the country whom they had not seen since last Show day came to visit and were always given afternoon tea.

The morning's chores had to be finished as speedily as possible and lunch was a hurried meal. By early afternoon we had to be dressed in our best ready to walk decorously down to the Show field. Our first visit was to the tents with their dark green light and damp, mossy smell, there to see who had won what. The trestle tables were covered with exhibits which were spotted here and there with coloured cards denoting who had won prizes and who had been highly commended. Great, though subdued, was our satisfaction when we learned that Auntie Isa had collected three or four cards, among them a first, for her efforts. Uncle Lin and Uncle Will also came in for their share: they were both keen gardeners.

The journey round the tents was slow, very slow. My aunts knew all the entrants and they felt themselves sufficiently knowledgeable about the various exhibits to pass their own judgement. All this took a great deal of time. Added to that, the number of acquaintances whom we met were legion. Each had to be spoken to. Sometimes we were acknowledged, sometimes not. For us, the being there was all important. For the rest, we waited patiently and spoke when we were spoken to.

After the tents we visited the 'horsey' events, the riding and jumping, then the farm machinery and finally, somewhat shop-soiled, we walked back to Grannie's where, naturally, those who had come to visit had tea first.

At night there were the shows in one of the fields. Normally, we did not go, but on one occasion Auntie Amy took me. She intended going with Uncle Will later, so this was in the nature of a preview. My worldly wealth was my Saturday penny which I was trying to save to buy something to take home. When we were about to leave, Auntie Amy said, 'You haven't been much fun. You haven't spent anything.'

'I was just looking,' I replied, 'to see what I liked best.'

'We're going now,' she said. 'You'd better make you mind up quick.'

I had been rather attracted to the roll-a-penny stall nearby.

'I'd like to try that,' I said.

We went to the stall and I sighed inwardly as I placed my penny in the slot and watched it roll away, for good, as I thought. It rolled on to the chequered table, curved, wavered a bit and fell in the very centre of a twopenny square. The woman in charge pushed the penny towards me and flicked two more in my direction. I couldn't believe it. In seconds I had trebled my capital.

'If I were you,' said Auntie Amy, 'I would play sticky to it. If you try again, you'll lose the lot.'

I was only too happy to leave, jingling the fortune in my pocket.

It seemed like perpetual summer when we went to Wooler, but, in fact, we were there at all seasons, even if only for a few days. Without our actually being aware of it, we got an idea of how much work there was on a farm for both men and women. To begin with, the week was seven days long and for most of those days there were signs everywhere that work was going on. There always seemed to be people about, in the fields ploughing, spreading manure, sowing, hoeing, weeding, singling, mowing, turning hay, hay-making, reaping, potato picking. Before the reaper went into the field, the edges had to be cut with a scythe. Fences had to be mended, hedges seen to and ditching done. Then there were the animals to see to, milking to be done and butter to be made. And these were only the jobs we could not avoid seeing done.

Now, in place of all those knowledgeable, weather-hardened men and women, all one is likely to see in the fields is a solitary tractor, the driver of which is hardly visible, protected as he is from the worst weather and entertained as he is by his portable stereo.

Chapter 4

Visiting

Visiting was the bond that kept both sides of the family together. Indeed, one was expected to call on every opportunity.

'I heard tell you were at Woodhorn last week. You must have passed my very door. What happened you didn't call?'

'I would have done but I was in a hurry. I had –'

'Hurry nothing. It wouldn't have taken a minute to pop in and let us see you were still alive. You didn't *want* to call. That's the top and bottom of it. For all we see of you we might be living at the Back of Beyond.'

As far as we were concerned, Grannie Summers was the focal point when it came to gathering and disseminating family news. Most of the time, for my mother's side of the family, we had to rely on our weekly letters and our visits to Wooler, Edinburgh and Alnmouth during holiday periods.

To visit Edinburgh was to visit a foreign country. The buildings were different, the shops were different and some of the food was different. There were, among other things, morning rolls and afternoon tea-breads together with shortbread and Auntie Nan's rock buns, all of which were absolutely delicious. I have not tasted their like since.

Alnmouth was, and is, a most delightful, quiet village which has retained its individuality without being in the least stand-offish. Here sea and country meet.

Up till about two hundred years ago, Alnmouth was a flourishing port serving the nearby town of Alnwick and its environs. In the seventeenth and eighteenth centuries it was a famous port for smugglers and, as such, was far from quiet, according to John Wesley. He visited there in 1748 and described it as 'a small sea-port famous for all kinds of wickedness'. In 1778 it was bombarded by the famous 'pirate', Paul Jones.

On Christmas Day, 1806, during a great storm, the river Aln changed its course as a result of which the harbour silted up. The links (or golf course) is the second oldest in England.

At the time of my visit, during an Easter holiday, Auntie Isa was staying with an elderly relative. I only knew him as Mr McDougal so that he was, most probably, a cousin of my grandmother. He lived in a turreted house, the Towers, which was linked by a passage to the very much larger Nether Grange, then the home of Miss Pease. Both houses were enclosed behind high walls. These walls seemed to shut out the twentieth century for, behind them, the nineteenth century still lingered. Here, there was an almost undisturbed, 'sleeping beauty' calm. The pace was measured, the clock ticked slowly and light filtered through modestly, anxious not to disturb.

Behind the walls, out of sight of passers-by, trees flourished and flowers bloomed among green velvet lawns. From a multiplicity of windows those who lived in Nether Grange and the Towers could look out on the world around, secure in the knowledge that no-one could see in. No coaches now passed through the archway that led to the Towers, but that didn't matter, their ghosts lingered, for this was where they belonged and the cars (or car) that now replaced them travelled not much faster and no less sedately than they, the coaches, had done.

From the moment I set foot behind those walls, I felt at home. The rooms in which I spent most of my time while I was at Alnmouth could not have been more different from those to which I was used. The sitting room had heavy velvet curtains that almost obliterated the light pleading to be allowed in at the window. The furniture, enough to furnish two large rooms with ease, was of dark wood with seats and sofas upholstered in stout plush. The walls were crammed with pictures in pronounced old gilt frames.

Heavy framed photographs of bearded men and well-endowed ladies stood sentinel along the passage which led to the bedroom in which I slept. The candle cast eerie shadows on the walls as I walked, shadows which came uncannily alive as the flame flickered. To an unseen, unheard tune they performed ghostly dances and yet I felt at home, my fear of the dark dispelled. It was the same in the large bedroom with its high Victorian bed, huge ornate wardrobe, wash-stand and wooden towel rail, where the soap-dish, slop-pail, wash-basin, ewer and chamber pot all matched. Over all were the framed words, 'Thou, God, seest me' and the picture of the Light of the World. In the cellars, apples were stored, singly, on shelves and there were cheeses and other goods enough to withstand a seige.

Across at Nether Grange, the cook, Mrs Pearson, took me into the large kitchen that I might see the huge burnished copper utensils used there long ago. I saw the housekeeper's room, the servants' hall and the rooms not being used the furniture of which was draped in dust sheets, the carpets covered in drugget and the light fittings sewn up in dust-proof bags. As I looked, I felt as if I'd already been there, but a long time before.

For the rest, we visited and were visited. Billy and I had a plethora of aunts and uncles and two great-grandmothers on my father's side of the family.

Several things went to make visiting then easier than it is today. Quite apart from the duty aspect which pertained, particularly among the women of the family, there was no television to engage our prior interest, there was little money available for daily entertainment and most relatives lived within reasonable walking distance.

On visits of an informal nature it was not usual to stay to a meal, even when asked. There was no such thing as a 'handed cup of tea'. This would have been considered as an insult. If the lady of the house said, 'You'll have a cup of tea?' or 'You'll stay for a cup of tea?' she meant a properly laid out meal taken sitting up at the tea-table. The same applied to supper time. 'You'll stop for a bite of supper?'

The reply to this was usually, 'Now it's very kind of you, but we'll have to be going,' and thereafter would follow the reason which would be sound enough, but the more important reason had to do with the state of pantries at that time. The time of which I am speaking, the late twenties and early thirties, were the years which followed the 1926 strike when, for most miners, short time and reduced wages were a reality. Admittedly, this was not true of everyone we knew, so that there was no absolutely hard and fast rule as far as we were concerned, but we were often told, 'Now, if they ask you to stay to tea/supper you are to say, no. They have enough to do to look after themselves.' Similarly, we were not allowed to accept money for doing jobs such as going messages (errands).

When I visited with someone other than my parents, it usually had to be established who I was.

'And which one is this?'

'This is Margaret's/Archie's lassie.'

'Aye. Yes. Well. Who does she take after?'

This was the cue for my person to be examined minutely for likenesses – eyes, nose, ears, mouth, chin, hair, height, weight. I didn't come out of it at all well. And why did they liken mine to the worst family features? 'She's got Tom's nose. And Em's hair. Em always had poor hair.' No-one, it seemed wanted to claim me as a worthy descendant. Thereafter, they had nothing further to say to me, or of me, nor did they try to think of anything. As a visitor I was something that had been brought and was just left there, like the newspaper parcel of produce they'd brought from the allotment. Generally, however, I was happy to sit listening unobserved and uncomplaining, uncomplaining because they nearly all had horse-hair furniture which scratched bare flesh something awful.

One particular house we visited held me enthralled because the relative concerned appeared to have been involved in an inordinate number of deaths which were spoken of in hushed sepulchural tones and many deep sighs made on the long drawn out word 'Aye'.

'Aye. I mind fine. I looked at him lying on the bed and I shook me head. Shook me head I did. I knew fine the minute I saw. Aye. Aye I says to meself not to upset anyone else, Aye, I says to meself. He's not much longer for this world. He's being sent for. Any minute'll see him breathe his last and I went forward and I says John I says its me Em. Do you know me? He opened his eyes. Aye. What a trouble it must have been to him and him so near the end. And he gave a bit of a smile. Em he says and the death ruttle was in his throat. Em. Them was his last words. Em. Just like that. Fetch the glass I says but I knew deep down the glass wasn't needed. Aye. And when Giv passed on....'

I enjoyed (if that's the word) these visits even though what I heard gave fuel to my nightly terrors. I was terrified of the dark.

Of my two great grandmothers still living, one was

Grannie Summers' mother, the other Grandad's. We visited Great Grannie Summers regularly. She lived with her daughter and son-in-law, Aunt Bella and Uncle Andrew and their children Archie, George and Eliza Hyslop. Great Grannie's territory was the front room, more particularly, either propped up by many pillows in the huge, high bed or, on her 'good' days, sitting supported in the multi-cushioned easy chair before the fire.

She had, by this time, sunken features which had not, as yet, become pointed. Her skin was pale and paper thin. She had grey eyebrows, faded grey eyes retreating into their sockets, sparse grey hair combed back into a bun and a benign, almost beatific expression. A knitted grey shawl and a white flannel night-dress covered her scant frame. When she sat up in the chair she had a knitted rug over her knees and knitted slippers on her feet.

We were expected to go forward to the bed and say:

'And how are you today, Grannie?'

Invariably she answered:

'Canny. Canny. I can't complain. God is very good.'

After that, we stood quietly by while the adults spoke to her. We didn't stay in the room long. The fact that she was in bed meant it wasn't one of her 'good' days.

When she sat by the fire we stayed longer. No doubt wishing to entertain us, she asked us two riddles.

'Little Annie Etticoat in a white petticoat.

The longer she stands the shorter she grows. What is she?'

And, 'As I was going to London Town I met a London scholar.

He drew off his hat an' drew off his coat.

Now what is the name of that London Scholar?'

I knew the answer to both for we had heard them many times, but I always pretended I didn't and she then said, 'Well, I'll tell you.'

The answer to the first was 'a candle' and to the second 'Andrew'.

'Now,' she would say, 'you'd never have guessed, would you?' and I always replied, 'Ee, no, I never would.'

On these occasions, her other little party piece was to get Aunt Bella or Uncle Andrew to tie the huge fire irons loosely together at the top. We then bent forward in turn while either my uncle or aunt put the string to our ears and shook the irons gently.

'Now,' asked Great Grannie, 'what do you hear?'

Actually I only ever heard the fire irons rattle, but I knew that wasn't the answer.

'The temple bells,' I said. In fact, temple bells might have sounded like fire irons rattling for all I knew. I'd never heard them.

After our visit to her, we went into the scullery where Archie set up his magic lantern for our entertainment. He and George hung up a white sheet after which we sat in darkness while Archie fiddled with the machine. I was an avid attender of lantern lectures, the free ones that is, and I had already learned that this fiddling about was mandatory. It let one know how difficult these things were to operate and how lucky one was to be there. I'm sorry I can't remember the programme. The church lantern lectures were usually about missionaries with whom, to me, lantern lectures are for ever associated. Invariably, one slide was put on upside down. I never knew whether or not this was an accident or whether it was deliberately done to inject a little live excitement into a serious subject.

Once Grannie Summers took me to visit her mother, Great Grannie Barnfather. It was one of those visits which leave a lasting impression.

Great Grannie Barnfather lived by herself in an upper flat, 8½ Acacia Terrace. Once we got up the stairs we almost fell over the pail of coals beside the door on the landing, it being invisible in the darkness. The room, when we finally got there, was lit by the glow from the fire and the feeble light from a window almost completely obliterated by curtains, and plants clambering to get out. My great-grandmother sat on a cracket (stool) as near the fire as she could get. She was completely shrouded in indeterminate, bunched-up black, far too big for her thin frame which seemed to be nothing but toughened steel wire. The fire lit up her profile and I could see that her face and the front of her sparse, grey hair was already kippered from the effects of her continually smoking a very short black clay pipe which had to be firmly planted at one end of her mouth or it would have burnt the end of her nose.

We stood trying to get accustomed to the semi-darkness. My great grand-mother shoved the pipe over to the other end of her mouth, turned slightly towards the fire and triumphantly ejected a stream of hostile spittle into the heart of the fire. The fire hissed angrily back at her and she responded with a second venomous, disdainful stream. In spite of the fire's furious response there was no doubt who was boss.

Throughout our visit my spirited great-grandmother demonstrated there was life and independence in her old frame yet and she still had the ability to laugh at herself.

Although it was sometimes difficult to sit quietly and there were other much more exciting things I could have done, I am very glad I visited my elderly relatives. When I began to realise I was only a link in a long chain and that these faded people had once been young like me, I began to have some idea of what had gone before. Several of my relatives lived until well into their nineties. This meant that I had living contact with people who were born in, or about, 1840.

The big family get-togethers usually took place at Christmas and Easter and on specific Sundays. On these occasions the best china and cutlery, including the slop bowl and the sugar tongs, were brought out and used. The best tablecloth was also in evidence and every cake plate had its frill of lace doyley coyly fluting the edges.

Before the tea and immediately afterwards, the sexes polarised, the men in one room and the women in the other if there were two rooms, the men round the fire and the women round the table if there was only one. Children were expected to amuse themselves quietly and not intrude on any adult conversation. If the company was very large, children were given their meals either after the adults or on a makeshift arrangement away from the main table.

When the women were together my mother had a certain cachet among them because she could read the cups and the cards. They took it all very seriously. For tea-cup reading the dregs were emptied slowly and carefully into the saucer, the cup turned upside down and turned three times clockwise while the person who was having her cup

A typical family party, this one at Uncle George and Auntie Lizzie's house in Second Row.

read made a wish. 'There's a letter here. I can't see who it's from. G. Would that be a surname? It's a bit off yet. Anyway, there's money in your cup. There might be a connection. There's a stranger here....'

Naturally these functions took a lot of preparation beforehand especially with regard to food all of which had to be made within forty-eight hours at most.

As these occasions also included supper, it was late when the gathering broke up. Children, who under normal circumstances would, by this time, be fast asleep in bed, found it hard to keep awake. Towards the end of the evening I found it very difficult, particularly at Aunt Martha's and Uncle Tommy's where, most often, there was only conversation by way of entertainment.

Sitting on the horse-hair sofa, the hum of voices became more individual and clear cut yet, at the same time, distorted. I was less aware of the little intermediate sounds. Then the voices and the furniture began to recede and I felt myself falling. I awoke with a sudden start then drifted off again till waking and drifting were both part of sleep.

'Wake up,' my mother said briskly. 'Don't go to sleep.

We're going home soon.' But it was impossible not to drift off again. This time I had to come a long way back to reach consciousness. After the warm room how cold it was outside! Fogged with sleep I felt chilled and pinched and miserable. I waited, stamping my feet while they said goodnight at the door. It took so long. There were things they'd forgotten to mention earlier. I ran ahead to the shelter of a doorway. Then we were together, a group, hunched up inside ourselves. The streets were almost deserted so that the footsteps of those still abroad could be heard in isolation. Moving from shadowy doorway to shadowy doorway, checking that all was well, were the dark forms of two policemen. They bade us 'goodnight' as we passed. The lamps swayed a little, moving the shadows. There, ahead of us, was home....and sleep.

Chapter 5

In Sickness. . . . .

I grew up with illness. My mother suffered from frequent attacks of what were then called sick headaches, later termed migraines. She went round carrying on with her work as long as she could, her face white, her eyes drawn so that it looked as though the skin between her eyes had been gathered together like the strings of a Dorothy bag. From the beginning I found her changed appearance worrying, even frightening. Sometimes she was forced to lie down when she told us to play quietly. When this happened and my father came home, he was always upset because there was nothing he could do to make her feel better.

When she could, my mother retired to the bedroom where the curtains were drawn against the light. Noise everywhere was kept to a minimum because 'it went through her head like a knife'. Her remedy was cloths wrung out in vinegar and water placed across her forehead. My guess is that this was a remedy used by the women in her family for many, many years. It was some years after we left 180 Station Road before Mother was able to get pills which gave her some measure of relief. These were called, as I remember, Fermagin, and cost eighteen shillings (90p) a bottle – a very great deal of money at that time.

My father also suffered, in his case in three ways. He had regular bilious attacks, sometimes called 'the bile'. His remedy for these was very strong, sugary tea and bicarbonate of soda. If he was not at work he sat up in the big armchair, his winter overcoat over his head so that no light penetrated. How he breathed I do not know, but apparently he couldn't lie in bed when he was thus afflicted. Every now and again he lowered his coat and his tousled head and sour expression appeared while he looked at the clock to see if he had to get ready to go to work. He never lost a day's work through illness of this sort. Of course we had to keep quiet. Mother, too, kept an eye on the clock till, finally, she would make a cup of strong tea, gently tap my father on the knee and say,

'Archie, drink this. It's time you were getting ready for work.'

Incidentally, in later years when the doctor told him it was imperative he give up smoking, the bilious attacks stopped altogether.

For neither of these two complaints of my parents was the doctor sent for.

Dad's other illnesses, however, were a different matter. He had been wounded in the war (World War One) when his ankle was shot away and he had been in a gas attack. He suffered from periodic attacks of bronchitis and, when he was upwards of fifty, emphysema. Each autumn, as the days began to shorten, Mother turned her thoughts to 'seeing him through the winter', when she prepared the first of her cough bottles, which preparation Dad took till spring came round again. The principal ingredient of this medicine was Store (C.W.S.) black bullets (sweets).

When he became ill, his suffering was painful indeed both to him and to those who watched. Every snorting breath was slow and agonising so that one was aware of its torturous journey from some remote place inside his being. And when the air was finally expelled the harrowing process began in reverse as new air was gasped in. Looking at him and sitting up with him at night, as we sometimes did, we feared for his life. Indeed, my mother was told, more than once, that he would not recover. In fact he lived till he was almost eighty.

His other illness was the result of his ankle injury. At first it was decided that his foot would have to come off but, happily, it was saved. Often he was in great pain which seemed especially bad when it seized him during the night. Not all the shrapnel had been taken out of his leg and, in later years, some pieces came to the surface and had to be removed. He spent two fairly lengthy periods in a military hospital where he saw people who suffered a great deal more than he. One was a man who spent all his life in a cradle. He had lost both his arms and his legs.

Indeed, my father's friend, Tommy Dodds, had fared worse than Dad. They had been great friends from school days and both had enlisted during the war, as a result of which, Tommy was now paralysed from the waist down

Tommy Dodds in his motorised spinal chair

and had to spend his days in bed. When he did go out, it was in a motorised spinal chair, provided by the coal company.

My brother was a fine, bonny lad who 'never had a day's illness'. He did, however, suffer from whooping cough at the same time as I. While we were ill my father was on back shift and I recall his taking us, warmly wrapped up, to where they were mending the roads that we might breath in the smell of tar which was supposed to be good for whooping cough.

The common ailments among children were chicken pox, German measles, measles, whooping cough and mumps. They were regarded as an inevitable part of childhood and I had them all.

There were other almost inevitable, unpleasant ailments that had to be endured, especially in winter, among them, chilblains on hands and feet. They itched terribly and boracic acid and Snowfire Ointment, however liberally applied, did little to ease the complaint. Chapped hands and lips were other winter hazards which could be extremely painful. Mercifully, I did not suffer from either of these last two. Boys wearing short trousers suffered chapped knees and keens on their ankles, this last caused by socks getting wet and chafing the ankles.

Another complaint I never suffered from was ring-worm. This was a highly contagious, very unsightly and unpleasant ailment that usually manifested itself in the hair. As the name suggests, it was a round or oval patch. Individual hairs had to be pulled out of this area while the remainder of the hair was shaved off, this because the infection usually spread. The contagion was treated with salve, a mixture of vaseline and sulphur. The unfortunate patient, when cured, had to return to school with a shaven head. In boys this was not thought to matter so much, indeed there was little one could do for them, but girls usually wore a home-made cotton mob cap till the hair started to grow again.

Rickets was also a fairly common, severe childhood ailment, often, though not always, connected to malnutrition. Then, the cure was massage and exercise in plenty of fresh, country air and a diet rich in butter, milk and cod liver oil.

The philanthropic society who sent emissaries to schools to give footwear to needy children, also kept their eyes open for those who were undernourished. These children were sent to homes in the country and to hospitals.

Unlike Billy, I was a sickly child and I succumbed to the smallpox epidemic. I was sent to the isolation, or fever, hospital as it was then known, at that time situated at Pity Me on the banks of the Wansbeck. A red cross on the back and the front of our house would tell the world that we had a case of small pox and were still in quarantine. Children passing the door would hold their breath in case they got the 'smit' and died. (Perhaps some adults did too). Children also held their breath when the fever van (ambulance) passed for the same reason.

My parents and Billy had to be vaccinated. They were all quite ill for several days and painful scabs developed on the site of the injection. To indicate they had been vaccinated and to warn people not to touch the vaccinated area, each wore a red ribbon around the arm in question. It was thought that the result of a scab knocked off prematurely would be dire indeed.

Also, on my removal to hospital, the house had to be fumigated or disinfected. This was done two rooms at a time. All bedding and furnishings were disinfected by steam heat or baking. For this formaldehyde and Lysol were both used. When the room was fumigated all air vents were sealed, all cupboard doors opened and all drawers taken out so that their contents were exposed to the fumigation. Formalin or a sulphur candle was placed in the centre of the room and lighted after which the sealed room was left for four hours or longer (in the case of formalin), then all doors and windows were opened wide and left like that for twelve hours. When a sulphur candle was used, the room was left for twenty-four hours before it was aired. In extreme cases the walls were stripped and washed with lime. All furniture was scrubbed with a carbolic solution.

Because of an accident, I suffered from recurring blood poisoning after I came out of hospital and I was, for a time, very ill. The blood poisoning usually manifested itself in a succession of boils and abscesses and once, a carbuncle.

Boils and carbuncles were unsightly things, most often seen on adolescent boys and young men. Boils began as a red pimple and gradually grew in size to a cone with a point on top. They were painful and had to be bathed constantly with very hot water. When they were 'ripe' they burst. After all the pus had gone, one had to get the core out otherwise another boil would grow on the same site. In fact, whether the core came out or not, it was more than likely there would be other boils for they came in crops, probably because the victim was reinfected from the seat of the original boil.

Carbuncles covered a wider area, had several heads and they were much more painful. Often these had to be lanced by the doctor in his surgery (doctors did minor surgery then), or at the out-patients department of a hospital. Usually the patient felt ill and was subject to bouts of shivering and feverishness, but it was rare he stayed off work on that account. The remedy for boils and carbuncles was either an iron tonic or quinine. At that time, quinine was taken for quite a number of illnesses.

In my case, I also had hot fomentations and hot poultices applied to my afflicted arms and legs. Hot poultices, which had to be changed fairly frequently, were used to bring inflamation to a head, to bring down inflamation or to ease pain. This last was probably psychological. It wasn't so much that the pain was eased, it was rather that the hot poultice provided the greater discomfort. Also, the thought that a poultice might be applied tended to make the sufferer reappraise the pain being undergone; it wasn't quite as bad as was first thought. The very sight of a poultice being prepared had the 'invalid' calling out 'Ooh! Oh! Ah!' in agony before the remedy even touched him.

The main poultices were bread, linseed (i.e. crushed linseed), sugar and soap, mustard and bran. The commodity chosen was mixed with boiling water, the water poured off and the very hot residue put on a piece of calico, the side being placed next to the skin smeared with cold cream to stop it from sticking, and the result slapped on top of the inflamation or pain site, covered with something woollen and the whole kept in place by a bandage.

A hot fomentation was used to draw a boil or abcess or to relieve pain. The lint or flannel was wrung out in boiling water, placed on the affected area and held in place by a bandage.

The lint often dried when it was pulled quickly off the sore, a very painful experience but all part of the cure. Usually salve was then applied. This ointment came in a box made of soft, pliant wood. In no time at all, not only did the box become very greasy to the touch, everything anywhere near become similarly affected. The rough side of a cabbage leaf placed on the affected part was a less painful way of trying to draw a boil. Plasters, already made up, consisted of a main ingredient such as belladonna, mustard, mercury, opium or menthol in a base of soap or oil. They were warmed first, either before the fire or by being held against a jug of boiling water. These plasters were not only placed on boils, they were used on the chests of those suffering bronchial complaints and on the breasts of nursing mothers to regulate their secretion of milk. Every dressing needed a bandage, some of which were used over and over again after washing. Sometimes clean rags were used instead of bandages.

In addition to the poultices, hot fomentations and salves I was given medicine which always tasted nasty. We were given to understand that the nastier the medicine tasted, the more good it was doing. When the time came for me to be dosed I would clench my teeth and shake my head, deaf to pleas and promises of making me better and the blackmail of a sweet to follow. Sometimes in desperation my nose was held and when I opened my mouth for air, the medicine was poured in and my jaws firmly closed till I'd swallowed it.

For lesser ailments and for bottles (medicine), we went to the doctor's surgery. Our practitioners were Doctors McLean, Muir, McPhereson, McFarlane and McPhee, all Scotsmen, I hardly need add. Dr McLean, head of the practice, lived in one of the large detached red-brick houses at the end of Wansbeck Terrace near where the road turned off towards Sheepwash. He was a familiar figure who went about on a large, upright bicycle summer and winter. Also, summer and winter, as though it had been glued there, he had a drop on the end of his nose. As I grew older I used to wonder if he cultivated it to keep his patients' minds off their afflictions. He was a very kind and caring man in whom we had the utmost confidence. He spoke with a soft, slow Scottish accent.

The doctors had their surgery in the end house in Laburnum Terrace. One walked up the garden which, while not being regularly attended to, was none-the-less respectable, like a child whose face has been rubbed with a flannel in preference to the good wash which would have served him better. The front door was always open when the surgery was on. Once one had closed the second door which marked off the tiny hall-way, one was in the surgery proper, and very dark it was. One had to stand a few minutes getting accustomed to the gloom which wasn't easy because the décor was of a dull greyish brown. Definitely not a place for any kind of hilarity. In the brief interval, some officious patient (nearly always a woman) would tell the latest arrival where to sit and just when his or her turn was.

'Just sit down there, hinny. There's room if everybody moves up. That woman with the bairn at the end is next, then there's him and him and then me and then everybody on this side, then you.'

At her bidding everybody squashed along to make room on the form that ran the length of the longest wall, coughing and sneezing as they did so and generously allowing their germs to shower over everyone else like confetti.

Once used to the gloom, one was at liberty to take in the rest of the surgery. Facing the long wall was the business part. Central to it were two narrow, high Victorian desks. Usually two doctors were in attendance, one to each desk. To the right of the desks was a small room and to the left was the green painted dispensary. The wall in between was completely taken up with shelves on which were huge bottles with unpronounceable names written in gold lettering on the outside, while inside they were filled with liquids in jewel colours, red, green and pink. There were also large jars filled with pills in different colours and underneath drawers like those in the chemist's also labelled with strange names in gold lettering.

The patient who wasn't particular which doctor he or she got, was attended to sooner than expected because one or two people were waiting to see 'the other' doctor. After the doctor had called 'next', the afflicted went up to the desk and in full view and hearing of all those present avid to learn why one was wasting the doctor's time, he or she stumbled through symptoms which, no doubt, did not seem as bad as they had been when the decision to go to the doctor's had first been made.

Those whom the doctor felt should be examined were taken to the little room at the side where there was a supplementary store of bottles already on view in the main surgery. There was also a brown leather couch and a trolley laid out with instruments at which one tried not to look and an antiquated gas fire which managed to burn with a great deal of hissing, the energy this took no doubt preventing it from giving out any heat. I must always have paid my visits there in the dead of winter because, after I'd removed my muffler, hat, coat, woollies and other layers of clothing, I was chilled to the bone.

After the consultation it was usual to wait for the dispenser to put up the medicine. This meant going back to the form, eyes glued to the little hatch waiting for it to open and the dispenser's disembodied head and hands to appear and call one's name and hand out the bottle, pills or ointment.

It was generally thought that if one got a bottle which had to be shaken so that white powder was suspended in the liquid, then one had stomach trouble; a thick brown 'bottle' meant chest trouble; a red 'bottle' anaemia; a green 'bottle' the doctor wasn't sure but it was serious; a blue 'bottle' – if the doctor knew he wasn't telling!

Usually, if men were in the surgery it was because they were on Loygeorge (sickness benefit – Lloyd George) and needed a note. We, as a family, were in the care of these excellent doctors because my father had threepence a week taken off his pay check. This threepence (1¼p) was shared between the hospital and the practice.

Not everyone went to see the doctor or called him in. There were many who could boast they'd never had the doctor in their lives. Some of these had no need of a doctor, others diagnosed their own illnesses and that of their near and dear, relying on remedies in which they had great faith.

Most people expected to have something wrong with them somewhere most of the time. Coughs and colds were prevalent. As few people stayed off work for a cold it was perhaps natural that they were widespread. Indeed, we all expected to have colds and coughs, especially in winter. Summer colds were not unknown. These were supposed to be worse than winter colds, possibly because they came when they shouldn't have done.

The trouble was that colds, not serious in themselves, could lead to something much worse such as bronchitis or pneumonia. It behoved the person with a cold to do his or her best to get rid of it.

Among the many recognised cures for coughs and colds both in children and adults were, rubbing the chest with goose grease, camphorated oil or wintergreen, soaking the feet in mustard and hot water and having eucalyptus oil sprinkled generously on one's handkerchief. Those children who did not possess handkerchiefs had to go round with 'candles' which they sniffed up from time to time. Others attempted to dry their sodden handkerchiefs out on the school pipes. Even worse, I think, was the child with a cold who had a handkerchief pinned to his or her person that he or she might not lose it.

To ward off colds, some children, including me, had their chests enveloped in Thermogene, a sort of pink cotton wool heavily impregnated with strong smelling substance that generated a great deal of heat. When it was taken off to be replaced, the skin thus exposed was as pink as the Thermogene itself. Some children wore a small muslin bag containing a block of camphor round their necks.

The cures for coughs were, swallowing a mixture of butter and sugar periodically, sucking a piece of hard Spanish liquorice and, for a tickly cough, drinking vinegar and sugar.

For sore throats, some people put their faith in an old sock, preferably unwashed, wrapped around the neck. Sulphur was blown from a paper bag into the throat of the patient. Glycerine was taken to ease not only sore throats, but those of singers and public speakers.

For adults, the recognised cure for all coughs and colds was hot toddy taken as often as was thought necessary.

Today the health-consicous person has a shelf full of vitamin pills and food supplements together with a neat First Aid kit. Then, somewhere in the cupboard or pantry, there was an old shoe-box, slightly greasy, full of half-used medicaments garnered by the woman of the house who, among her other duties, had the care of the household's health. Her medical lore included the use of arnica and comfrey leaves for the relief of sprains, bruises and rheumatism. Rubbing butter, or butter and sugar, on a bruise was a more common remedy as was steak for a black eye, while some still kept leeches to suck out the bad blood from a bruise. Zambuk was used for cuts and grazes. Those who suffered from arthritis and rheumatism were advised to drink cod liver oil daily to oil their joints. For the rest, there were smelling salts and sal volatile for faintness, dandelion tea and nettle tea for anaemia, castor oil and salts from the chemist for worms, bicarbonate of soda for a bad stomach and nettle beer for kidney trouble. Keetings

Powder was used to get rid of bugs and other unwelcome visitors.

To save time and energy and a visit to the doctor, some people put all their faith in one cure-all. Uncle Will (Wooler) took castor oil for everything. He didn't bother with a spoon, he drank it from the bottle. Incidentally, medicine bottles then were graduated in relief down one side to indicate the dosage.

Castor oil was also high on the list of cure-alls for children. It cleared the blood and kept the bowels open, wide open. Other bowel openers were senna tea, gregory powder and liquorice and slippery elm. Adults seemed to have greater faith (or more likely, found them more palatable) in salts, Epsom, Enos Fruit, Kruschen or Andrews Liver. With Seidlitz Powders (one blue, one white) not only were they bowel openers, they were the antidote for being 'off the crooks', 'all egg shells', 'right shabby' or 'bonny and hard up' all euphemisms for not feeling well. Beecham's Pills (worth a guinea a box) and Bile Beans were common aperients used regularly by adults.

When Uncle Jack felt 'off the crooks' or had a bilious attack he had one way of dealing with it.

'I get up and force myself to eat a big breakfast, bacon, eggs, fried bread, the lot, and then I starve myself till I feel better. It always works.'

Other cure-alls were garlic syrup (when those who drank it were advised to chew parsley afterwards to ward off the bad breath), Milk of Magnesia and Snowfire powders.

Those thought to be tubercular were advised to go out in the early morning, find a snail and swallow it.

A general tonic was egg white beaten stiff added to which were two teaspoonfuls of brandy and a pinch of sugar. Spring medicine, taken to get rid of the poisons accumulated during winter, was made up of two lemons, some cream of tartar, as much Epsom salts as would cover a sixpence and boiling water allowed to cool.

To bolster what was termed a weak constitution I was regularly dosed with Virol, cod liver oil and malt and Parish's Chemical Food, all of which were considered tonics. Chemical Food was rather nice to take, but it contained iron which was said to rot the teeth.

'If it rots me teeth what,' I tearfully wanted to know, 'will it do to my inside?'

Among the very serious illnesses which often resulted in the death of the victim were diphtheria, the fevers, rheumatic, scarlet, enteric, typhus and typhoid and consumption (TB).

'Well now, Aa've been right shabby. Not that Aa'm complaining. It wouldn't do any good if Aa did. Not a soul came near to say 'How are ye?' So Aa just got on with it. Did ye hear tell the Smith's lass got away on Saturday. Poor soul. Aa saw her in the Store just before Christmas. She had a church-yard cough (TB) if ever Aa heard one. And thin! No more than flesh and bone. Aa said then she might last till the summer but Aa had me doubts. And Aa've been proved right. Eh dear. Take care of yourself and wrap up well. Aa know the nights is gettin' longer but we're not through the wood yet an' you're not gettin' any younger. Just think on. None of your lot's ever made old bones that Aa mind on. Not one has lived to a decent age. An' ye know what they say. A green Christmas makes a full church-yard. Aa've never known a greener nor last year. Well. Aa'll have to be off. Aa've enjoyed your crack. Mind what Aa say an' take care. Ye have a right shabby look.'

During long illnesses the doctor was a regular and very important visitor. The patient was freshened up, the bed and the room made to look tidy and the woman who was doing the nursing felt constrained to change into a clean pinny. Both patient and nurse would be on their best behaviour, the former who might have been fractious and groaning in agony before, putting a brave face on his/her illness.

Once, after the death and funeral of a middle-aged friend, I went with her son whom I shall call Tom, to thank those who had helped her during her last illness. Tom had moved away from his home area.

We came to the last port of call, a young couple who had just moved into the district and who were, virtually, next-door neighbours. Tom thought it politic to tell them he was going back to his digs and to leave his address in case they needed to get in touch. It was a Sunday evening. He was wearing his best clothes (and he was in mourning), black homburg hat, dark tailored overcoat, white shirt, dark suit.

A tousle-haired woman, dressed in a pinny, opened the door to our knock. She didn't open it far. When she saw my friend standing there she gave an audible gasp that developed into a shriek as she shut the door hurriedly. The door opened straight onto the kitchen and we could not avoid hearing frenzied activity. Presently the door opened again and the young woman, now very subdued, had smoothed her hair into some sort of order and removed her pinny.

'Come in,' she said respectfully.

We went in to a sort of *tableau vivant*. In the corner was a bed with the top sheet smoothed. In the bed was a young woman looking somewhat flushed and cradling a very young child. A young man still damp and glistening from a hasty rub over with a wet flannel and an even hastier attempt at combing his hair, sat bolt upright in a Windsor chair, the cushion of which, struggle though it might, could not cover the recent influx of papers and magazines it was its duty to hide. The woman who had let us in stood uncertainly by the fireplace. I thought she was undecided whether or not to curtsey. Except for the baby, they looked as one towards my friend.

'Good evening,' he said soberly. 'I hope I haven't called at an inconvenient time, but I shall be leaving tomorrow and I thought it best to leave my address in case, for any reason, you want to get in touch with me.'

The two women looked at each other in bewilderment. The man tried to look as if he wasn't there. Then, finally,

'Oh,' said the woman who had let us in, 'where?'

'Back to Gloucester.'

'Gloucester!'

'Yes. I came up for the funeral.'

'Funeral?'

'Yes. My mother's.'

'Yer not – ' began the woman who'd let us in in disbelief, 'yer can't be. Ye mean yer not the doctor?'

'No,' he said.

Visibly the starch inside the two women crumbled and they were left with cotton wool.

'Well,' said the woman in bed. 'Well I never. D'ye hear that?' she said, looking across at the man, 'It's not the doctor.'

'Eh!' he said, pulling at the tie that was obviously choking him.

'Ee,' she went on, 'Mary made sure ye were the doctor come to see me and the bairn. He was only born last week. We weren't at the funeral. We thought fancy him coming on a Sunday and us like this and you're not him. What a turn you gave us. I was sitting up with me hair in curlers. I had to get them out, give me face a bit rub and lowp into bed. He had to tidy hissell up and put a tie on and wor Mary tidied up. An' aal for nowt,' and she laughed.

Among the minor ailments for which we did not seek the advice of the doctor were earache and toothache, both of which seem to have been more prevalent then than now. In the case of the former, to ease the pain warm olive oil was placed in the ear and, against that, a thick pad of some material which had been previously heated. The patient's head was then swathed in a thick woollen scarf to keep the pad in place and keep out the cold.

Gumboils (which, for some reason, were regarded as funny when one became the butt of jokes – 'Fill your mouth with warm water and sit over the fire till it boils') were also more prevalent then. For both toothache and gumboils the affected area was rubbed with oil of cloves and then kept warm as for earache. For the gumboil, the pain subsided when it burst. Toothache usually merited a trip to the dentist. Generally speaking, the toothache started in the middle of the night and had gone by the time the dentist opened his doors, but there was no reprieve. When the offending tooth had been removed, the patient could be seen coming out of the surgery pale of face and swaddled about the head in the inevitable thick muffler which covered the mouth. Between the mouth and the muffler the edges of a blood-soaked handkerchief were visible that all might see how the afflicted had suffered. Indeed, coming out of the dentist's thus muffled was almost obligatory.

Neuralgia, from which my mother suffered, was also very painful but very little could be done to ease the situation other than give a nerve tonic and keep the patient as warm as possible. In my mother's case, she took quinine and put hot fomentations against her face to act as a counter-irritant. In the end it was decided all her teeth would have to come out.

Generally speaking, the only reason one visited the dentist was to have a tooth extracted. It cost two and six (12½p). When my mother-in-law went to have a tooth extracted when she was young, there were two prices, one with cocaine, the other with nothing at all. She had to have the cheaper extraction. It was an experience she never forgot.

Regular dental hygiene for children was in its early stages. Many young people had had all their teeth out by the time they were in their early twenties. Thereafter they had to go round toothless for some three months to allow the gums to harden. In the early stages they ate only soft milky foods (pap) and broth.

Dentures had to be paid for. Often this lengthened the period of toothlessness. One young man repeatedly saved up to buy these necessary appurtenances but when he had the required sum he could not resist having a night out on the beer to celebrate with the result that, yet once more, the saving had to start again. As far as I know, he never did get his teeth till the National Health Service played Santa to him in this respect. Another man managed so well without his teeth, he kept his dentures in a glass on the scullery window sill most of the time, only wearing them at weekends when he went out dressed. Even then he took his teeth out to eat. And I remember hearing of one man whose gums were being hardened off passing a tomato to a friend equipped with teeth and saying, 'How lad, start this off ferriz.'

When milk teeth had to come out, the extraction was done at home. One method was to tie the tooth to a door handle by means of thread. When the door was closed sharply, the tooth came out. Instead of closing the door, some took a shovel of burning coals and pushed it towards the child's face, so that he/she stood back sharply thereby losing the tooth. I never ever heard of the tooth fairy and, certainly, neither Billy nor I were given any sort of compensation for the loss of a tooth. It was just part of life.

Among the chemists in Ashington was Mr Cawthorne, a man of many parts, indeed, some might have thought of him as a benefactor. He extracted teeth and sold a special black 'bottle' reputed to be effective against unwanted pregnancies. A modest notice also informed the initiated that he sold rubber goods.

Also concerned with the health of Ashington's population was the herbalist, Mr Billy Hume of High Market. He had a considerable following.

Illness in the house was the woman's affair. For those who read magazines and other journals there was a great deal written about sick nursing in the home. Housewives were expected to be competent nurses able to add the duties of the sick-room to all their other duties.

Ideally, the sick-room was isolated from the rest of the house, a very difficult thing to do when large families lived in small accommodation. If the illness was infectious then a sheet soaked in disinfectant was suspended over the entrance to the room, all mats were removed and the floor scrubbed with disinfectant. All cutlery and crockery used by the patient had to be washed in carbolic. Chloride of lime was used liberally in the disinfecting of bedclothes and the clothes worn by the patient. (Even today, when I smell chloride of lime, I am immediately back in the isolation hospital.)

Almost every cookery book of the day devoted a section to invalid cookery. In it, the writer expressed the importance of serving meals daintily and regularly to patients and stressed the inadvisability of asking them what they wanted to eat beforehand. In their weakened state, it was unlikely the patients would know. It was, therefore, better to stick to what the doctor ordered.

Milk (always boiled) was the all-important food especially when it was made into dishes that also contained arrowroot, cornflour or ground rice. The popular dishes (not necessarily from the patient's point of view) were, gruel, (milk and oatmeal), boiley (milk, bread and sugar), curds and whey (junket), beef tea, oatmeal tea, chicken broth, lightly cooked eggs, raw meat juice, steamed fish, toast soaked in hot water, boiled tripe, lentils, barley water, soda water and the jellies, beef, calves' foot, lemon and chicken. In preparing these dishes, a great deal of cooking, pounding and straining was called for. All food had to be served up at body temperature because it was thought that cold food had to be heated in the stomach before digestion could begin.

In these days of instant mashed potatoes, instant coffee and the answer to erstwhile laborious long division sums given in micro seconds at the touch of a button it is difficult to appreciate the length of time illnesses lasted and the repetitive, exacting work they entailed at a very anxious time.

Long illnesses were followed by a long convalescence. The patient got better by slow degrees, sitting up in bed followed by being wrapped up and sitting up in a chair for gradually increasing periods then, finally, coming downstairs for short stays which lengthened as the patient got stronger.

Normally, bedrooms were like Greenland for eleven months of the year but, in the case of severe illness very often a fire was lit which, of course, added to the nurse's duties. I only once remember having a fire in the bedroom and I thought I must be dying.

There were two sorts of pneumonia, pneumonia and double pneumonia. The former meant that only one lung was affected, the latter two. Both had a crisis. This invariably seemed to happen in the middle of the night. Crisis point was near when neighbours were able to tell each other, 'They're sitting up at night with him/her now.' When the patient passed through the crisis it meant he or she was on the long road to recovery. Death was the other alternative. My maternal grandfather died of pneumonia at the age of thirty-four. My paternal grandfather also fell victim to the illness. He was what was termed 'a man's man'. He liked his whisky, his beer, his flutter on the horses as well as everything else synonymous with masculinity. As he lay ill, he decided to reform if he got better (so I'm told). He did get better but the decision to reform must have been part of his delirium.

Fairly long stays in hospitals or sanitoria were relatively common. When a relation or friend was in either institution food and drinks (barley water) were taken in rather than flowers, unless the flowers came from someone's garden when they were an added gift. The most popular food were eggs (marked with the patient's name in pencil) fruit and small home-made cakes or sandwiches.

Hospital discipline was much more rigid then. Beds had to be lined up, locker tops cleared and counterpanes smoothed into the accepted pattern for the daily visit of the matron or doctor. Visiting times were shorter and the rule of not more than two visitors to a bed was strictly adhered to.

Sanitoria were cold places. Usually the patients there suffered from consumption (TB) when the regime was abundant fresh air and abundant nourishing food, plenty of milk, cream, butter, fat bacon, suet, bread, calves' foot jelly, eggs and cod liver oil.

Like many girls of my generation I had no preparation for the discomfort which would be mine during the greater part of my working life. I knew *something* happened but beyond that I could not get. Some months before I left school, one of my friends was absent. When she returned after two days, naturally we asked, 'What was the matter?'

'I haven't to talk about it,' she replied soberly and somewhat depressed, 'but, from now on I haven't to get my feet wet and sometimes I won't be able to do Games.' And there the matter ended. It was a Mystery. From then on, she regularly had a day's absence, the reason for which could not be divulged.

After I started work, one day I went over to the cloakroom set aside for female staff. When I opened the door I saw a girl, white faced and in obvious distress, leaning over the huge iron radiator so that her abdomen lay on the hot pipe. Two friends, very much concerned for her, were standing near. They could do no more than offer sympathy and the news that, in a few hours, she would be home.

'What's the matter?' I asked.

'She's got the curse. She's always like this the first day,' they said.

'How long have I been here?' the suffering girl asked.

'Just ten minutes,' her friend replied.

'I'll have to go,' she said. 'I'll have been missed.'

Little bit by little bit I acquired a vague motion of what

81

the curse was. (It was so called because it was supposd to be a curse on Eve, and subsequently all women, because she ate the forbidden fruit.) It was about half-past-ten on a Sunday morning when, having gone to the toilet, I saw drops of blood. I didn't go to church, saying I didn't feel too well. Throughout the day I tried and better tried to tell my mother what had happened. When we were alone and the opportunity offered, I had not the words; when I thought I'd worked out what I was going to say, there were others present.

We were clearing the supper table, both in the pantry, when I muttered, 'When I was across the road, I saw some blood.'

'Oh,' said Mother, 'then I'd better tell you –'. I thought she was embarrassed but, possibly, what I saw was my embarrassment projected onto her.

'I – I know all about it. It's all right,' I said.

'Oh,' replied Mum. 'Come upstairs, then, and I'll get you something.'

And there began and ended my sex education. My ignorance in that field was abysmal.

Thereafter I suffered absolute misery and discomfort on the first day. It was something that had to be endured. At no time did I lose any time at work. As my periods were erratic to begin with I couldn't make sufficient preparation and was often caught out at work. White-faced, heavy in body and spirit, enduring as best I could a pain which is like no other pain, I got through the day. Finally I carried round with me the necessary protection and a packet of Veganin, the most effective pain killer I knew.

One morning, in the second winter of the war, on a bitter day of snow and ice, I set off for work having detected the early signs of my imminent 'visitor', a heavy sluggishness in my body, the beginnings of a headache and a marked feeling of depression. I had already had two Veganin.

'Here,' said my mother, 'take this,' and she handed me a flask of hot Ovaltine. 'Have it with two more pills at about half-past ten. It will keep you going till dinner time and the hot drink will make the pills act faster.'

At ten o'clock I stood in my Dickensian office under-the-stairs from whose black pipes no heat, as yet, emanated. I was doing the invoices, standing at the sloping side of the high Victorian desk. The effects of my earlier dose of Veganin was beginning to wear off. Thankfully I poured out a thermos-capful of the steaming Ovaltine preparatory to taking my tablets. I took an appreciative sip of the hot liquid to test its temperature and, as I did so, the Boss came into the office.

'Miss,' he said. 'What's this I see? Drinking when you should be working?'

'I'm still working,' I began.

'No,' he replied. 'You're not. You cannot do two things. You are paid to work, not to drink. Now pour that back into the flask and get on with your job, and, just in case you're tempted again, I'll take the flask with me and give it you before you go home.'

I did as I was told. He was not a hard man, nor an unkind man, but Rules were Rules. In no way could I have told him why I wanted the drink. Nor was he affected by my white face or the temperature in which I worked.

Ashington Coal Company's float for the hospital Carnival Week.

Considering the climate of the day, I thought we did very well in Ashington for medical care. I was never afraid of the doctor, nor did I resent my stay in hospital, perhaps the most unpleasant part of which was the sickness one felt

83

when coming round after an operation.

On the whole, when we went to the doctor's surgery, we had simple things, or we thought of them as simple, wrong with us, chesty cough, beat back, stomachache, spots, chill on the kidneys. We expected the doctor to do something about it in the shape of a bottle, some pills or some salve/ointment.

The doctor was always on hand. There were very few telephones. When the doctor was needed one had to go to his house on foot to request him to come and he always did. When we needed to go to the surgery we just went and waited. The surgery didn't close till all patients had been dealt with.

Many people lived into their eighties, some of my relatives among them. Two of my male relatives asked that I might go and see them before they died. In both cases their dignity and presence of mind was greater than mine. In bidding me 'Goodbye' both shook hands with me, gave me a blessing and wished me well. Very unfortunately, there was nothing I could say I reply.

Chapter 6

. . . . . and in Health

Playtime for children was not a right, it was a privilege given after one had fulfilled one's responsibilities. These last were usually domestic chores, messages (errand-going), or, in some cases, school homework. Usually the time allowed for play was specified. 'You can go out for half an hour.' It was the council clock that rang the curfew on lots of our games.

The strictures were more likely to be on girls than on boys. Boys usually went out earlier and stayed out longer. In fact, boys went 'out' as soon as they could and, very often, over-worked mothers were glad to see them go. They were noisy and, if there was a big family, the kitchen was full and the children would have to eat in relays when the boys would be served first.

We took the actual 'playing out' for granted, once we were outside, not realising how precious was the freedom we had to play in the streets, or even wander further afield, say to the park. This was especially true in winter in the 'dark nights'. We were not taken to the Store classes, the Brownies, Cubs or Guides, nor were we collected there-from. Our parents did not worry about what might happen to us on the way there or back. Nor did we appreciate freedom of another sort, the freedom, perhaps born of necessity, to use our imagination when playing. And, of course, there was the freedom of being able to play in the streets. Traffic then was much lighter and slow moving. Indeed, at nights there was very little traffic in the back rows and streets.

There were skates, scooters, tricycles and children's bicycles but few had them. Those who had skates probably only had one. A large toy, such as a scooter or a bicycle, was often shared between siblings. Most often those who had bicycles got them for winning the scholarship to the grammar school.

This bicycle, however small the child, was an adult bicycle which, when the seat was lowered to its utmost extremity, was sometimes still too big. Then wooden blocks were screwed onto the pedals. Bikes were grown into just as clothes were. Some children rode men's bikes through the cross-bar i.e. they passed the right leg under the cross-bar and rode in this lop-sided fashion without benefit of a seat to sit on. The cheapest bicycle cost about £5, for most, at least two weeks wages. The most popular were Raleighs and Rudge-Whitworths.

A boy with a pocket full of marbles, among which was at least one penker, a top and whip and a pack of tab (cigarette) cards was sufficiently well equipped for any number of games with his contemporaries. Marbles consisted of 'chalkies', the most commonly used, 'glass alleys' thought to be rather effeminate, and penkers, known as 'killers'. A prize penker was known as a three hole killer. It was so strong it could actually break other marbles when it cannoned into them. Some boys did not allow penkers in their games. It was a common sight to see boys playing marbles in the gutters on the way to school. If, as sometimes happened, a boy was playing with a penker and it fell down a drain, he lifted the cover, put his hand down into the drain and fished about till he found his precious marble.

Tab cards were used in a game where the participants flicked their cards towards a central point. Any card flicked in such a way that it merely touched another card allowed the owner to pick up his card and the card that had been touched. Cards were also collected to form a specific collection in a particular series so that some cards were kept specially for swaps.

Some boys still had gourds (hoops) although these were not as popular as they had been.

Those boys who owned a cricket bat and a ball were fortunate. They found themselves rich in friends who wanted to join them in a game of cricket when they, the owners of the bats and balls, could expect to be both captain and umpire. As umpire, his decision not to put himself out when batting went unquestioned. To question it meant he would go home taking his bat and ball with him. Few had stumps. These were easily catered for and were usually chalked up on any convenient wall or door. The boy

In the garden at 16 Ashbourne Crescent. Jack Tocher with Mother, John, Charles and Billy.

who owned a real leather football was similarly fortunate. In this case, two largish stones or two piles of discarded outer garments did duty as goal post.

Other games played outdoors by boys were, 'Moont the cuddy' (High Cockalorum) and 'Jack shine yer low' (light). This game, a type of 'Hare and Hounds' was played on dark, winter nights when one boy (girls played too sometimes) was allowed time to run off, carrying with him a shaded light, usually a candle in a jam jar.

Duck stones (a stone placed on top of a mound to be knocked off) knocking down cans (row of cans placed on top of a wall to be knocked down), Hare and Hounds, French cricket (using legs as stumps and a soft ball) and Hot Rice were all games one could play with the minimum amount of equipment. When a game got out of hand or, in the case of football or cricket, when the person with the ball went home, then the others banded together and walked round singing, 'Billy Billy Buck, the game's broke up,' after which they all went home or decided on another game. Usually for girls, if a game got out of hand, say tiggy (tag) or hide and seek, a few who felt this to be the case shouted, 'All in. All in,' when those taking part came back to base and the game was discontinued.

Most girls' games were singing games. I never saw the words of singing games written down yet, in common with others of my age, I knew them all by the time I was old enough to 'join in'. The words for nearly all games were on one theme, the getting and marrying of a young man.

The two essentials for a girl were a skipping rope and a good stotty (bouncing) ball. Most also had a top and whip. The skipping rope could be a bought one with painted handles, but it rarely was. The best ropes were those that had been cut from the end of a clothes line, particularly a line that had been used for some time. A short rope was used by a girl skipping alone but long ropes were most common.

Just as singing games were played all year round, so were hitchy dabber bays (hopscotch) and ball games. For hitchy dabber bays it was handy to have a piece of chalk, but not necessary. If one had a piece of chalk then the bays could be marked out on a concrete surface, other than that, one girl took a sharp stone or something similar and drew out the bays on an unmade road.

The most popular games played with stotty balls (the best of which came from Woolworth's and cost sixpence – 2½p) were 'Piny' and the game where one had to go through a series of actions while stotting (bouncing) the ball. 'Piny' was played on a gable end.

'Five Stones' or 'Chucks' could be played with an ordinary bouncing ball, but a small one was better. Usually this was played with girls sitting on the kerb-side. 'Five Stones' could be bought, but most just picked up small stones from the road side. As the ball bounced the stones had to be picked up in turn.

Although most children played in the rows and back streets some boys did play in the main street when they hung on to the backs of moving carts. The idea was to get on when the driver wasn't looking and hang there by the fingers, feet up on the back of the spring or any other convenient protrusion, for as long as possible. The driver would shout at them to 'gerroff' and sometimes even use his whip, for it was a dangerous game they played. The winner was the boy who held on longest and went the farthest. A similarly dangerous game was 'last over' in front of cars and buses. It was played so often there was a warning on the backs of the red exercise books we bought at Woolworth's and other shops 'DO NOT PLAY LAST ACROSS ANY ROAD OR STREET'.

We did not always play out. This was especially true of the worst winter weather and when one was convalescent after an illness or one had a cold. I never found evenings spent at home dull. Like my father and my brother, I was reader and, if nothing else presented itself, my having read my own books and Billy's till I knew them by heart, I could always ask for a book out of the book-case, most of which were very dull to my young eyes, but they did have pictures and conversation bits.

Reading while someone else was working was almost a crime. Work-wise, it was rare that there was absolutely nothing to do in a house so that one had to be prepared to stop reading to do an errand, 'Linda, just run upstairs and get my slippers', 'Just stop what you're doing for a minute and lay the cloth. Your father will be in in a minute and if he sees the cloth on the table he thinks the meal is ready!' 'Just bring in that shovel of coals, the one standing underneath the one on top of the pail furthest away from the back door.' 'While you're doing nothing (Doing nothing! I was sobbing my heart out, if they but knew it, with Beth lying there stricken with scarlet fever and likely to die) just wind some wool for me. You can hook it over those two chairs.' I soon learned that the quickest way to get back to the book was to do what I was told as speedily as possible and without any fuss. Complaining got me nowhere, kept me away from my books all the longer and upset the atmosphere. Even today I read as one divided, part of me deep in the story, but an even greater part alert to what is going on around.

Often we were invited to play in someone else's house. When this happened we usually took a board game with us. We had to play quietly. During the week the kitchen was the focal point of activity in nearly all the houses we knew, thus we had to consider there were other people present.

Apart from Guides, Scouts, Brownies and Cubs there were a number of other things to which young people could belong among them the 'Sons and Daughters of Temperance' where one was expected to sign the pledge, i.e. promise to abstain from drinking alcoholic liquor throughout one's life, the 'King's Messengers' and the 'Band of Hope'.

There were also the lantern lectures, usually about missionaries or wild life. I wasn't wildly enthusiastic about either, but they were free and there were pictures. The best lantern lecture I ever attended was the one where a young lad from the Hirst secreted one of his father's banties (bantams) into the lecture hall under his jersey. He released the banty from its prison just after the lights went out before anyone had got used to the dark. It was difficult to tell who made most noise, the frenzied banty or the shaken women. It took nearly all night to catch the banty and calm the womenfolk down. As the lecture was free, there was no question of anyone demanding money back, but people from near hand brought in some tea. They said that from the noise they thought the Last Trump had sounded for the Primitives. The lad concerned got a hiding from his father, with the pit belt. It was every bit as bad as he expected. It was a prize banty and the father said the lad had given it the fright of its life and God alone knew what harm had been caused it. From where I was (on the window-sill) it looked as if the banty was having the time of its life. 'Every dog has its day' they say. That banty certainly had its night.

Wash-house dramas were also a feature of childhood. Indeed, the first thing I ever wrote for public acclaim was a play to be performed in a friend's mother's wash-house, a building that had the edge on a telephone kiosk – just. The play depended on the costumes I could get. My friend, Mary, had been in a school play where she had taken the part of the king in a costume her mother had made from red crepe paper. The costume was somewhat skimpy because her mother refused to buy two rolls of paper saying there would be too much waste, one would have to do. Naturally, as it was her wash-house she had to have the best part. My mother wouldn't supply a costume so I had to go to Grannie Summers who gave me a bed valance. I tried it on behind the hen cree, that is, I wound it round and round my person.

'You look', said Lizzie, another friend who also wanted to be in the play, 'like a hula-hula dancer.'

As I had no idea what a hula-hula dancer was, I had to take her word for it. Of course, Lizzie who couldn't act for toffee apples, wanted to be the queen, clinching the part by saying her mam would see to it that she had a costume. So that left me the hula-hula dancer.

I wrote the play in the lavatory, the only place where one could get real peace and quiet. There was trouble from the start. The king said the hula-hula dancer had the best part and it was her wash-house. The queen said you couldn't call it acting lying on a cold floor in a wondrous daze catching her death. Also she didn't think her mam would like them words, they were strict Methodists. Mary's little sister, four years old, turned out to be a right pest. We put her out but she came back with her mam who said unless she was in the play we'd have to find another wash-house and while she was on about it, she wasn't going to make another costume and would we put the poss barrel back where we'd found it. So I had to put their Connie, the sister, in and make her a wicked varlet dressed in the mangle cover.

The play I wrote was about a king who had come home from the club somewhat the worse for wear. He'd had a row with the queen after which he'd fallen into a deep sleep and dreamed of a hula-hula dancer. The wicked varlet did her competent best to muck this up for him too.

The next night we got a bit of slate and chalked up, 'Play tonight. 2 pins to get in' and we propped it on the wash-house window sill. At half-past six Mary's mam came across to see that nothing happened to her wash-house. Lizzie's mam had lent her one of her old dresses that was split under the arm so she came to see that nothing more happened to the dress. Nobody even thought of paying the two pins. Mary forgot what her mother had said about not moving in the costume because she wanted to keep it for their Connie when she was made a king, the school wouldn't want to waste the costume. Anyway, Mary split her costume and her navy gym knickers ballooned through so she had to keep her hand on her behind after that.

Lizzie's mam wondered where I'd got all my ideas from considering we were supposed to be a good-living family, but, of course, we were Church, all right on Sundays when the vicar was there but the least said about the rest of the week, the better. She said the best part of the night was when Mary split her costume that was too small any way. Mary's mam said some folk would laugh at their grandmother's funerals and Lizzie's mam took the huff and took Lizzie away saying, 'You're not playing with them no more. I never heard such language in all me life.'

Mary's mam stayed till we had put the wash-house back to rights. I took the valance back to Grannie's.

'I took good care of it, Grannie,' I said.

'Ee, pet,' she said. 'It would have been all right. It's nearly ready for dusters anyway. Was the play all right?'

'Canny, I suppose,' I replied. 'But it didn't turn out the way I thought.'

'Aye,' she sighed. 'You'll have to get used to that.'

Money was scarce, but we were all in the same boat. A few children did get money for sweets during the week, but Billy and I were not among them. Nor were we among those who dashed into the house to get a slice of jam and bread to stave off the pangs. Eating between meals was liable to put us off the food offered at the table.

However, in common with most children, we did get a Saturday penny and what a choice we had before us. Sweet shops were just that. Most sweets, even bars of chocolate, were unwrapped, thus chocolate melted and boiled sweets stuck to their jars and to each other. They had to be prised apart with a 'steel' kept for that purpose and, as far as I could see, never washed. The main sweet shops for children were Orde's and Mossman's in High Market, Nixon's in Middle Market and, beyond that a number of ice-cream shops till, at the Grand Corner, next to Stanley Cook's, Armstrong's sweet shop.

Something else on which one could spend one's Saturday penny were Billy Stampers. These were transfers costing a half-penny a sheet to be stamped on arms, backs of hands or other appropriate area of flesh. One spit on the transfer, pressed it on to the flesh then peeled off the transfer to see how much remained. It took quite a bit of practice to get a perfect transfer. Other popular purchases, especially for boys, were caps for bombs and pistols.

Crazes of various sorts had their brief lives. Among those were the making of bead flowers. Tiny glass beads in all colours could be bought in half-pennyworths. Somehow we girls managed to get little boxes (usually pill boxes) in which to keep our store. With lengths of very fine wire we fashioned flowers and brooches.

When yo-yos were popular somehow everybody seemed to acquire one. It wasn't just a case of allowing the yo-yo to spin up and down, one had to be able to do all sorts of complicated moves.

Autograph albums also had their share of the limelight. I still have mine, one of Woolworth's best (nothing over sixpence), given to me at Christmas.

When it came to play children used what was available and improvised, using their imagination. An old tin and a spoon made very satisfactory mud pies. One woman I knew put an old sofa out into the yard to send to the sale rooms. She allowed her children to play on it till it was collected. When she saw the fun her children got out of it (a ship, a bus etc.), she couldn't let it go. At best, she said, she'd only get two shillings for it (10p).

Perhaps the common denominator between the world of childhood and that of adults was 'the pictures'. In all there were five picture halls in Ashington and Hirst, the Miners' Theatre (later the Regal cinema), the Buffalo, the Wallaw, the Pavilion and the Hippodrome, also known affectionately as the Hip or flea pit. There were regular penny matinées for children on a Saturday afternoon. I only ever attended once. This was no reflection on the matinée. It was during the time when I felt almost permanently below par with a persistent headache. I waited with the vast majority of Ashington's young population, an eager, restless body waiting for that moment of moments when the doors opened and Johnny Allen, the manager, stood to shepherd us in.

This would be a silent film, yet the noise in the cinema was deafening in spite of the presence of Mr Allen aforesaid who, when things got out of hand, was liable to stop the film and even put people out. For Saturday matinées, however, he allowed things to transcend the normal permitted noise level. For those who could afford it, bags of monkey nuts sustained the constitution of the committed picture goer who was anxious to finish his quota before the picture started. In those days monkey nuts came in shells which gave off a very satisfactory cracking sound. They could be hurled playfully at other picture goers, stamped and crunched underfoot and kicked. When the film started, the bad and the good were easily distinguishable as were the funny men. The good were loudly cheered, the bad were booed and hissed and the funny people were laughed at uproariously. To rise above all this the pianist had to play louder than ever. By the time I got home I was quite ill and the matinée was blamed and so I missed out on Tom Mix. I also missed out on the 'Talkies' which arrived at about that time.

Kate Gardiner often acted as relief pianist at the Piv (Pavilion) and she tells me that she could exchange places with the resident pianist, taking up the tune without a note ever being missed.

I was finally admitted to that knowledgeable sect, those who went to the pictures, some time after I started at Bedlington School. This was a treat indeed given for some co-operation on my part, probably for helping with the Spring cleaning coupled with the fact that it was my birthday. This film was *Rebecca of Sunnybrook Farm*. With my threepence clutched in my hand I ran all the way to the Buff to be there when the doors opened. What did it matter that, because I was a child and on my own, the usherette had directed me to the very front row so that, when the curtains parted and the entertainment began, I had to lean back to see the distorted and very large features of the gods and godesses paraded for my enchantment? No matter. I was there. I had joined the ranks of those who could say, 'I went to the pictures last night'. The plush seats, the plush and gilded décor, surely the epitome of high living, and the gathering audience, of whom I was one, all waiting to be transported to another world, was magic. That delicious moment when the lights dimmed, the curtains parted and the adverts began. We got a lot for threepence – Adverts, Pathé News, a travelogue, a 'B' picture and the big picture.

When *Rebecca of Sunnybrook Farm* ended, I was still lost in another world, my eyes wet with tears I had shed in the sad parts and those brought on by my laughter in the funny parts. The lights went up. Those who had come in late sat on. I did too, although I'd been given strict instructions to go home as soon as the first house ended. The girl came down the isle with her tray of chocolates and sweets. Of course, I had no money to buy any, nor did I take this amiss. I had done very well to get there.

The second house started. We were nearing the end of the 'B' film when a message written in white imposed itself over the action on the screen. 'If Linda Summers is in the house she has to go home now.' (They did that sort of thing then.) I got up and went, enveloped in the radiance of what I had just seen and with a new hero to worship, Ralph Bellamy. Now I could go to school and say, 'Did you see Ralph Bellamy in *Rebecca of Sunnybrook Farm?* Wasn't he marvellous?'

Quite a number of girls got the *Picture Goer* every week. We devoured everything the magazine said, avid for stories of the stars, every one of which we believed utterly.

Film Fan was another, less popular, magazine dedicated to the lives of the stars.

At the pictures, or flicks as we sometimes called them, all girls were beautiful. They had perfect teeth, lovely smiles, elegant figures, flawless hair and exquisite clothes. I hated it when the picture ended, their world demolished by the gunshot sounds of the tipping up of seats as everyone raced to the exit before the first note of the National Anthem sounded, only one foot out of the auditorium and you had to stay, both feet just on the other side and you could go.

The person who brought us news of the forthcoming attractions at the various cinemas was the bill-poster. He arrived with his curiously shaped, narrow, oblong bucket and long-handled, narrow brush to paste up the huge posters that decorated the boards outside the cinemas. Watching his deft movements was fascinating. He was an artist at his job.

A good film, such as *Rebecca*, would be shown for a week. Sometimes this was extended. The most popular picture nights were Wednesdays and Saturdays, but only on Saturdays were there two definite houses where the cinema was emptied after the first house. To be sure of a place at the second house on Saturday nights, it was better to book. The prices of admission were threepence (1¼p), sixpence (2½p) and ninepence (3¾p). Those who booked their seats paid a shilling (5p). There was usually a queue for both houses on a Saturday night. It was a friendly crowd that waited for the doors to open, or for the first house to come out.

The theatre managers walked round their houses regularly during performances to see that there was no unruly behaviour in which case they were within their rights to stop the film. Usherettes, too, were persons of authority. They put one where *they* thought one should go. And they had good memories. It was no good trying the change into a better seat. They soon returned the recalcitrant to his or her original seat with the very real threat of any more of that and he or she would be put out. The usherette could, if she liked, put paid to any little illicit liaisons she though inappropriate.

With her knowledge of human nature gleaned during the execution of her duties, she would assess any given situation for herself. Thus a too-young-to-be-courting couple who had, with great subterfuge, gone into the cinema after the pictures had started, the girl first telling the usherette she wanted a back seat because she had to leave early and the boy following quickly afterwards before the usherette had time to get back to her post that he might get the seat next to the girl, were given short shrift. She, the usherette, would either indulge their young love and allow them to sit together while making them aware she would keep a vigilant eye on them, or she made sure they sat in the body of the cinema or, even, that they did not sit together at all. The back seats were for courting couples who got two for the price of one in that they had somewhere to kiss and cuddle while they got the gist of what was being shown on the screen. To make sure matters in the back row did not get out of hand (no pun intended) the usherette regularly flashed her torch over this area as she walked and down the aisles.

In spite of all this watchfulness, there were daring young lads who crept up to the front and, putting their hands in front of the strong light coming from the projection box, made shadow pictures on the screen to cries of 'geroff' from those whose evening they were spoiling. They were always back in their seats before Johnny Allen or his counter-part got down to the front.

'The next time,' said the voice of authority, 'the picture's off till we throw out the one who did it.'

When, later, I become one of the world's workers, threepence was ear-marked most weeks for a trip to the pictures. As my earning power increased, and with it my pocket money, I graduated to the sixpenny seats. The first lad who booked seats for us for the second house on Saturday night made me feel I'd arrived. I felt like Royalty swanning in to the dress circle.

It was pleasant to go with company, but I was also happy to go on my own. As soon as the picture started I was lost in a world where people did and said the right things, young people having the sort of conversations I wanted to take part in, but never did. I came out, still part of the picture, hoping that something would happen to me as it had happened to the girl in the film, but knowing it really wasn't possible.

Chapter 7
High Days and Holidays

It was at the weekend that leisure time came into its own. Most people saw to it that what money there was for spending on leisure pursuits was available on Saturday nights.

Saturday morning was the time for preparing for Sunday, at least at home. All the loose ends had to be neatly tied. Cakes were baked for the weekend, the yard swilled, the kitchen (cleaned thoroughly the day before) had to be given a final dust and polish, any necessary shopping completed and all before Saturday tea-time when the best fender and fire irons were brought out to replace their weekday fraternity now banished to the glory hole under the stairs.

For the woman with a large family, too much work and too little money, it was enough that the food was in and she had managed to get through the week and had enough energy to prepare to get through next week. She was grateful that she could change into a clean pinny and stand at the yard gate, her hands busy with knitting, watching the world go by. To her, a trip away for even half a day was so far from her ken she did not even think about it.

I was in the Store grocery one fairly busy day when the staff were bustling around under the watchful eye of the Boss, and several customers were standing at both the dry goods counter and the bacon counter. Suddenly a stout woman, flushed of face, eyes alight, worn hat slightly awry, opened the door and just stood their looking round.

'Ee,' she said. 'You'll never guess where I was yesterday. Wait till I tell you.' Everybody turned to look at her. 'You know,' she went on, 'Wor Mary's laddie, him that went away. Well, he got himself a car and he come up to see his mother and yesterday afternoon I was up to me eyes cleaning out the glory hole when in he comes. "Put your hat and coat on, Aunt Ellen," he says, "and I'll take you for a drive in me car." Well. You could have knocked me down with a feather. I says, "Like this?" "Aye," he says. "Just as your are. No-one'll notice." So I did.'

'Where did you go?' somebody asked.

'Ee. I can hardlies tell you. Everywhere. We went from wor house to Woodhorn and round by Lynemouth and Ellington and back to the road ends on to Longhirst and Pegswood and back home. Ee, it was lovely. I felt like a queen and me in me old things and not even time to wash me hands and face.'

It was a very moving and unforgettable moment. She was a cheerful, hard working woman who never got into debt and who had brought up a big family. The journey she had been on was fifteen miles maximum and it would have taken three-quarters of an hour to complete at most.

One leisure time occupation that cost nothing was a walk up the street to look at the shops. In winter the lighted shop windows on the Main Street were a magnet.

Here there was a variety of shops, from Oglethorpe's the chemist at the bottom end, to Russell Cook's and Arrow-smith's at the Grand Corner and, beyond that, the Store Arcade. On this walk one passed greengrocers, grocers, hardware stores, butchers, bakers, milliners, haberdashers, drapers, dress shops, shoe shops, men's outfitters, stationers, sweet shops, ice-cream shops, and Woolworth's, each shop different, each cramming as much as possible into their windows so that there was plenty to look at and comment on. The window shopper did not have to pass window spaces full of cardboard stands or windows plastered with huge posters. Most shops were family concerns which had been established for many years. What banks there were carried on their lofty transactions between solid walls, sitting amid polished mahogany and brass with their bright, brass shovels for money and their gleaming delicate scales, symbols of their stability.

Also, shops stayed open much later then, summer and winter. I remember one girl telling me she worked in a shop that did not close till ten o'clock on a Saturday night, after which they had to clear up. She thought herself lucky if she got to the dance by a quarter to eleven so that she could dance away the last hour.

For those who went to the cinema, especially those who went to the second house, there was the added treat of calling in at the fish and chip shop on the way home, or even Porky Orman's, real name Irhmann (I think). Here a gastronomic delight could be had for as little as one half-penny. The 'hapny dip' was a bread bun dipped in delicious gravy and wrapped in a pale grey paper which soon became saturated with gravy and thus part of the bun. A penny dip consisted of the bun and gravy and a filling of sage and onion stuffing with a smigeon of pork crackling. A twopenny pork sandwich was a meal. The bun contained a good helping of hot roast pork, some crackling and a generous helping of stuffing. Dips, sandwiches and fish and chips were all the better for being eaten out of a paper, in the case of fish and chips, newspaper.

Dances, whist-drives and socials of all descriptions finished before midnight that the sabbath might be respected.

I loved Sundays. First of all domestic work was kept to a minimum and I wore my best clothes. Also I loved both church and Sunday school. Ashington's Church of the Holy Sepulchre had greater seating capacity then than now. When I attended, the Sunday school filled the entire centre body of the church.

Sometimes, on winter evenings, (perhaps for economy's sake) some of the lights were put out during the sermon. This changed the atmosphere of the church giving to the air of sanctity a certain eeriness as deeper shadows filled the corners.

I early learned to sit still and cope with long periods when adults were occupied in a way that held no interest for a child. In any case, the very air of the church, the smell of hymn books and cassocks, of incense and Sunday clothes, that, over the years since the church was built, had mounted up and taken possession, pervaded my soul.

Then there was the imperceptible shift in the atmos-phere. The sermon was almost over. Any second now the vicar would say, 'And now to God, the Father......'. Had Mrs Davison coughed ever so slightly? A cough that, in our reverie, we had not heard, but it had subconsciously alerted us to the here and now?

Whatever it was there were throat clearings and rustlings and a turning of leaves as we looked at the board to get advance notice of the next hymn.

Soon we were out of church and standing near the gates talking to friends and asking after their health before setting out on the almost obligatory Sunday evening walk.

For some, Sunday was different in that there was no reading other than the Bible and Sunday Stories, no playing games, no sewing or knitting, no frivolity of any sort. At home and at Grannie Summers', apart from going to church and Sunday school, we were allowed to do the things we normally did except that we had to be extra careful of our Sunday clothes.

Once I was confirmed I was expected to attend early communion at eight o'clock in the morning, not having had anything to eat. Mother, as ever, was concerned for my welfare, especially in the winter, and her ideas of what constituted nothing to eat or drink were a little blurred.

'You're not having breakfast, you're just putting a lining on your stomach to keep out the cold (winter) or to stop the wine upsetting your stomach (summer).'

After I started work, things became more relaxed at home as far as I was concerned and one Sunday I was allowed to oversleep when I went to eleven o'clock communion. At the end of the service I was approached by a church member who asked why I had not been to the earlier service.

'I slept in,' I replied.

'You ought to be ashamed of yourself,' she admonished. 'At your age not being able to get up to go to first communion to meet your Maker!'

I didn't feel ashamed but I did feel a sense of guilt, particularly as I'd had something to eat before I went to church. Added to this was a feeling of resentment that I should feel this way. The net result was that I stopped going to Sunday school.

I had, by this time, sampled other religious denominations and I still attended some evening services at the Central Hall Methodists. No-one stopped me from going, but there was an unspoken feeling that, when it came to churches, the C. of E. was in the 'A' section. Not only in the 'A' section, but top thereof. It would have been very unchristian to have voiced this opinion, but it was there.

We did not doubt that those who went to other churches were devout, but their devotion wasn't of the same calibre. It was just that little bit lower. Top of the 'B' section, perhaps. And there was something a little singular about them for which one had to make allowances.

'Ah, well, you see, Margaret, Martha's chapel. They don't just see things the same way. I'm not saying anything about them, or about Martha. She's a bonny good worker for that chapel. A hundred and fifty pinnies for the Sale of Work last Christmas. Not many can say that. But there's just that Something.'

At Wooler the Presbyterians stood higher. They were at the top of the 'A' section. Like the Liberals. References to other churches were never actually voiced but the feeling was there that, in the eyes of the Almighty, the Presbyterians were on a higher plane, like the faint trace of smoke that lingers however wide the window is opened and the air wafted to get rid of it.

At a personal level, I was torn between the two. I liked them equally with the result that, as far as my most devout relatives were concerned, I never made the 'A' section in church or in chapel. Perhaps this was because, although I enjoyed Sundays and all they meant wholeheartedly, during the week I tended to ally myself with sinners who had more catholic tastes and were more durable.

Very often on Sunday evenings in the summer, a brass band played in the park and thither many of us went to listen, standing around in groups, nodding and smiling to acquaintances – a sort of prototype al fresco cocktail party without the drinks or the eats.

The Church's social activities and the pictures apart, other entertainments included concerts, operas, operettas and amateur dramatics. All of these had an air of festivity about them as we waited for the performance to begin, this even after cinema going was established. The stars of these amateur performances were all local people well known to us and, as we waited, experience having made us indifferent to hard chairs and what might be termed as other minor discomforts, we looked forward to the evening ahead. Fortunately, no-one expected perfection.

A day's outing was another thing long looked forward to,

principal among which was a day at the Town (Newcastle). For girls and women, this meant looking at the shops in the afternoon, while for men, the majority of whom went on a Saturday, it meant going to the match in the afternoon. Thereafter, for both men and women, (usually single men and women) it was a ninepenny tea at Lockhart's or Carrick's, and a very good tea it was, hot pie and peas or fish and chips, scones and cake with a pot of tea. This was usually followed by a trip to the Empire to see a show (variety) or to the Palace in the Haymarket to see Music Hall. For those who wanted to dance, there was the Oxford Galleries and Josh Q. Atkinson. All of these entertainments would be followed by a drink in a pub or club and, or, fish and chips either in Newcastle or at Ashington. The basic cost of the day would be three and six (17½p) or four shillings (40p).

Most people, children and adults, managed at least one day at the seaside during the summer. Bathing costumes were becoming more common but for plodgeing (paddling) up and down along the water's edge, they weren't necessary. All I did was tuck my dress inside my knickers. Women tucked their dresses in the elastic of their knicker legs. Boys still wearing short trousers turned them up to make them shorter. They kept on their caps to protect themselves against the treacherous sun. (We were for ever on guard, protecting ourselves against something.)

Men turned their trouser legs up to plodge and, in doing so, they usually gave an onlooker a glimpse of their linings which also had to be turned up. As the suit they were wearing was likely to be their Sunday suit, then they would also be wearing waistcoats which, in a spirit of abandon engendered by the health-giving sea, they unbuttoned so that their watch chains dangled from waistcoat pocket to waistcoat pocket.

Both men and women had white legs. Trips to the seaside were infrequent, however good the summer. For the rest, even in the hottest weather men and women kept their legs decently shrouded. Not till the Second World War did women walk around with bare legs. Even at the seaside in baking heat, we still tended to be warmly clad. One never knew.

Aunt Bella and Uncle Andrew at Newbiggin with George, Eliza and Archie Hyslop.

Plodgeing on a warm day is a very pleasant exercise of itself, but, for some, it was almost sinful to give oneself up to pleasure. They plodged because the sea water 'strengthened their ankles'.

At the far end of Newbiggin sands (we stayed at the end where the Horseshoe Steps used to be) there were donkey rides and, occasionally, a few roundabouts. We never rode on either. We had gone there to enjoy ourselves, not to spend money.

Some people brought their own food to Newbiggin but bought hot water, probably from a café, to make their own tea. There were also ice-cream carts on the sands and at least two ice-cream shops near at hand. At Cresswell there was practically nothing but the dunes, the sea, the sand and, at a distance, rocks where one could pick winkles. Most people picnicked among the dunes. This gave them greater privacy.

The sea meant summer and sun. I never saw it in winter till one winter's night Mr Pumphrey took me to Cresswell to the Colliery Farm and, while he was busy, I ran to the dunes. I looked out over the vast expanse of Druridge Bay. It was immense, lonely and awe-inspiring. The continual roar of the waves as they crashed on the shore, the faintly luminous moon, the long, bare stretch of sand and the black dunes. It was wild, mysterious, exciting. It defied the cold. I was entranced.

I could hardly call the cat's whisker set they had at Grannie Summers' entertainment. It seemed to be a very delicate, tetchy instrument that needed careful handling to produce screeches, wails and faint voices. The wireless which replaced it was much better although it never dominated the domestic scene as television was later to do. The set was switched on for specific programmes, listened to and then switched off. Among the programmes we listened to were *Children's Hour, Band Wagon,* and *Saturday Night Theatre.* We listened intently. It was never just a background of noise.

Holidays with pay came in before the Second World War but during my early childhood they were not so common. There was no mass exodus of people from Ashington, leaving the village denuded of all life. The few who went on holiday were hardly missed. Those who did go away tended not to travel far. Usually they booked one room for a family, the going rate of which was ten shillings (50p) per week. They brought their own food with them and gave it to the landlady to cook for them. Very little money was spent other than the basic cost of the holiday. It was enough that one had gone away for a holiday. I remember a family going to Blackpool. I listened enthralled as I heard of the marvels to be found there, the cafeteria system, the dancing in the Tower Ballroom, the Golden Mile, the various rides in the pleasure grounds. Very soon going to Blackpool and to holiday camps and joining the ever-growing queues at the main railway stations, everyone dressed in their best, was going to be commonplace, but then, when I first learned of these things, it had an Arabian Nights quality.

There was no television then to water down our individuality, no vast commerce to ensure that shops in places far apart such as Edinburgh, Newcastle and

Birmingham sold the same things and looked the same. People who went away on holiday to other parts of the country came back with stories of the odd way other people talked and the strange way they had of doing things. The shops were different too and the holidaymaker was able to bring back small mementos to prove this.

My parents bought a car in the middle thirties and we toured Scotland and England in successive years, camping. The car was a new Morris Eight tourer. A 'powder box' from the pit was converted into a clothes chest for four and it was fastened onto the luggage grid at the back of the car. Above it were strapped the two tents. Mother made covers in a strong holland material to fit over the front seats. These covers had compartments into which specific things went. The two primus stoves were housed on the floor. Everything we needed for that week's touring was neatly stowed away in the car. It was a marvellous experience. The further we journeyed north, the narrower grew the roads and the sparser became the traffic. And how courteous and friendly everyone was. There was a sort of instant fraternity among drivers then, regardless of the make of car. The A.A. scouts helped. They drove round on motor bikes with sidecars and, as they passed, they saluted the driver of the car carrying an A.A. badge, a handsome brass affair. This was to indicate to the driver that all was well with the car he drove.

Similarly, when we found a spot where we wanted to camp we were never refused permission. Many were glad of our company and welcomed us into their homes in the evening after we had cooked our meal. They plied us with eggs and fresh vegetables for which we had great difficulty in getting them to accept payment. Among the photographs taken on that holiday is one of me with my father and mother. We are walking down the middle of the main street in Wick, almost the whole of which is in view. Ahead of us is a grocer's delivery bike propped up against the kerb. There is no other sign of traffic or, indeed, of life. I am wearing sand shoes, tennis socks, shorts, blouse and blazer. My mother is wearing her best navy blue outfit complete with summer fur trimming. My father is in a grey threepiece suit and grey homburg. The day would be

Thursday or Friday and the time late July.

When, the following year, we toured the south and west of England, the roads were much more crowded and there was much less general camaraderie although the people on whose land we camped were as friendly as their counterparts in Scotland. When we got to Land's End we found that, for every car there had been at John o' Groats, there seemed to be a hundred at Land's End.

There were no parking problems with that first car, even on the rare occasions when we went to Newcastle. The car was never used for frivolous reasons such as taking Billy or me to keep an appointment and picking us up afterwards. Nor did my father use it to go to work, nor yet to attend the weekly board meeting of the Store, although he was often pressed for time and had a mile to walk both going and coming. Mainly, the car was used for trips to Wooler, occasional trips to Edinburgh, runs on a Saturday or Sunday afternoon when we always invited one or two of our relatives to go with us, and for holidays. The acceptable

Linda and the family car.

reason for our getting a car in the first place was that Mother was a bad traveller and she wanted to visit Wooler more often.

That car was cossetted. It was treated like a dear but delicate member of the family. The hen crees at the bottom of the garden were sacrificed and the hens moved to the allotments that we might build a garage to house our motor. After each journey, especially if it had rained, the car was carefully washed, dried and polished before it was 'happed up' (covered with old blankets). Internally, it was added to the list of things that had to be cleaned thoroughly each week.

Two people were required to start the car, one to turn the handle and one to operate the choke and the accelerator. The former had to be pulled a little bit in or out while the latter had to be tickled at just the right second when, all three working in harmony, the car leapt into throbbing life. Great was our concern during the next few seconds as a delicate hand continued to operate the choke and a gentle foot the accelerator pedal. Would the car continue to throb, or would it die on us? The starting handle, too, had to be treated with respect. It took offence easily. A starting handle out of humour was no light matter. If it kicked back, it could break an arm or a wrist unless the person concerned was aware of the danger.

The car had a very fine Klaxon bulb horn adjacent the windscreen, a running board and, at the back, the luggage grid. There were no automatic indicators so we used all those elaborate hand signals which meant so much. Drivers often waved to each other in friendly greeting as they passed. To pass a car of similar make merited a wave and a toot on the horn.

In winter, after a journey, the radiator was emptied and the car, the bonnet in particular, was smothered in blankets and other warm cast-off covers that it might not risk hypothermia. If this was the return journey, to make doubly sure, a small oil lamp, suitably guarded, was kept burning in the garage during the bitterest weather. Thus, when we started out on a journey, the radiator had to be filled with hot water and the covering rugs removed. There was no heating in the car so that passengers had to wrap themselves up as for a sleigh ride across the Arctic, furs, hats, scarves, gauntlets and Otterburn rugs. At our feet, underneath the rugs, we had hot water bottles. We also nursed them on, our laps.

I recall my parents once offering a young lady a lift when we ourselves were returning from a Christmas visit. The distance she had to go was approximately twenty miles. Giving her a lift would save her having to wait for a bus and also save her a walk at the other end. Loaded up with rugs and hot water bottles, we set off. As a family, we were, by this time inured against the drawbacks, setting a naught the risk of frost bite and exposure to cold. As the car had a hood and side curtains it was by no means draught-proof.

When we arrived at the young lady's home we met with a forthrightness we had not hitherto encountered.

'I won't thank you for the lift,' she said. 'I've never been so cold in the whole of my life. I'm frozen to the marrow bone. Coming by bus would have been a hundred times better. In fact, I think I would rather have walked. Goodnight.'

Apart from its day to day nursing, the car had to be periodically decoked and decarbonised. It repaid all this care by serving us loyally for almost fourteen years. Even then, there wasn't a scratch on its body work.

From time to time 'the shows' came to Ashington, Hirst or Wooler. Billy and I were never taken there during our early years and, certainly, we were never taken to Newcastle Town Moor during Race Week to see the marvels there.

For a small place Ashington did very well for shows. Just seeing the chair o' planes going round and round was enough for me so that I felt no loss at not being able to afford a ride on any of the roundabouts, including the 'shuggy boats'. I didn't like freak shows of any description, however, at about ten years of age, I was lured into a tent where a woman without any head was being kept alive. The price of admission was sixpence which, of course, I did not have. But the idea that such a thing was possible interested me greatly. How could this possibly be? I hung around the tent so long, trying to get a free glimpse of this phenomenon, that the man outside, who was endeavouring

– not very successfully – to attract custom, became angry.

'Come in, or get away,' he said.

'I can't come in. I haven't enough money,' I replied.

'How much have you?'

'A penny.'

'Give it here and get in. It'll be worth it to get shot of you.'

There weren't many of us and we were kept well back from this human wonder, a lady sitting in a chair minus a head in lieu of which various tubes ran from her neck to various jars filled with different coloured liquids which bubbled at various speeds. According to the man she had been abroad somewhere in a country much more advanced than ours. While she was there, she met with an accident which decapitated her as clean as a whistle, leaving the rest of her body intact. Fortunately, at that moment, there were those at hand who not only had the know-how, they also had the equipment to keep her alive. They acted with miraculous promptitude and this was the result.

At the command of the showman, the woman raised an arm or a leg. More, he started a conversation with her and asked her questions. She replied in bubbles through one of her jars and the showman very kindly interpreted what she said for the benefit of his audience ignorant of bubble language. I didn't believe a word of it. I just didn't. How could anybody be there at an accident with all those trappings at the ready? I tried to get a closer look and tried to get the showman to be a little more forthcoming as to detail (after all I'd paid enough – one week's pocket money non-refundable) but he wasn't having any and I was put out for being cheeky.

I didn't much care for Punch and Judy shows either. They seemed a quarrelsome lot, for ever angry and shouting and hitting out.

These, then, were the high spots of our day to day living. The other red letter days were the Bank Holidays, eagerly looked forward to and much appreciated as oases in the desert of our working lives.

The New Year was ushered in with a great deal of noise. As soon as the pit buzzers stopped blowing, first-footing started and many and fervent were the wishes exchanged that the following year would be a happy, healthy and prosperous one for all. Tradition had it that the first-foot should be male and dark. Fair men were better than no men; women brought bad luck. Tradition also had it that the first-foot brought with him a bottle of spirits, usually whisky, and a lump of coal. The latter was thrown on the fire, the former offered to those present. Only the men would accept the whisky, often only the host. For those who did not drink the first-foot's whisky, the host provided other drinks usually ginger wine for any children present and for some women who did not 'drink', and port wine for those who did. At that time port was more popular than sherry.

Children were usually got up to see the New Year in. I found this very frightening at first. The noise of the buzzers, the unaccustomed hand-shaking and kissing and the toasts. The strangeness of it all. We were returned to bed but first footing went on through the night as group after group came to welcome in the New Year before going on to another house. Not only were we expected to have sufficient drink to accommodate our visitors, we were expected to have enough food on the table to offer sustenance to all, principal among what was on offer being Christmas cake, shortbread and ham and pease-pudding sandwiches. By six o'clock those revellers still going the rounds were rather sick of Christmas cake and shortbread and looked for something savoury. If we were the last port of call my mother made breakfast, after which the first-footers went home and my parents turned out the lights and went thankfully to bed. Occasionally we were visited by guisers but these were becoming less popular.

We children woke up to a bleak morning on the first day of the new year. The kitchen had that grey, empty, tawdry look about it that betokened a night of revelry now over, only the litter remaining. Little fire remained in the grate and the room was cold, the air stale. Tousled parents would make an appearance later in the morning, not noticeably refreshed from their recent slumber. Both my father and my mother were tee-total but they still looked the worse for wear.

As I grew older I didn't like New Year for another reason, I hadn't yet finished with the old one. But that's been one of my problems. I always have a backlog of years that I don't feel I've used up.

We knew about having to take the Christmas decorations down by the 6th of January. I did not know then that this was Epiphany. Once, during the first week of February, I visited a house which was still hung with Christmas decorations, now dusty, and very much an anachronism. Christmas cards obliterated the usual ornaments on the mantelpiece and the chest of drawers, and how they looked out-of-place.

'I mistook the date,' said the lady of the house. 'I thought it was the sixth and it was the seventh so we've had to keep them up.'

'Till next Christmas?' I asked, astonished.

'No, no,' she said tetchily at my stupidity, 'only till pancake Tuesday. I have to put them on the fire and cook the pancakes on them as they burn to get rid of the bad luck.'

We had pancakes on Shrove Tuesday and recognised the beginning of Lent. The only thing we could really give up was the Saturday penny which was added to the collection plate and we did without sweets. On Ash Wednesday those who went to the C. of E. were allowed to come to school late if they'd been to church in the morning when the vicar dipped his thumb in the ashes of the previous year's Palm Crosses and made a cross on the forehead of the supplicant, a method of showing grief or mourning. In the main, it was only the Catholics who followed this rite.

During Lent we also followed the practice of eating fish on Friday's.

We did not keep Mothering Sunday as such and certainly there was no Mother's Day, but it was still the custom in some areas for sons and daughters living away from home to return for a visit on that day. What we did have was Carlin Sunday. Carlins were grey peas usually fed to pigeons, but, a fortnight before Easter they were elevated and prepared for human consumption. They were soaked overnight, boiled, then fried in butter and sugar and very tasty they were. Clubs and pubs served them liberally as did any house one happened to visit. The aftereffect of all this was a certain discomfort for which Flatulent Monday would be polite euphemism. The custom derived from the story that, long ago, a ship carrying these grey peas was wrecked nearby and the cargo was washed ashore. At that time the people living in the vicinity were starving and they considered the ship-wreck to be an act of God designed to save their lives.

Palm Sunday ushered in a very quiet week underneath which was the rush to get everything ready for the weekend. I don't remember being given a palm cross on Palm Sunday, but I do remember being given some pussy willow (hazel catkins). On Maundy Thursday the church was stripped of all ornaments including the altar cloth and on Friday there was a three hour service in church from mid-day till three o'clock when there was no music, no bells, no flowers. Most people who went did not stay the full three hours, but Grannie Summers always did and so did Aunt Bella. I usually went for part of the service, but once, when Grannie asked me to go with her, I stayed the three hours. A great part of this was spent in prayer. As far as we were concerned, there was only one way to pray in church, on one's knees on the hard form without benefit of the hassocks which hung from hooks suspended at intervals along the backs of the benches in front.

Not all people went to church. For those who gardened, and most miners were good gardeners, Good Friday was considered a good day for planting potatoes. My father managed to attend both church and garden. At home, the spring-cleaning had been done, very often the last place of all having been finished around midnight on Maundy Thursday. The day, Good Friday, was like Sunday only more so. All shops were closed and the pits were idle. The only treat we had was hot cross buns, home-made and utterly delicious dripping, as they were, with butter.

On Easter Sunday morning the church bells pealed cheerfully, the church was filled with flowers and the altar was adorned with the white and gold cloth. Those children wearing new clothes had a few coppers to jingle in their pockets. For all children there were pace eggs, hard boiled eggs in 'bonny colours'. We dyed ours with onion peelings, our attempts to produce masterpieces with coloured cloth or a paint brush having come to naught. The good thing about using onion peelings was that, if the egg cracked, which it often did, it could still be eaten. Relatives and friends gave the children they knew a pace egg at least. Most also added an orange, a large, sweet, juicy Jaffa. A few also added a penny to their largesse, and, possibly, even a silver threepence. There were a few chocolate eggs to be had but not many children got them. I only remember being given one, a sixpenny one, unwrapped, with my name on in white icing.

On Easter Monday, unless the day was a total disaster weather-wise, it was the children's day for a picnic at Sheepwash and thither families (most often minus the father) could be seen walking with their baskets of food and drink and their pace eggs. Sheepwash was tailor made for this project. There were banks of grass and turf absolutely right for 'boolin' eggs. There were little hidden pitfalls and obstacles so that it was difficult to roll an egg in such a way that it survived unbroken, and thus able to challenge other 'boolers'.

Ascension Day, now hardly mentioned, was like Ash Wednesday in that those who wished to go to church were allowed to come late to school. As on Ash Wednesday, those who did, arrived looking very self-important. One school I knew of attended church *en masse* after which they had the whole day off.

On Whit Sunday we wore our summer clothes and, sometimes, we shivered but, whatever the temperature we persevered. Whit Monday, like Easter Monday, was a picnic day for children, this time a seaside picnic. Most went to Newbiggin, many either by bus or train. We were among those who walked. Those who elected to go to Cresswell had to walk at least part of the way.

With Harvest Sunday came the thought of evenings by the fire, the Harvest Socials and Harvest Suppers.

My mother, who was a country-woman, still spoke of Michaelmas otherwise I should not have known about it. She used to say that all blackberries should be picked before the 29th of September which was Michaelmas Day.

Throughout my school life we had a special lesson or service on Empire Day, 24th May. At Bothal School particularly, our attention was drawn to the pink areas on the shiny porridge-coloured map that hung on the wall. These pink areas marked the extent of our Empire. Mention was made of the various races of people who made up the Empire. We were also told of the variety of Empire goods which helped to fill our shops.

Similarly, on the 11th November we recognised Armistice Day when we were reminded of the 1914-18 War and the enormous death toll resulting therefrom. We had a special service and kept the two minutes' silence at eleven o'clock.

The other pleasanter and much more exciting annual event connected with school was Sports' Day when we lined up in our various school yards ready to march behind a brass band to the park where groups of miners sat behind trestle tables handing out a penny, a bun and a bag of sweets to each child. Afterwards we ran races for prizes. This special Children's day was funded by the miners themselves.

I have no particular memories of any August Bank holiday, then the first Monday in August. Of course, it fell during the Summer holidays which would lessen its importance for children. From then till the Christmas holidays was a vast desert of time which Guy Fawkes' Day did little to brighten. As a family, we celebrated this in a very modest way.

A lot of women who lived in the Rows had reason to be thankful when Guy Fawkes' Day was over. Young, high-spirited lads spent what money they had round about the 5th November on squibs. They waited till it was dark, secreted themselves in the shadows, and waited a while longer for some woman to 'go across the road'. When they could assume she was safely in the nettie, engaged in what she had gone there to do, they lit a squib and threw it into the area designed to receive the end product of her efforts. After that, they ran away at speed, the screams that followed being sufficient reward for their financial outlay, one supposes. Sometimes they were caught, when corporal punishment was meted out on the spot. If they were sufficiently well-known for their parents to be informed, they got another lot of punishment at home.

Occasionally there was a party, most often a twenty-first

115

party. On this important occasion more people than could be accommodated were asked when they all had to be shoe-horned in somehow. The all-purpose kitchen table would have been augmented, if not supplanted, by trestle tables which, once they were up, would not allow doors that led in and out of the kitchen to be freely opened or closed. Thus they, the doors, had to be propped open or firmly shut once everyone was in and sitting down. This meant one either sat in a draught or 'scumfished' in increasing heat. Before everyone was actually seated, there was the business of the chairs to be got through. All available seating accommodation including the cracket and the cane chair with the bottom out from upstairs was pressed into service. In spite of that, there still weren't enough.

'How many are we short now? Why, lad, I made sure there would be enough last night. Are you sure you can't get one more on the form? And are all the bairns sitting three on two chairs? Who's sitting on the Smith's cracket? It's bigger than ours. I can balance meself on the end of that. Well that's good of you, Mary. But as you're one of them that's pouring out the tea, it would be better if you just stood by the oven door and ate your tea there. Jinnie can pass you what you want and you'll be able to see who wants more tea better. Right? Are we all sitting down. I didn't say "Are you comfortable?" Just mind what you say, young fella-me-lad or you'll get your ears clipped, party or no party, and you'll stay in the yard till everybody's finished.'

Apart from the twenty-first birthday cake, there was little different between the food provided for this party and that provided for wedding teas and funeral teas.

Parties consisted of a mixture of ages and sexes. No parents would dream of leaving the house to allow a group of young people to have a party in private. In addition, everyone knew they were at a party and parties meant games, Trencher, Forfeits, Winkie, Sardines, Postman's Knock, Passing the Parcel, Musical Bumps (no room for chairs) and singing round the piano or listening to a tune from Uncle Fred on his concertina.

Wedding breakfasts were still held in the home of the bride when, once the meal was over and the bride and groom had gone to the Town for the day (honeymoons were still in their infancy), the two families split up, his side going to the groom's home where they were better able to discuss the events of the day without having to mind what they said. In fact, all the weddings I attended where the reception was at the bride's home, were excellent affairs where the festivities went on till the evening.

Christenings were, naturally, much more restrained affairs. For children, or rather, for one lucky child, the best part of the christening was the amice. It was unlucky for a child to visit a house before it was christened, just as it was unlucky for a mother to visit before she had been churched, so that the christening followed as soon as possible after the birth. When the christening party left home for church they took with them a small parcel containing salt (for savour), a candle (to light the child's way through life), some money, usually a silver threepence, (so that the child would never be poor) and a piece of bread or cake (that the child might never go hungry). If a girl baby was being christened, the amice went to the first boy they saw after leaving the house, if a boy, the amice went to a girl. To a child whose total income was a penny a week, threepence at one fell swoop was a gold-mine.

Christmas was the crowning event of the year and was much looked forward to. In the vast majority of cases, the only toys children got were those they got at Christmas. Often, too much was expected of this season of the year. We were expected to be happy because it was Christmas so that the disappointments with which one could easily have coped at other times, seemed so much worse then.

Preparations for Christmas began on or about 1st December. Indeed, December 1st was sometimes referred to as 'stir up day' because on that day Christmas puddings were made when each member of the family was supposed to stir the pudding mixture and make a secret wish. I did not realise till many years later that this time of year was called Advent which meant 'preparation for Christ's coming'. Thus, beginning our preparations then was in keeping with the church calendar.

From the beginning of December till Christmas Day, the delicious smell of dried fruits and nuts was hardly ever out of the house. After the Christmas puddings were made, the currants, raisins and sultanas were washed and dried and added to the cherries and nuts which went into the making of the Christmas cake. Thereafter, it was mincemeat. For each of these, pudding, cake and mincemeat, there was a try-out, a small sample of things to come. For many, this was perhaps the most memorable part of Christmas, the preparation and the eating of Christmas food. Presents were modest. There was too little money around to be lavish in this respect. Christmas clubs which operated all the year round were, most often, for food. The exceptions were clubs for children's annuals and selection boxes.

At school, during that final month, there were Christmas cards and decorations to be made and, perhaps, a Nativity play to perform.

During the last few days before the day itself, the cake was iced and the secret storage places were filled with dates, muscatels, apples, oranges, figs, nuts, tangerines, sweets, chocolates and little gifts. Decorations were not usually put up till Christmas Eve so that, for young children, seeing the decorations was part of the wonder of Christmas morning. A few people bought fresh Christmas trees, but many got two hoops from the Danish butter barrels and, crossing one inside the other, wrapped the hoops (gourds) in coloured paper and suspended them from the ceiling. Christmas baubles were then hung from the 'tree'. Year after year the same toys came out, carefully preserved. In fact, some trees represented a social history of the family because the baubles spanned two or three generations.

To get Santa to call on Christmas morning, a child had to be good, that is, he or she had to be obedient and well-behaved.

Except for one year, Christmas for us meant going to Grannie Summers'. We went for mid-day dinner, tea and supper with, in between, nuts and apples and sweets. The adults all played 'New Market' on Christmas night but we children were not allowed to join in. How much fun they seemed to have and how I would have loved to play. They promised I would when I was older but that actually never materialised.

On the first Sunday on which my father was on the right shift we had a family Christmas party at our house when all my Ashington uncles and aunts, together with my grandmother and grandfather, came to tea and supper. There were no games as such, but most gave a turn of one sort or another and there was a great deal of laughter and singing. We had a wind-up gramophone and a piano. Auntie Anna played the latter and my father wound up the former and put on the records, 'Charmain', 'When the red, red robin', 'I'm forever blowing bubbles', 'Twas on the Isle of Capri', 'Bye bye blackbird' among them. While the gramophone played one of us stood by to push the needle over the scratchy bits.

The Christmas we went to Wooler stands out in my mind. We went the day before Christmas Eve in time to see the shops decorated in tinsel and glitter, the hoar frost on the windows sparkling more vividly even than their simulated counterparts. The air was sharp and clear, the country roads rutted and hard on the feet, little glassy puddles frozen hard, the sun shining, the stiff grass coated in sugar and steam came from our nostrils when we breathed. A real live Christmas card. My mother and father were expected for Christmas dinner so that they were not there when we opened our stockings. It was my best Christmas ever as far as my memory went. Billy and I each got watches, his a gold plated one, mine a silver one. More than that, I also got a pair of kid gloves, both of these presents I'd wanted for ages. I cannot remember what else Billy got but we asked each other the time every alternate minute as we walked towards Walker Wall to meet Auntie Amy, Uncle Will and John who were also to be members of our family party.

We left the following day because of Dad's having to go back to work. For me, however, the holiday was far from over. That year I had been invited to four Christmas parties, those of Ruby Lowry, Topsy Siggins, Betty Watts and Winnie Douglas. And I had this lovely lemon party dress and a silver watch and pair of kid gloves. Life had nothing more to offer. However, I did feel at a disadvantage in that I wasn't having a party of my own to which I could ask my friends in return. I decided to redress the balance in part by entertaining my hostess and her guests in some way and, to that end, went to Woolworth's where a fat book entitled *Foulshard's Complete Party Entertainer*, or something similar, was to be had for sixpence.

I hadn't got sixpence, but I looked critically through the book as though I were considering buying it and finally came up with one trick guaranteed to bring the house down. It was called 'The disappearing penny' and it entailed borrowing one's hostess's *best* tumbler (nothing less would do), a penny and a thick newspaper. One covered the penny with the upturned tumbler, placed the paper over the tumbler, grasped it firmly, shook it back and forward so that the audience could hear the penny rattling, lifted up the paper to see if the penny was still there, rattled again, lifted up the paper and tumbler again, put it back but, instead of rattling one brought one's fist down hard on the best tumbler. This was guaranteed to bring gasps from the audience because, undoubtedly the tumbler would now be broken. The trick was to drop the tumbler on one's lap and only replace the newspaper which had taken on the shape of the tumbler.

I practised and practised at home till I got it every time and, full of confidence, I performed it first at Betty Watts' party. Unfortunately I hadn't taken into consideration a slightly higher table, a slightly lower seat and the difference between my thick winter skirt and my silk party dress. The tumbler, gathering momentum, dropped to my lap, slid off my dress and crashed on the lino covered floor!

Usually Christmas did not last twelve days. When we left Grannie Summers' on Christmas night it was all over. By Boxing Day the anticipation and the excitement had gone. This Christmas was different. It lasted the whole of the holiday despite the tumbler fiasco.

Holidays and treats were so widely spaced that their advent meant that, for a short time, we dwelt in a modified Garden of Eden. There was bound to be a small snake there somewhere. At Christmas there was the fact that it might not live up to expectations. When it came to trips and holidays there was the 'coming back' when absence had not fulfilled its promise. Every excursion away from the daily round had its quota of extra work beforehand in preparation. The burden of this was considerably lightened by the anticipation of the delights ahead.

Once back home, lost time had to be made up and it was usually females who did the making up. Males were above both the preparation and the aftermath. As far as we were concerned, when we had been away for only one day, on our return the fire was low and needed a great deal of coaxing back into life and the coal pails were empty. The house itself sulked because it felt itself neglected. Added to this, we had probably returned later than was planned, the original time having been fixed because, either my father was due to go to work shortly or he was due back from work. In either case, there was a meal to prepare for him, a fire to coax into sufficient life (with the aid of a blazer, a sheet of newspaper and the draught from the door) to boil a kettle or cook something and the place to freshen up.

Before we could begin our making up for lost time, time spent galivanting, we had to rush upstairs and take off our best clothes, substitute them with old ones and put the former away. It was back to 'auld claes and parritch' with a vengeance. Coming back from holiday was worse. Any lingering signs of carefree abandon had to be exorcised immediately in favour of bringing back to life and routine our dusty, neglected house.

Was it worth it? Of course it was. As Auntie Nan used to say, 'The hotter the war, the sooner the peace.' The sooner everything was back to normal, the sooner could we recount what a good time we'd had. For we did appreciate these deviations from routine. A trip to Rothbury, say, would today merit little interest, it probably having been a spur of the moment decision. Not so for us. It was long anticipated and long talked of afterwards. For, in spite of the fact that we worked hard, we had more time to talk to our relatives and friends. There was no time-consuming television and the world's disasters were not daily brought into our sitting-rooms and kitchens. Thus we talked of the things in which we were interested, parochial though they were.

Chapter 8
Clothes

We took care of our clothes. Cleaning garments was not the easy matter it now is. Once clothes were cleaned the 'body' was taken out of them and they never looked the same again. Besides, cleaning clothes cost money. Clothes were meant to last. For children, all new clothes had to be grown into so that, when they were bought, they were too big and too long. In addition, they had to have hems that could be dropped, seams that would let out and cuffs that could be turned up. Boy's short trousers had to have fullness and, when they were new, they most certainly covered the knee, again to allow for growth. In fact, children's clothes did not fit really well till the newness had gone from them and they were on the downward spiral, for almost all new clothes started out as Sunday best and were relegated to second best after which they became old clothes, clothes to sit around at home in, to play in or to work in.

While they were doing housework women always wore old clothes covered by a pinny (pinafore) and sometimes a bratty (sacking) apron. This was because there was so much dirt and dust to dispose of. Then, no housewife could do her housework all dolled up as today's housewives seem to do, if television is to be believed. In some cases 'old clothes' and 'second best' were synonymous, thus expressing the limits of the wearer's wardrobe.

As far as children were concerned, serviceability usually came before fashion and so it was possible that there was still some goodness in clothes that had become too small. When this happened, they were handed down to a younger sibling or relative, or made into something else. Before that happened everything possible had been done to extend the life of the garment in question. It would have been patched or darned if necessary. A jumper was often resleeved or had an extra bit added to the welt. Sometimes this was done skilfully, but, very often this spare-part surgery was half in pulled out wool and half in new wool always just the wrong

122

shade. The effect of this was especially noticeable if the repairs had been done at different times. Home-knitted socks were almost always refooted when the original feet had become a mass of darns, gnarled or otherwise. (Nearly all miners' pit stocking were home-knitted). Shoes were cobbled (usually at home) and the soles liberally covered in segs to increase their life span. Newly cobbled shoes were uncomfortable to wear till they had been walked back into shape.

Dresses had new sleeves put in and false hems added when the too-short dress had already been let down to its extremity. Sometimes a piece was put in at the waist. Success depended a great deal upon the skill of the dressmaker. The cuffs and collars of shirts were turned or replaced. To provide material for these replacements or for patches in places where it showed, bits were cut from the long tails of the shirts both men and boys wore at this time.

Thus, almost every kitchen had a sewing machine and certainly every kitchen had a darning and mending basket. Rarely, if ever, were these last two receptacles empty. Darning and mending took up a great deal of the housewife's 'free' time in the evening. In addition, almost every glory hole contained a shoe last for cobbling.

When washable clothes or materials were bought, the question was, 'Will this wash better than that?' Even those clothes which were washable did not see the inside of the tub as often as necessary. Washing took the goodness out of them. Cotton dresses and blouses faded with too much washing and woollens felted. Socks and stockings made of wool were washed as infrequently as possible and certainly not after every wearing. When buying clothes, of more importance than the fashion, then, was, 'Will it fade? Will it show the dirt? Will it go with everything?'

For those clothes which could not be washed Fuller's Earth, a soft clay-looking substance, was used to remove dirt and grease from woollen material. A more common method was that of putting brown paper over the offending spot and ironing the paper with a very hot iron. The paper was expected to soak up the melting grease. Milk was used to remove ink stains. Lemon juice and washing soda were also popular cleansing agents.

At home, on fine days when there was a slight breeze, we regularly put out-door clothes on the line to air and to discourage moths who were supposed not to like sunlight. Those heavy coats in need of a clean were put into a large bag containing oatmeal and the whole lot thoroughly shaken. I knew of one woman who regularly washed her husband's suits in cold water. They certainly looked no worse for the experience.

When clothes were absolutely no longer fit for wearing they were turned into clippings for the next mat. Old trousers, coats, thick dresses and the like were cut into strips three inches long and an inch wide for proggy mats. Woollens were cut into long strips for hooky mats. Depending upon the material of which they were made, underclothes were turned into dishclothes, floor cloths, dusters, rags and bandages while tablecloths, worn in the middle, were cut up for tea-towels or napkins. Sheets worn down the centre were cut in two and turned sides to middle. The next time they were vandalised by scissors they joined the ranks of dishcloths, floor cloths, dusters and rags.

Clothes were *never* replaced simply because they had gone out of fashion (they could be altered) or because the wearer had grown tired of them. Whatever the feelings of the latter, clothes were deemed to have nothing wrong with them if it could be said there wasn't a break in them or there was a lot of goodness in them yet.

A new born baby had a layette. This included a pram, a cradle or bassinette, blankets for both and, for best, in the case of the pram, a satin coverlet and pillow adorned with satin ribbons. Clothes-wise, there were six of everything, binders, long petticoats, short petticoats and barricoats, all made of flannel. This last was a long cross-over garment tied with tapes at the side in which the infant was swathed at night. The barricoat was long enough to tuck under the feet of the sleeping child. Included in the layette was a long Christening robe, long dresses for the first weeks and short dresses to be worn after the baby was 'shortened'. For convenience both boys and girls wore dresses but the custom of keeping the former in dresses till they were three or so years of age when they were breeched, had died out by the time I was born. The last, and most necessary, items of the layette were two dozen terry-towelling napkins, known locally as nappies or hippens. Matinée coats, bootees, hand-knitted leggings and hats were usually given to the new baby by the close family who had also been preparing for the event.

As it was expected that this new arrival would have brothers and sisters in due time, then, as he or she outgrew each stage of the layette, it was carefully put away.

For a number of years Mother kept our layette in a kist (chest) in the kitchen. It kept company with the ostrich feather, the white silk stockings with fancy clocks up the side and a dress, (all of which she had worn on her wedding day) and Billy's first tussore silk suit, each item carefully wrapped in tissue paper. Only the ostrich feather survived the move to Ashbourne Crescent. Indeed, I still have it. The layette and suit were handed on and the dress was made over into a dress for me and a blouse for Mother.

Generally speaking, during the summer, little girls wore white dresses on Sundays till they were six or seven. Underneath they wore their best white petticoats and knickers both of which were trimmed with crocheted lace. When Billy and I were dressed for going out, once we were ready we had to sit absolutely still till the adults were ready. This was so that we were still clean and spotless when we went out.

After the age of seven little girls wore summer dresses in pastel shades probably made in art silk or levisca. Cotton dresses were not considered proper Sunday wear.

Sunday summer hats for girls were very pretty. They were made of straw and garlanded with artificial flowers and satin ribbons. After I went to grammar school, on Sundays I wore a white panama similar in shape to my school hat. It didn't stay exactly the same shape long. Panamas had a tendency to flop very easily. All girls' hats were kept on by a piece of elastic that went from ear to ear via the chin. When the elastic was new it cut into the skin but it was chewed so much and pulled so frequently that it soon became gnarled and slack when it was knotted to make a better fit. One piece of elastic was expected to last the hat out.

Kiltie shoes were very popular. I liked the patent leather

ones best, but they only looked nice when they were new and uncreased. When I got my first pair, I walked stiffly, my body rigid, to stop my feet from bending and cracking my shoes. After I'd been told several times to walk sensibly, my mother said firmly, 'That's the last pair of patent leather shoes you'll get,' and it was.

Sometimes I had both a summer coat and a winter coat but, most often, my summer coat was thick enough to have pieces of fur tacked on to the collar and cuffs, thus, with the addition of a woolly underneath, making it warm enough to withstand the weather.

The seasons were clearly marked, weather-wise, and we had to wrap up well in winter. We walked everywhere undeterred by the falling temperature, snow, ice, wind, rain or sleet. We were prepared to be cold in church, school and Sunday school. We didn't go to these places to be pampered. Summer socks had been changed for woollen stockings, in my case hand-knitted. These stockings were kept up by elastic garters or the suspenders that dangled from liberty bodices, a sort of fleece-lined vest which reached to the buttocks and which buttoned down the front. This liberty bodice was worn over woollen combinations, an all-in-one garment reaching almost to the knees with short sleeves and round neck. It buttoned down the front till just below the navel where there was a convenient opening from there to the small of the back. It was thought essential that one should wear wool next to the skin. For me these combs (as they were called – to rhyme with bombs) had all the comfort of a hair shirt until they'd been washed several times when they were a little less misery making. Fleece-lined gym knickers had a little pocket in the right leg, supposedly for a handkerchief – a dichotomy. Any little girl who kept her handkerchief there would have to lift her skirt to get at it and this was thought very rude. The combinations had done away with the need for red flannel petticoats (red flannel was thought to ensure good health) so that the petticoat worn on top of these garments was of white, thick, serviceable linen material with a draw-string neck.

Sunday dresses were made of velveteen, velvet, serge, wool or stockinette in dark colours sometimes lightened by a lace collar or Sunday beads designed to go with anything.

Winter hats for girls were plain round velours or felts or, less frequently, felts or velours similar in shape to summer hats except that there were no streamers and very little adornment.

Young children wore gaiters made in felt or leather. They were strapped under the soles of shoes and buttoned up the sides to well above the knee. A button hook was needed to fasten the buttons. Gloves or mitts in wool, leather or fur were secured to each other by a piece of cord which passed, via the sleeves, from one glove or mitt to the other. On very cold days a small child might be mummified in a huge muffler put on top of all his or her other clothes.

In wet weather, summer and winter, we wore mackintoshes and wellingtons. The former had a very distinctive smell. Wellingtons were supposed to 'draw' the feet and, certainly, the tops tended to chafe the legs.

Clothes worn for the first time were always admired, whatever the private opinion of the admirer. The clothes one paraded in for the first time were those one was going to wear every Sunday for at least a year, either continuously or on two consecutive summers/winters. Very often one's wardrobe was so arranged that one got a winter outfit one year and summer outfit the following year. Children wearing new clothes for the first time were often given a penny by an adult or relative.

Although not all the clothes I had were to my liking, I loved Sundays and the feel and smell of wearing best clothes. Sunday clothes were also worn for Christmas Day, parties, socials and weddings. Thus, there was never any question of what one should wear on these occasions. By the time Christmas came around everyone knew what everyone else was going to wear so that there was no fear of being unexpectedly upstaged.

On Mondays, Sunday shoes were cleaned, returned to the box in which they were bought and put away in the bottom of the wardrobe till the next wearing. Dresses, coats and suits were carefully brushed and also put away, sometimes covered in a bit of protective sheeting. Hats were returned to their hat bag and placed on top of the wardrobe. Incidentally, if a hat was too big, or the crown too deep, it was stuffed with paper so that it did not fall over the eyes of the wearer.

Once one had returned home after church or Sunday school, because it was the Sabbath, one could not change and sit around in old clothes. Instead one was shrouded in an apron or pinafore and told (commanded) to be careful.

I had little choice in the matter of my clothes. My mother dictated my wardrobe and made all my dresses and some of my coats till I left school. Apart from my school uniform, the clothes I remember with the greatest pleasure were a particular dress and coat.

My best loved dress was a pale yellow silk with a round neck, plain bodice, puffed sleeves and a full skirt falling in soft folds. It was made originally as a party dress for the grammar school second year Christmas party. It saw me through that summer, the following Christmas and the next summer when it had been let down and out to its furthest extremity. In fact, it did duty as a best dress until I was confirmed when I had my first bought dress. After confirmation, it was dyed blue when it became my Sunday dress.

The favourite summer coat I had was a navy one made by the Store tailor, Willy Weatherson. According to my mother's account books still extant, it cost £1.4.*s*.6*d*. (£1.24p). At that time I was probably nine years old. On the whole, I was much more fortunate with my summer clothes than I was with my winter ones.

I longed for a dark red winter coat with fur collar and cuffs and a black velours hat to go with it. I longed in vain. Apart from the navy coat already mentioned my mother made my coats till I went to the grammar school. Some were better than others, particularly an astrakhan coat which I wore at about five years of age. The worst, however, the most awful monstrosity that gave rise to many, many silent tears (shed by me), was a sort of sludgy light mud-coloured figured face cloth creation made over from a coat of Grannie Summers' which she declared was too good to be cut up for a mat; it would make into a nice coat for Linda (me). I hated that coat with an all-consuming hatred and the thing I hated most about it was its principal adornment, a large round button in the same sludgy light mud-colour with a mother of pearl centre. It was firmly sewn onto a sort of simulated self-material belt dead centre of my person.

Well. There was one thing I could do. I could get rid of that button. All during the catechism at Sunday School I picked and picked at it. I went off by myself on the way home and, in the safety of the plantation next to the church, I had a go with a bit of twig. The button stuck with touching tenacity to the coat, but my blood was up and I was determined to separate them. Finally I did – throwing the offending button into oblivion among the trees. I felt I had conquered.

My mother was not noted (as my father often remarked) for replacing buttons the minute they fell off. But as soon as I walked into the house she looked me up and down.

'What's happened to the button on your coat?' she asked.

'Eh – button?' I said aghast and stupified. I hadn't prepared for this.

'Yes. Button. The one that should be there,' and she pointed to my middle.

'I – I don't know. It must have come off.'

'It was there when you left the house. Now go back the way you came and find it. And don't come back here till you do find it. I haven't got money to waste on buttons. You've been fiddling with it. That's what you have been doing. It wouldn't have come off otherwise. Now, back you go this minute.'

Tearful, crestfallen and feeling wronged by the whole world I went back to the plantation. It wasn't a big place: it shouldn't have taken long but, could I find the button! Of course, being the colour it was, it was easily camouflaged among the damp earth and dead, fallen leaves. Another fear took hold of me. The light was fading and the church yard was no distance away and who knew what moved around this very plantation in the darkness. I only found the button when I stood on it. I was grateful that I'd found it unscathed but by no stretch of the imagination did I rejoice. When I got home, my mother sewed the button back on again. Firmly.

Shopping for those children who were going to a school where wearing a uniform was obligatory was done the week before school began. In common with many others, I took my uniform off as soon as I got home, brushed it and hung it up ready for next day. I then wore old clothes in which to sit around, do homework or play out.

Boys, generally, had smaller wardrobes than girls but they, too, had Sunday clothes. My brother wore a navy suit on Sundays with short trousers, a white shirt, grey socks with elastic garters and black shoes. Most boys held their trousers up with snake belts which were very fashionable at the time. They wore caps and, as they grew older, they were taught to lift their caps when they met a woman whom they knew. In winter they wore overcoats although the all-purpose gaberdine mac was becoming more popular. When they were too old for gaiters some boys suffered from chapped knees from the cold. While he was at Bothal School, like most other boys of his age, Billy wore a jersey with a collar underneath which was knotted a knitted tie in two-colour stripes, the same two colours that were in the snake belt.

In Summer, for Sports' Day, boys wore grey flannel shorts, new white sand-shoes and white open-necked cricket shirts. I expect Billy wore off his Sunday trousers at school, but, as few boys wore a jacket to school, it is probable his Sunday jacket was 'handed on' once it became too small. At the grammar school, when he went there, the uniform was grey short trousers till he reached the fourth form, grey socks with the school colours on the tops, grey shirt, school tie, navy blazer, school cap and navy gaberdine coat.

The great divide for boys was when they went into 'long 'uns' (long trousers). This usually happened about the age of fourteen, then the school leaving age. Indeed, many boys got their first pair of long trousers when they started work. Once they went into long 'uns a boy no longer played children's games. They tended to hang around in groups, go for bike rides (those fortunate enough to have a bike), go to the Tute (Priestman Institute) or the Rec (Miners' Welfare Recreation Ground). They also began to plaster their hair down with brilliantine so that it had a patent leather look, and they frequented Bothal Bank on winter Sunday nights there to make a great deal of noise to attract the lasses who had gone there, giggling, to attract the attention of the lads. An added spice to this activity was the fact that the lads weren't old enough to have lasses and the lasses had been forbidden to talk to the lads.

When a boy went into long 'uns for the first time, a small gift of money from each of his elder male relatives was almost obligatory. Those who were still at school when they went into long 'uns wore flannel trousers which soon lost their crease. The turn-ups soon had to be let down after which the trousers started creeping up to their ankles. Sleeves and blazers got shorter too.

Not all children were so well off for clothes. Some wore sandshoes summer and winter unless the Sunshine people came to school distributing boots to those in need. Some wore shoes with holes in the soles when an inadequate cardboard sole was inserted to attempt to make good the discrepancy. Also, not all shoes were waterproof. Shoes were made of leather, but it was said that cheap shoes were made of cardboard designed to look like leather.

At the other end of the scale, there were those who had many more clothes than I have mentioned. One of my

Billy in his first pair of 'long-uns'.

friends went regularly to Newcastle for her clothes. Apart from her uniform she had a fabulous wardrobe, or so it seemed to me. In it was a black leather coat, then the height of adult fashion. Imitation leather called 'leatherette', was sometimes used for coats.

There were no clothes specifically for teenagers. (The word had not then been coined.) Boys went through a gawky period when their clothes rarely fitted. Girls wore children's clothes till the clothes were 'too young' for them when they changed to adult fashions which were often 'too old' for them.

As far as the avante-garde were concerned, brassieres (bras) were replacing chemises, bust bodices and camisoles. Directoire knickers were being superceded by French knickers, very wide legged and usually made of satin with lace insets. Underwear was very much lighter in weight and matching sets of French knickers or panties and petticoats or slips in delicate colours were becoming very popular. For the very avante-garde, satin pyjamas were popular as evening dress and pyjama parties had a brief popularity.

When I first became aware of adult fashions, bobbed and shingled hair was in vogue as were very short dresses, some made in gossamer voile – then very popular. These dresses were usually sleeveless and the fashion was to wear a gold slave bangle entwined with a silk handkerchief, on the upper arm. Fancy garters were worn just above the knee. Flesh-coloured stockings, strapped shoes in light colours and long, leg-hugging Russian boots zipped up the sides were de rigeur. The Charleston was still the rage as were ukuleles. There were Bright Young Things, even in Ashington. I remember an older girl trying to teach me, in the street, how to do the Charleston.

The flesh-coloured silk, or art silk, stockings would only be worn for best. At other times lisle thread stockings were worn. As they, too, had to last a long time, all holes were darned, even in places where the mending could be seen.

The tubular dresses of the day demanded a different type of corset from the suffocating, creaking stays hitherto worn and, for the young, the corselette, a straight up and down garment with shoulder straps became fashionable. This garment was made in mercerised cotton front and back with elastic sides. The corselette flattened the bust so that it appeared non-existent. Underwear was lighter in weight and more scanty; directoire knickers with shorter legs, French knickers, cami-knickers and Princess slips. Knowing no better, we called this 'linggery' (lingerie). With these dresses went short, straight coats and cloche hats.

Whalebone stays which clamped the body, emphasising the waist and pushing up the bust so that it had a 'shelf' appearance, were still with us. They came in long narrow boxes labelled Desbeau Corsetry, at least they did if one shopped at the Store. They were worn by those who could not be called Flappers by any stretch of imagination, perhaps the same people who still called knickers, bloomers. The corsets were boned and fastened down the front with hooks or clips. After they had been worn for some time, this front curved in at the waist and out over the stomach. The backs of the stays were laced so that they could be adjusted to fit the wearer who always assumed she was much slimmer than she was. Some women wore short stays from the waist and added a boned bust bodice. In this case, they had the added discomfort of being cut in two. As a child, to be clasped in embrace by someone wearing stays was like being suddenly fettered in iron. No wonder the wearers sighed with relief when they removed this scaffolding before getting into bed.

Drawers, sometimes called, locally, heckboards or duckboards, were still worn by some of the elderly. These drawers were the later models of the original pantalettes which were two independent legs brought together at the waist and tied with tapes. These later models were in one piece fastened at the waist either by tapes, or, more commonly, by linen buttons, these last so that the garment could go through the mangle without the buttons breaking. The drawers reached to the knee or below where, for best, there was a wide lace edging. The best drawers were made in white linen or lawn, while those for everyday were made in a grey material called Linsey-woolsey. As they were for common wear, they had no adornment whatsoever. In appearance, the drawers resembled men's plus-twos except that, at the back, they had a wide opening, rectangular in shape, anchored at the small of the back with three linen buttons, this, of course, for a convenience that may be conjectured at. When one considers the wealth of heavy floor length garments worn, it must have taken considerable effort to unbutton this garment, even to get at it, especially in an emergency. It seems natural to assume, therefore, that most its life was spent unbuttoned.

Ladies who wore these garments were loyal to the fashions of their youth and indifferent to the fashions of the day. Thus they still wore ankle-length coats and dresses. Widows still tended to wear black as a matter of course. My maternal grandmother, Grannie Gallon, was one such. She outlived my grandfather by fifty-eight years and, after his death, she never wore anything other than 'deep' black, possibly even keeping to the fashion prevalent at the time of his death. Her coats and tailored skirts were made by Colville of Chatton (the place where my grandfather died) throughout her life. Her blouses and dresses were dressmaker-made in Wooler. Her coats were made of smooth face cloth, plain in summer, fur-trimmed in winter. On Sundays she wore black silk. The clothes she had to buy, such as hats, came from Paxton and Purvis of Berwick. I remember going once with Grannie and Auntie Isa to buy Grannie's new summer hat. By this time, the choice available to her was not large and the only suitable hat had a little bit of purple in its trimming. There was a long discussion as to whether, it being too gaudy, the entire hat should be retrimmed. In the end, it was decided she would wear it once or twice and, if she still felt the trimming was not to her taste, the hat was to be returned for refurbishing. Some milliners still bought only the hat shape, preferring to trim their hats themselves.

Occasionally, too, Grannie wore a face veil, also out of fashion. Personally, I was rather sorry about this last because I liked to see women in face-veils. A face-veil made them look prettier somehow. Those who wore them drew them up and anchored them on the brims of their hats when they were out visiting and were required to eat or drink.

With her outfit Grannie wore tight-fitting black gloves in fine kid. They were always put on very carefully, each finger caressed into place before the wealth of little pearl buttons were fastened. They were taken off just as carefully and smoothed out before being put away. Almost all the family shoes were bought at Pringle's of Wooler (people tended to be loyal to one shop in those days).

At this time there were no effective anti-perspirants or deodorants. In an attempt to counteract this problem dresses had guards, semi-circular pieces of material placed under the arms to prevent perspiration discolouring and rotting the material.

My mother kept abreast of fashion but the edges of what was decreed in good manners were blurred when it came to distinguishing between one generation and the next. Throughout her life, my mother wore a hat when she went out, even if it was only to feed the hens or put out washing. When she was visiting, she took her coat and gloves off, but never her hat, even when she'd been asked out for a meal. (Grannie Gallon did likewise, though none of Mother's sisters did.) Mother also clung to the dictate that only real jewellery should be worn and very little of that. Throughout my childhood, on Sundays and other high days, the only jewellery she wore, apart from her engagement and wedding rings, was a gold bar brooch inset with a sapphire flanked by diamonds.

Clothes, when they were new, were bought as complete outfits. First of all, the colour had to be decided upon. There were fashionable colours then as now, but, in general the fact was borne in mind that the colour chosen should be one that could withstand wear and not show the dirt. We looked at fashion magazines, and, later, the *Picture Goer* to see what the stars were wearing. Having seen these fashions in magazines we could then expect to see them worn at church, on Sunday walks, at weddings and other celebrations, because there were always those who felt they had to have a new outfit. Today, we seem to see a proliferation of fashion shows, but rarely do we see the fashions in everyday life. The ubiquitous jeans, T shirts and anoraks took over years ago.

An outfit consisted of a hat, coat, dress, gloves, shoes and handbag, all in one colour except for the shoes and bag. In summer, the dress and coat might be replaced by a costume (suit) in which case the blouse would be

Mother feeding the hens.

in a contrasting colour.

If there was to be a wedding in the family, the buying of new clothes was delayed so that everyone had something new for the wedding. Apart from her wedding dress and going away things, the bride had a trousseau. This included several sets of underwear, possibly all hand-made in art silk, milanese, celanese or crêpe de chine. She also had as many new outer garments as she could afford because, after marriage, the likelihood of her getting new clothes in the immediate future was slim indeed. All girls gave up their jobs on marriage so that the young couple had to live within the limits of one person's wage. It was more than likely, too, that a baby would put in an appearance during the first year. In fact, often the trousseau, together with the going-away outfit and the groom's wedding suit, had to do the couple for best for many years when, no doubt, they began to look very dated, though not in the eyes of the wearers. There was something about recognised 'best clothes' that defied fashion. Just to be putting them on meant the occasion, or the day, was special, even if it was just an ordinary Sunday.

There were one or two women who scorned any fashion completely. Actually, I only knew of one first-hand. She wore men's boots (her husband's old ones), a shawl over her dark skirt and blouse and man's cap skewered into place by hat pins. Age had given her outfit a certain uniformity in that, whatever colour each individual item had been originally, they were, collectively, now all dust coloured.

Incidentally, the white bridal gown was supposed to be indicative of the bride's virginity. If the bride was already pregnant, when, no doubt, the wedding date had been brought forward, if not actually instigated, then it was deemed she had no right to wear white. In fact, if the bride was already pregnant, a quiet, early morning wedding was thought to be more seemly and decent.

In our family we had two early morning weddings for a very different reason. The weddings had already been planned for two dates in February but Aunt Maggie had died the previous December so that the family was still in full mourning. Because of this, neither bride could wear white. Auntie Anna wore a grey costume and Auntie Jean wore a navy one. Both weddings were celebrated quietly at eight o'clock on a Saturday morning.

Clothes-wise, funerals were very sombre affairs. The immediate family went into 'deep' black. I am given to understand that the manager of one shop, Shepherd's (ex Russell Cook's) kept his ear to the ground as far as impending funerals were concerned. When he realised there was a death and the purchase of mourning was likely to come their way, the staff were forbidden to close the shop at 6 p.m. as was their custom. Nor were they allowed to do the preliminary tidying up. Many people paid into a Burial Club of one sort or another and possibly there was collusion between the manager and the one who paid out the money on this melancholy occasion.

'Old Mr Smith has passed on,' the manager informed his staff. 'They're paying out after tea-time. If they're coming here they should be here by half-past-six at the latest,' and, sure enough, in they all came, red-eyed as the occasion demanded.

Naturally, they started off in the men's department which was always downstairs, near a discreet door so that men who had to go there could sidle in and out as quickly as possible. Providing for the man would not take long, perhaps a new dickie, if he wore a Union shirt summer and winter, and a black tie. After that he was released and the women were at liberty to attend to their own wants. They began on the upper floor in the mantles department, first for a dress, then a coat. From there they progressed to the millinery department where the hats were set out on long stands or hidden in huge, deep drawers. Then it was downstairs to the haberdashery for black edged handkerchiefs, black stockings and black gloves.

When the manager's eyes was not upon them, the assistants did their best to prepare for this event by coercing each other to keep the choice down to a minimum.

'Just show them two styles of gloves and say that's all we have in or we'll be here all night.' The most popular style in gloves then was the gauntlet in leather, or leather with fur backs. For those who wished to pay their respects to the deceased (i.e. attend the funeral), men were easily catered for. Most had a bowler hat, a black tie and a dark suit. Black bands did the rest. For women it was different. Some had their own black which defied fashion, some borrowed and others dyed blouses and even dresses, not always successfully. Full mourning lasted a year and a day, followed by half-mourning when a touch of white, grey or purple was allowed to brighten the unrelieved black. During the period of full mourning the immediate family were not supposed to attend parties, outings or other convivial get-togethers.

When buying new clothes, those who could afford to shop at Fenwick's French Salon or (further afield) Marshall and Snelgrove, had their dresses and coats wrapped in layers of tissue paper and packed in large oblong serviceable but attractive boxes, embellished with the firm's name in silver or gold. Hats were packed in very fetching hat boxes. As hats were still universally worn, for those who travelled a hat box was almost a necessity.

Boxed new boots and shoes were thought to be of much

better quality than those bought at shops where the footwear hung on long strings like hands of bananas. As they were made of leather, new boots and shoes were very stiff and had to be wraxed (stretched). When my grandfather got new boots, before he wore them he gave them to one of his sons who had bigger feet than he and said, 'Wrax them shoes for me.' The uncle concerned had to walk around the house wearing these boots till he had stretched them and softened them up to my grandfather's satisfaction. Fortunately, boots and shoes were made with left and right feet. Some years earlier this was not the case; it was up to the wearer to walk the shoes or boots into the shape of his or her feet. When new footwear squeaked as the wearer walked, it was said it hadn't been paid for.

My father's wardrobe was dictated by my mother and he was very happy to have it that way. There are several photographs of him as a young man, extant. On them he is wearing a straw benger, wide tie and narrow trousers, which, I suppose, were the up-to-the-minute fashions of the Ashington youth of the day. Perhaps it was his mother, Grannie Summers, or his sister, Auntie Anna, who kept him in fashion, or perhaps he was anxious on his own behalf and, once he got married, he saw the overseeing of his wardrobe as part of a wife's duty.

Underneath their rather long shirts most men wore woollen linings and body shirt. The former reached to the ankles while the latter was buttoned to the neck and had long or short sleeves depending upon the likes or dislikes of the wearer. Dad tucked his linings into his woollen socks, depending on this arrangement to keep his socks up. Younger men wore sock suspenders, fastened below the knee. Usually they wore fancy socks with clocks up the side. When they sat down and hitched up their trouser legs to preserve the crease, it was possible to see their suspenders. The crease in Sunday trousers particularly was the result of that garment spending from Monday morning to Sunday morning between two sheets of brown paper under the mattress.

Dad wore a fairly wide brimmed trilby during the week, even for work. In his last years he found it very difficult to come by new replicas. On Sundays he wore a bowler till they went out of fashion when he wore a black or dark grey homburg, by which time he wore a black jacket and waistcoat and pin stripe trousers for best. He wore the same weight of clothing summer and winter except that, in winter, he wore a thick muffler and an overcoat. Once when they went on holiday, Mother persuaded him into a tweed jacket, grey flannels and open-necked shirt. Not even in the coldest weather would he wear gloves. He considered these very effeminate.

For some years men's gloves were made in pale lemon chamois leather. Very often, the most noticeable thing about a young man wearing these were the gloves themselves. I can also just remember men wearing Oxford bags and carrying cane walking sticks. White silk scarves for men were popular for many years as were plus fours these last originally intended for those who played golf. They were worn by men, young and old, who never went near a golf course or links.

All trousers were made to finish at the waist (for small men they almost went up to the arm pits), when they were kept up by braces or a thick leather belt with a buckle. Some men wore both.

Boots for men were becoming less popular, black Oxfords and brown brogues being more often worn. Men who rode bicycles wore bicycle clips round their ankles.

The most important thing was to be decent when one went out. In fact, it was considered good manners to look one's best. All shoes were highly polished in spite of the fact that many roads were unmade and clarty. Some even polished the insteps. White sandshoes were also cleaned after each wearing – either with a special whiting or pipe clay. Because of the state of the roads, almost every house had a scraper embedded in the cement near the outside door. Before entering the house, one scraped the soles of one's shoes to get the worst of any dirt off afterwards rubbing the soles of one's shoes on the coco-matting that lay just inside the house door. Shoes and boots were cleaned by the spit and polish method which was thought to give a better shine.

Even on the sunniest day most people were prepared for a sudden change in the weather. Men carried a neatly folded mackintosh over one arm and women carried a mackintosh and an umbrella. They might also carry gloshettes, a transparent, plastic-type overshoe.

I never had any real dilemma when it came to what to wear at any given time. My mother dictated my wardrobe which was not large and was strictly graded, school uniform and old clothes during the week while I was at school, work clothes and overall and I left. For going out at night there was second best and, for Sundays and occasions, best. When I had been out at night during the week, say to the pictures or to a weekly dance, as soon as I came home, I changed into something I could sit around in.

In the interests of my developing figure, I stopped wearing a vest once I left school, although I took great care to keep this information to myself. To leave off a vest at any time of the year meant one would catch one's 'death'.

After I started to work, my wardrobe grew by slow degrees. Most of my dresses were dressmaker made. My first dressmaker lived on a diet of pins and, being a compulsive eater, she always had a mouthful which impaired her speech. Clamped to her wrist was a velvet porcupine of pins to supplement her diet. Round her neck dangled a tape-measure the end of which was chewed (an unexpected dearth of pins? The pin harvest had failed that year?) so that she always had to remember to add half the length of her thumb nail. Obviously she never had the time to make any clothes for herself or do any tidying up because her person was covered in little bits of thread and faded dust from all the materials she had cut up. The upper part of her body was a reserve well-stocked larder for her desserts, needles. Needles threaded in every imaginable colour were stuck all over her bosom. Round the walls, from the picture rail, partly finished garments hung dejectedly waiting their turn to be completed, hope long since gone from their ageing hearts.

Yet, she was full of lively hope and promise. When I went to keep my appointment for a fitting, the dress was no further forward than when I was last there. Just as she was about to sew it, she'd had an idea about a different neck-line that would suit me better. Finally, I gave up. I realised that, however much I liked her and sympathised with her, if I was ever going to keep abreast of fashion I was going to have to change my dressmaker. I did, and Isa Foster became my sempstress from then on, and an excellent dressmaker she was.

Chapter 9

A Man's Job – Women's Work.

A man's job. Women's work. There is no doubt which was considered the more important. The tasks assigned to women were unworthy of men. There is no female equivalent of the word 'workmanlike'. Men and boys working inherited a common birthright. Their patrimony, as of right, was an inbuilt superiority. Beyond question they were, or would be when they married, Head of the House. The sentiment 'a man must be Boss in his own house' was often stated lest the principle escaped notice. It wasn't that they were despots or tyrants, it was just that they assumed a Divine Right. This was the way things were ordained. They were to be feared as God was feared. In some cases the fear referred to was correctly interpreted as respect. It was for me as far as my father was concerned.

As head of the house or breadwinner, a man's fads were indulged and he was served first at table. Also, wherever he sat was Head of the Table. The mother, on the other hand, sat at some convenient place where she was ever-ready to get up to go to the pantry to get something she'd forgotten, or that her husband wanted that wasn't on the table. She was also available to get the teapot from the oven door where it was keeping warm. Some men did not have to ask for a refill or have something passed to them. Their wives kept a vigilant eye on their cups/mugs and the state of their plates, anticipating just when a refill was needed, adding the milk and sugar and stirring the result. As her husband finished one course, or piece of bread, cake etc., something else replaced it till the wife judged the husband had had all he wanted.

At various times I stayed in two houses in particular where, in each case, the man of the house came home for his dinner (lunch). In each case, having eaten in relative silence, the man sat back in his chair to have 'forty winks' and we children had to sit quietly (nor were the women allowed to clear the table) till the man awoke, dusted himself down and went back to work.

In fact, if it had been said that a man was 'king in his own house', it might have given a better idea of the situation for, like royalty, men could do no wrong. They could see a woman fatigued from overwork and sit back and do nothing because to help domestically would be to diminish their masculinity.

Many, perhaps most, children went to Sunday school, but, when boys reached the age of ten, eleven or twelve and began to 'speak up for themselves', quite a number stopped going to church altogether. In adulthood, it was the women who were the most regular church-goers. My grandfather did not go to church at all. Grannie, on the other hand, was a regular church attender. She went to early communion every Sunday before she began her day's work, for, although Sunday was a day of rest for her men-folk, the same could not be said for her. There was no fixed breakfast time in their house. Each man got up when he felt like it and was catered for individually in this respect, Grannie making whatever he wanted for breakfast in between her preparations for the day's gargantuan dinner with a similar sized tea to follow later in the day.

Most of the women on both sides of my family were regular church attenders, but, among the men, only my father, Uncle Jack, Uncle Andrew, Uncle Will (Wooler) and Uncle Tommy were to be seen among those present at church. I think this state of affairs applied to many families, yet, in churches and chapels, it was the man who had the offices, the priest or minister, the church warden, the all-male choir in Ashington Church of England till they could no longer get men and boys in sufficient numbers, the Sunday school superintendant, the treasurer, the sidesmen and the elders were all men. In the main the menial tasks were left to women.

From their earliest days, the rôles they were to take up in adulthood were seen and absorbed by children. It was the mother who was given advice on how to please men.

'The way to a man's heart is through his stomach.' 'Keep him in a good humour. Do not contradict him.' 'Make him think he's right even when he's wrong. Men don't like to think they're in the wrong, especially from a woman.' 'Remember he works hard and brings in the money. always have a welcome for him'.

As one mother said, in heavy tones, to her daughter on her wedding eve, the advice highly Bowdlerised, 'NEVER deny him whatever you feel like. Remember he's a man. Give him what he wants and keep his eyes at home.'

However big the family, like his father, no boy would do any domestic chores, although he might be required to 'fill the coals', that is, keep the pails that normally stood just inside the door, filled with coals for the fire. He would also be expected to work in the garden and to shovel the load of coals into the coalhouse when a delivery had been made. My father was the eldest of eight children, the first four boys, but he grew up, as did his five brothers, without ever having to do a domestic chore.

Girls had a vastly different up-bringing. A boy would grow up to his responsibilities. He was expected to do well at school and get a decent job afterwards. When he married, he would be responsible for his wife and children. A girl grew up to duties — a bleaker outlook. If she had any inclinations of her own, she soon put them to one side in the interests of others. It was a daughter's duty to put her parents' and her family's wishes first. This was especially true if she were the eldest, or only, daughter.

Education was considered important for a boy, but not for a girl. This in spite of the fact that as many girls as boys went to the co-educational grammar schools now springing up. 'Educate a boy and dress a girl', was a maxim still prevalent. Girls should be pretty and docile. The dichotomy regarding the first requisite was that, although girls were expected to take great pains to appear as pretty and attractive as possible, yet, to tell her she was pretty or attractive would be to flatter her vanity. It seemed that young men looking for brides only considered those who were pretty and nicely dressed. To be considered plain meant one had little or no chance in the marriage stakes, for marriage was what it was all about. With this in mind, girls had to be seen as good daughters so that they could expect to become good wives.

A good woman was selfless. She never spared herself when it came to looking after others. She did her duty without complaint. Wherever she stood on the social scale, her rôle seemed to be to attend to others, to suppress any talents or abilities she might have which were outside the bounds of domesticity, to endeavour to please at all times and in all circumstances, to tolerate male behaviour and not notice when she was being exploited. Those who showed abilities or inclinations other than what was acceptable were ridiculed in an effort to belittle their talents. It was a world in which, generally speaking, only Marthas qualified. Marys had a hard time of it. An unmarried woman who showed ability, worked hard and kept down a decent job with a reasonable wage had priced herself out of the marriage market. No man would stand for it, or be expected to put up with it, even though the reasonable wage was a half or two-thirds of what a man would earn doing a similar job. A 'career girl' was destined to become an Old Maid or spinster. She belonged to the discard pile. A bachelor was a different matter. He had escaped the net.

At the same time, a woman who had merited a good job would be expected to give it up without a backward glance if she was needed at home, usually because of the illness or death of one or other of her parents. If there was an unmarried daughter available, hitherto perfectly capable women and men were thought to be unable to manage on their own after the death of their spouse.

A boy growing up was expected to make his way in the world, learning to stand on his own two feet. A girl had to depend upon her father and later, her husband, for her life-style. She had to learn to be self-sacrificing and supportive. Any job she did after she left school was only a time-filler. In this interval between leaving school and getting married, some mothers indulged their daughters, urging them to have a good time before they settled down. Experience had taught the mothers they (the daughters) were unlikely to get it afterwards. Quite a number of young people were told that from the age of sixteen or seventeen till twenty-one would be the best time of their lives.

Once a couple were married, especially after the first baby was born, they went about together less and less. The man usually went out with his mates and other male members of his family. The woman most often went to her mother's. At that time, no man would ever be seen wheeling a pram, just as no man ever, or hardly ever, went shopping.

In most cases it was the woman who operated the household expenses using what money her husband gave her. Normally this was his wage from which he was given pocket money, his to do what he liked with. On the remainder, the woman fed and clothed the household and paid all other bills. Some men, however, operated 'keepy backs', that is, the wage they gave to their wives was deficient by the sum the man thought fit to retain without telling his wife.

Most women were good shoppers. They assessed, valued, considered the cost and the quality and whether or not what they were buying was absolutely necessary.

Men, on the rare occasions when they did go into a shop, did so self-consciously, anxious that no-one should see them, their idea being to get out as soon as possible. They asked no questions. They plonked the money down without asking the price, made no complaints but just took what was offered. Most shop assistants thought they could palm anything off onto a man.

If, when he got home, his wife was not satisfied with the purchase then that was her look-out. She should have gone herself. It was yet one more good reason why he shouldn't shop. He had a similar aversion to letter-writing. The woman of the house wrote the letters and sent the cards.

For both sexes, marriage was the only way to get a home of one's own. To leave home before marriage was inconceivable. After marriage, the young man was now free to take on the rôle already exemplified by his father.

The wife, for her part, had exchanged one form of dominance for another. It was her father who had handed her over to another man at the marriage ceremony. Small wonder that mothers wanted a 'good' man for their daughters, a good man who would, if possible, give her a 'good sit-down'. (They would have a little more than enough to live on.)

Once they were married, the couple remained married. Their parents had done their work. The mother could congratulate herself that she had a daughter safely married.

Separation and divorce never entered their heads. What went on inside the marriage was the affair of the couple concerned.

There was a brotherhood among men, sometimes so strong that it seemed they were banded together against women. Men met daily at work, at the allotment, at the club, depending upon their interests. There was nothing similar among women. It seemed that men could come and go in a way that women could not. A man went to his club, a Working Man's Club (which was a male stronghold from which women were debarred), there to drink, to talk with his marras, to discuss the things that interested him. There were associations for women, mainly the Mothers' Union, the Sisterhood and the Co-operative Guild. All of these had, at their core, the betterment of the lives of others.

In the absence of the father, a grown up son temporarily took over his mantle. When I was thirteen I attended an evening class at Hirst, or the Hirst as we said. Among those present was a girl whom I shall call Mary Smith. When I say 'those present' I am exaggerating rather. She never turned up till just before the class ended. Nor did she just turn up. She made an entrance. The night was Tuesday and yet she always came dressed as if it were Sunday and she was about to visit one of the more progressive chapels of which there were none in Ashington or Hirst that I knew of. I say this because under the brim of her hat several spit curls were clearly visible. One just could not have faced the Reverend Samuel Davidson, let alone Mrs Davidson, with one's visible hair in spit curls. Matching her hat she wore a wine coloured coat with a high fur collar. The coat was much longer than fashion decreed which was just as well. The stockings she wore did not accord with her stylish outfit. On her feet she wore up-to-the-minute strapped shoes.

'Oh,' she panted as she stood in the doorway of the Store Hall where we were all seated just beginning to pack up, 'what a time I've had getting here. I'd no sooner got out of our house when I saw this lad waiting for me. What cheek! You know. I told you about him last week. Him from Newcastle with the motor bike. His father's a bank manager and I don't know what all. I nearly died. Just fancy. Waiting for me right outside our house. The cheek. I just gave him ONE LOOK. He was right upset. He says, "If you get on the back of me bike I'll give you a lift." I says. "I wouldn't get on your bike if you was the last man on earth. I think more of meself than that...." ' And so it went on. It seemed she couldn't get moved for lads seeking only a smile or a kind word from her tangee-red (orange actually) lips.

On Valentine's day three of us scraped together a half-penny and bought the sickliest card we could find adding to the saccharine words others of a long held admiration and undying love and the chance just to speak to her. Would she be at Arrowsmith's at half-past-seven where her admirer would be waiting. We went to the class early and put the envelope with her name on on the teacher's table saying, when he came in, a young man had left it.

Originally the idea sprang from the fact that we were rather tired of these weekly late entrances and, perhaps, if she waited for a non-existent suitor, we wouldn't, there-after, hear so much about the others.

At first, as we watched from our vantage point, we giggled, but somehow, seeing her standing there, I began to think it wasn't so funny. She was still there when we left. As the week advanced I began to feel a bit ashamed of my part in the episode and to compensate and because I was interested, I decided to seek out her address and call for her that we might go to the next class together.

I hadn't the least idea where she lived and the Hirst was a fairly big place largely made up of rows and rows of near identical houses. However, the task ahead was not arduous. One simply went to the first house that seemed likely and asked. In this case I picked out a house where both the yard and the house doors were open and I could hear sounds of people talking. I knocked on the door.

On occasions like these, the member least capable of answering one's question is sent to the door to see who it is.

'Please,' I said to the small girl who stood there, 'does Mary Smith live here?'

'Mam,' yelled the child although the short passage was adjacent the kitchen and there was no intervening barrier, 'there's a lass here wants to know if Mary Smith lives here.'

'Eh'

'DOES MARY SMITH LIVE HERE?'

While this dialogue was going on the child at the door was joined by two others slightly older. Finally the mother came.

'Mary Smith. No, hinny. Nobody of that name lives here. Were you given this address?'

'No. I just know she lives somewhere at the Hirst.'

'Bill,' shouted the mother, her head turned towards the kitchen, 'do you know anyone called Smith round here. They have a lass called Mary. There's them Smiths in the middle of the next block but except for two lads their family's up and away. Them five doors up has kin called Smith on the Avenues but there's not a Mary among them. There's Jinnie and Marget and Betty but they've never been a family for Mary's.'

By this time the mother had moderated her tone a little because the entire family, including the father, were crammed into the passage, cudgelling their brains to ferret out the whereabouts of Mary Smith. When, between them, they had disposed of all the families and their kin in a five hundred yards radius, I was sent two streets up to number 19 to ask there.

At number 19 not only was I given explicit directions on how to get to the Smiths, I got a run-down on their circumstances. The father wouldn't be in. He worked nights and he liked to leave early to get there in plenty of time. The mother was one of them gan-aboot-kind and she was a great one for the Guild. She wouldn't be in either. There was one lass married. She lived at the Winning. Another one was still at home but she had a job at one of them picture houses and Mary would be leaving school before long.

I found the house and knocked at the door. Mary opened it and when she saw it was me standing in the shaft of light the open door afforded, she hissed,

'Go away. Go on. Gerraway.'

'Who is it?' a man's voice called.

'It isn't anybody,' Mary replied.

'I SAID WHO IS IT?'

'It's only one of me friends come to seek me for the class.

150

I said I'm not ready.'

'Tell her to come in.'

I went in reluctantly, wishing with all my heart I'd never come. I didn't like the sound of the man's voice. Making myself as inconspicuous as possible, I stood just inside the kitchen door-way. A man in his mid-twenties was sitting at the table in his shirt sleeves eating. He neither looked at me nor spoke to me. Mary stood back a little way from the table, her eyes on the food her brother was consuming. When he was almost finished, she cut a piece of bread and handed it to him. He mopped up the remains of his meat and gravy with the bread and sat back still chewing. Mary took away his dirty plate and replaced it with a large dish of pudding that had been keeping warm in the oven. As her brother gulped this down, she made a pot of tea from the kettle now coming to the boil on the fire. She stood gently rotating the tea-pot in her hand until her brother pushed back his empty pudding plate when she filled a pint mug with tea, added sweetened condensed milk from the jagged edged tin on the table and stirred the tea.

'D'you want anything else?' she asked in subdued tones.

'I would have said if I did, wouldn't I?' he replied testily.

'Can I clear the table, then?'

He didn't reply and she took the dirty dishes away and busied herself in the pantry. I kept on standing there and the young man decanted his steaming tea into a wide saucer, blew on it, put the saucer to his lips and with a loud suction noise drew up the liquid from the saucer. This method of drinking cooled the tea still further. Mary returned and waited quietly till he had drained his mug when she took it away and came back to rub down the American cloth that did duty as a tablecloth.

Her brother got up from the table, put a cigarette in his mouth and, picking up the fireside tongs, he extracted a piece of red hot coal from the fire. With this he lit his cigarette and sitting in the Windsor chair, he stretched out and put his feet on the fender.

Mary watched him and when he was settled she said quietly, 'Can I go now?'

He leaned down and picked up a pair of mirror-bright shoes.

'D'you call them clean,' he said and, throwing the shoes towards her he commanded, 'Do them again.'

She went to the glory hole under the stairs and brought out the blacking and brushes. Kneeling down, she opened the tin of blacking, spit into it and recleaned the already shining shoes.

'Will them do?' she asked after her considerable exertions. He didn't answer. His cigarette was almost finished. Finally he threw the cigarette end into the fire and said, 'You can go.' Leaning back, he stretched out and closed his eyes. Mary put away the cleaning things and taking a worn coat from a nail behind the back door, she put it on and we went out.

'What did you want to come for?' she said crossly when we got outside. 'I'll be late. He wouldn't have made me clean them shoes again if you hadn't been there.'

Instead of going out of the yard, she went into the wash-house which was adjacent their house, fumbled for a second, struck a match and lit a candle standing in a tin candle-stick. From her pocket she took a little bit of looking-glass, a threepenny (1¼p) tin of Snowfire powder and little tube of tangee lipstick.

'What are you doing?' I asked, aghast at this further waste of time.

'Minding me own business,' she replied, as, her hasty make-up session over, she liberally coated her fingers with saliva and plastered strands of her hair like cup hooks across her forehead. Then she took off her coat and from under the mangle cover she produced her normal Tuesday night garb.

'Where did you get those?' I asked.

'You've got eyes haven't you? I brought them down before he came in. They're me sister's Sunday things. She'll never know.'

'What if somebody catches you? You'll get into awful trouble.'

'Nobody will. He's fast asleep now and he'll be gone before I get back and the rest'll not be in,' she said as she buttoned the straps of her sister's shoes. Those shoes were going to slow down our progress considerably.

'Unless we run we'll not get to the class before it finishes,'

I said, as we let ourselves out of the yard gate.

'You can run if you like,' she said. 'I'm not going. You know that Valentine. I'm seeing him tonight. He's real posh.'

'I'll run on then,' I countered, 'but it's a pity about the class. The teacher will miss you. I think he has a bit fancy for you.' (If she could lie, so could I.)

'Gerraway,' she began but quickly recovered. 'Yes, I know but I thought he'd kept it secret like in case folk talked. But –'

'I'll run on,' I cut in, 'and I'll not tell anyone I've seen you. Honest. Cross me heart.'

The class was beginning to think of packing up when I panted in and not even the teacher was interested in my garbled reason for being late. Before we left Mary arrived, two bright spots of tangee lipstick having been applied to her cheeks in place of rouge. She had eyes only for the teacher as she told him how she'd shaken off her latest conquest.

She didn't stay the course. I'd like to be able to tell you she changed her name to Gloria Divine and became a famous film star, but Hollywood producers and their talent scouts, together with their British counterparts, tended not to come to the Hirst – at least, not to the Store Hall on a Tuesday night. Her history was much more prosaic. She left school and was needed at home. To help with her keep she got domestic work half-days. Thus they got two full days' work out of her for very much less than the price of one.

As men grew older and were less able to do the heavy work entailed in working on the coal face, they were given a light job on bank (i.e. not underground). Thus the pattern of their working lives changed.

That of women did not change so markedly. True, the family grew up and married and her child bearing years ceased, but the pattern of her days remained the same and she gave a hand in the running of her children's houses and the looking after of their children.

One day I met a man who had retired the week before. I nodded to him in passing and said, 'Enjoying retirement?'

He stopped me.

'I've just had a grand bit of good news,' he said. 'It's the club trip next Monday for the Old Folk and because I've just retired I didn't think I'd qualify but they've just told me that me and the wife can go. I'm going to keep it as a surprise till the last minute.'

I thought about him on the Monday. It was a glorious day. About a week later I saw him again.

'How did the trip go?' I asked. 'You had a wonderful day.'

'Don't mention trip to me,' he said. 'It was awful. Never again. I didn't tell the wife till Sunday night when she started filling up the kit from the yard with cold water. "What are you doing that for?" I says. "For the washing," she says. "What else?" "There'll be no washing for you," I says, "I've got a real surprise. I've been keeping it up me sleeve. We're going on a free trip with the club." You should have heard her. She nearly hit the roof. "Up your sleeve is the best place for your surprise," she says. "What about the washing?" "Do it another time," I says. Women never think. They're not like men. They can't work things out. "What about me other work?" she says. "What other work," I says. "Just leave it." She went on and on, you wouldn't believe. There's no pleasing some folk. I had an awful job getting her to go and she grumbled the whole way. The weather was lovely and the company was grand. We got fish and chips free at Amble. They were champion. Then we had a bit of free time and a slap-up tea at Wooler afore we come back to the club where we all got tickets for free drinks. What better could anybody ask for? But hor. The whole day she kept saying, "I could have had me washing out by now." "I could have had the sheets in and mangled." "I could have had everything starched." "The ironing would have been nearly finished by now." She never stopped. And when we got to Wooler she says, "I don't know what we've come here for? There's nothing here. Wasting time. When I think of what I could have done this day. It's been one of the best washing days we've had this year." Never again. I tell you, man woman, it was awful.'

These clearly defined roles of men and women, boys and girls, and the structured lives each followed in fulfilling their rôle expectations made for security, but it also inhibited personal growth and put up barriers between the sexes when it came to relationships. There were those of both sexes who were very happy with things the way they were. There were others who thought that God, himself, had ordained things this way. Women especially, who thought this saw duty as a divine attribute. Those who carried this idea to extremes made themselves into doormats on the premise that the more they suffered in the cause of duty, the greater would be their ultimate reward. Any personal inclinations they might have had were suppressed to such an extent they no longer had an entity.

Women, however good they were at their jobs, had to give up paid employment on marriage. No man would allow his wife to work.

To assume one holds the reins of authority as of right, entails a terrible burden of responsibility. Men were expected to be right always for no other reason than that they were men. 'Don't argue with your father.' What happened to their integrity when they were discovered to be wrong and could not be contradicted? Were they, themselves, ever attacked by doubt or uncertainty? If they were, it was not noticeable. They never agonised.

There were men who had doubts, I'm quite sure, but, in the home especially, they learned to dissemble. This led me to think that men had no real feelings. They were not troubled by nerves, uncertainty or worry. Nor could they see any given situation in anything other than their terms.

As I saw it it was a boy's and a man's world. I didn't envy men, but I *did* envy boys. How I envied all the things they were allowed to do. They seemed to be gods. They had passports that allowed them to go anywhere, do anything, come in when they liked, go where they liked and no-one asked them searching questions as to what they'd been up to. I didn't have to bother about their feelings. I didn't think they cared enough to be hurt or upset, that when I turned down a date or an invitation to a dance, they felt nothing at this rejection but simply went and asked someone else. I was expendable. I did not consider that young men could be hurt or diffident or lacking in confidence. I thought confidence was synonymous with

155

masculinity. I never dreamed that any boy or young man might have suffered on my account – or even considered me as a valued companion. Years later I learned, painfully, that I had been wrong, sadly wrong on my blanket opinion of all men, young and old.

My male relatives all seemed to be big men and those who were taller than average appeared giants. My grandfather was of average build but I thought of him as a giant. The infant that had pulled herself up in her cot, pointed at Grandfather and said, 'Bo o' wicky' had long since disappeared. I was afraid of him, his bulk, his voice, his authority. He, more than any man I knew, coloured and inhibited my relationship with the adult men in my family. I think this pertained because they were all so deferential to him. I felt awkward and ill-at-ease in situations where my uncles were really trying to be relaxed and friendly and I giggled nervously at their teasing.

Not all men were so inflexible in their outlook. My father wasn't, nor was Uncle Kit, Uncle Andrew or Uncle Tommy, but there was still this barrier between men and children. When one went visiting without prior arrangement, if the man of the house was not in, it made little difference to the visit. If, however, the woman was not in, the house was empty.

Although men and boys were not supposed to do any domestic work, yet, possibly some was done without it being spoken of. When my father was on day shift or night shift he often turned the mangle for my mother on washing days. Moreover, he did this as though he was used to the exercise, so that, in his youth, he might have performed this act for my grandmother as a matter of course on her washing days. In addition, I often heard Will Coombes, a family friend, admit to helping his mother by 'double possing' with her on wash days. (They had two poss-sticks and they thumped the clothes in harmony, one coming down as the other went up.)

Would that I had had a much closer relationship with my father. Together with my mother, he wanted to give Billy and me the things he had been denied, principal among those being a good education. Thus we both, went to grammar school. In the climate of the time, this was considered right and proper as far as Billy was concerned, but not as far as I was concerned. I am more grateful than I can possibly say that my parents gave me this opportunity.

I now realise my father and I had much in common, but the invisible wall was a barrier that made for constraint and the taboo on tenderness, together with the rules of the day, prohibited a closer relationship.

Chapter 10

Food

We ate a basic four meals a day – breakfast, dinner, tea and supper. There were no such things as mid-morning breaks, elevenses or an afternoon tea-break. There had to be a good and noble reason for drinking a cup of tea between meals.

'There was some tea left in the tea-pot keeping warm on the oven door and it was a shame to throw it out'. 'My head was bursting fit to split so I just had to take an aspirin'. 'I felt a bad turn coming on so I just says to myself, you'll have to sit yourself down for two minutes and make a sup tea and it'll pass off. I made up for it after.'

The speaker was always careful to say she hadn't stopped work when she had her tea.

The actual meal times and the contents of the meal depended upon the man of the house, the work he did and the shift he was on. My father worked a seven day week on a shift system so that he came home at about two-thirty in the afternoon, ten-thirty at night or six-thirty in the morning.

In Grannie's case, throughout her married life, whatever shift my grandfather was on, she got up and cooked him eggs and bacon. Or, more likely, ham. They kept two pigs, one in the pantry (i.e. ham & bacon) and one in the sty. My grandfather liked eggs and bacon before he went to work.

As far as I know, all men who worked at the pit took bait with them. This was really a packed meal carried in a bait tin specially designed to cater for slices of bread. Like the cold tea which was carried in a tin bottle, the food was protected from the mice which lived on the coal face. Most men liked two thick slices of bread with a filling of either cheese or jam.

Bread, the staff of life, was made on a Tuesday. In our house, any old bread still remaining in the bread bin was either turned into a bread pudding or crisped up in the oven to be flattened by the rolling pin or churned up in the mincer, and thereafter used as bread crumbs. We had a huge earthenware baking dish in which the bread was made. Flour was taken from the big flour bin and riddled before it fell into the baking dish, this to get rid of anything undesirable that had found its way into the flour bin. The end product of baking day, as far as we were concerned, was sufficient loaves to last us through the week, tea-cakes to last us till the week-end and grannie loaves which were not in the least like the rather pale efforts one buys today. Ours were thick with dried fruit.

Nothing equals the smell of a house on baking days. The bread, fadges, stottie cakes, tea-cakes and grannie loaves were cooled on any surface that lent itself to propping up the finished products. Window sills were often used and, coming home from school, one often got a foretaste of what to expect at home as one smelt, and saw, newly-baked bread cooling.

I don't think anyone associated stomach upsets with the way food was looked after and prepared.

'You've got to eat a peck of dirt before you die,' I heard said more than once when a housewife, taking in a cooled loaf that had collected a smut, wiped it over with a pinny she had worn for at least two days. Once cooled, the bread was housed in a bread bin, but most other food stood uncovered on the pantry shelves, an open invitation to flies. Some people did have a meat safe, a sort of wooden box with at least one side made of perforated metal sheeting.

The subsidiary baking day was usually Saturday morning when scones, buns, tarts and cakes were made against the week-end, the great stand-bys (at least in our house) being gingerbread, ginger snaps, seed cake, sandwich cake, rock buns, queen cakes and rice cake, my father's favourite. All of these had a reliable, solid appearance. Cakes they might be, but they were filling cakes, for the great thing about food was that it had to be filling.

The highlight of the week was Sunday dinner. This consisted of a joint of meat of the sort that few people buy any more. Housewives then knew all the various cuts of meat and what they should look like. Depending upon the season, legs of pork or lamb and fillets of lamb alternated with the available cuts of beef. With the meat went Yorkshire pudding, potatoes, other vegetables and gravy.

At Grannie's every Sunday without fail, they had rice pudding to follow. I liked rice pudding. Mum rang the changes. We seldom had rice pudding. Instead we had vermicelli, tapioca (frog spawn), sago, semolina (lumpy), ground rice pudding, cornflour pudding (also lumpy) and a quite dreadful (to me) barley pudding.

On the whole, I just did not like dinners so that I was a Trial. A real Trial. I must have made Sunday dinner times at home a misery on many occasions. Children were not pandered to as far as food was concerned. (Or anything else for that matter.) We sat down to table with its white cloth, best cutlery (it was Sunday), best cruet plus the ubiquitous huge glass salt cellar in which rested a shining salt spoon. As at Grannie Summers' this last was never used. Those who wanted salt used the end of their knives to dig up a small pile. They then carefully positioned the knives over their dinner plates. Gently moving their arms so that the knife eventually passed over the plate area, with the fingers of their other hands, they tapped the blade of the knife near the handle, thus sending a little shower of salt evenly over their food.

Mother served the food. My plate was put before me. The meat had fat on it which I hated, but it was good for me. The potatoes were mashed, but not to the creamy consistency which would have made them at least edible as far as I was concerned. And then there were the vegetables which, as was common in those days, had almost had the life boiled out of them. I looked down at my plate. I had to eat it all up. I would get nothing more to eat till it was finished. It was good food. Many would be glad of it. (I only said, 'They can have it for me,' once.) It just wasn't fair. Why could the others eat so heartily? Why was it that I so disliked something which they so obviously enjoyed? Why was it that all the food I didn't like was the very food that did me so much good? 'Linda will eat any rubbish.' Why, oh why was what I liked rubbish? And why couldn't I just say 'No thank you'? Adults did. In the mean-time the food was getting colder. By the time they'd finished pudding the fat was beginning to congeal on my plate. Tears, sobbing tears, were of no avail. I had to do something.

I nibbled at the food while they were all eating, taking the bits that could be gulped down without chewing. When they had finished I knew they would leave the table and Mother would set about clearing up preparatory to washing up. I wore gym knickers into which I often put bits of paper. While Mum was out I transferred the meat to my knickers' pocket (protected by the paper) pretending to be chewing the meat when she returned. I dumped as much as possible of the remaining food on the soil of the plant housed in the yettling, to be disposed of later, and gulped the rest down. Of course, after that there was the pudding, now cold. I could manage to eat all but the vermicelli and the barley. I gulped these down with a bit of jam to take the taste away. Sometimes, before I was finally released from the table, I had to give thanks for the food I'd eaten. What I really gave thanks for was that Sunday dinner was over for another week.

All men were expected to be big eaters. Their plates were piled high with potatoes at dinner times. Potatoes were an obligatory part of this main meal. When I was a very young child I heard 'Now give him more potato. He's a big man. He'll take a lot of filling' so often that I thought men had lids on the tops of their heads into which food was ladled until their bodies had been completely filled from the toes up.

For the rest of the week, on Monday, wash-day, dinner was cold meat and a fry-up of all that remained of Sunday's potatoes and vegetables with cold rice pudding if there was any left, and tea and left over cakes from Sunday if there wasn't. Tuesday saw the last of Sunday's joint turned into pan haggerty or rissoles, both of which I liked, mercifully. Dinner-wise, Wednesday, Thursday and Friday generally weren't too bad. The bones of the weekend joint were boiled, together with bacon bones, to make stock for broth. These bones came from the bacon counter at the store. When the bacon man boned a side, he threw the discarded bones in the direction of the box kept under the counter for their collection. Most often he hit the box, but sometimes he didn't and the bones landed in the sawdust. These were later retrieved by an apprentice who put them, complete with sawdust, in the box with the other bones.

The broth was made in a huge iron pan from which it was served. As it was reheated on successive days, so it got progressively thicker. With the broth went a filling pudding, usually a clooty pudding of which nothing could be fillinger. Clooty puddings were made with suet, wrapped in a cloth and boiled. The most popular was spotted dick, a suet pudding thick with currants. It was eaten with sugar and milk or custard. The runners up were jam roly poly and treacle pudding. Another favourite was a thick suet crust with fruit inside. This was either boiled in a cloth or steamed in a basin. Ginger pudding and boiled rice and currants were also popular.

Instead of broth, hot-pot, leek puddings in a suet crust or stew and dumplings were common mid-week dinners, as were fish (usually herrings which were cheap) and mince.

On Saturdays we had a tea-dinner, that is, one easily prepared and very like a tea. This was the only dinner I really looked forward to. When she did her Saturday baking Mother made delicious meat mince pies for the dinner. With these, we had peas and grannie loaf to follow.

Because we had hens we occasionally had a fowl for Sunday dinner. The bird sacrificed was one who had laid its last egg and whose useful life was thus over. Experience taught us to kill these birds at night; they were easier to catch. The deed having been done, they had to hang for a few days before they were plucked and drawn. Mother did the plucking. She went into the scullery, back-end or wash-house, depending upon which house we lived in at the time, closed all the doors, shrouded her hair and clothes in suitable bits of material and set to work. It took quite a bit of strength to pull out all the feathers. Usually the carcase was dipped in boiling water first to make the job easier. Wings feathers were put aside to be used as supplementary brushes for getting at awkward corners of the fireside. The big feathers passed to Billy to add to a paper Indian head-dress and the small feathers were put into a bag to help make the next pillow. Once the hen was plucked and drawn, it was singed all over with a lighted bit of paper. In spite of all the feathers that had been collected, there was still a fair residue distributed over the room. Nothing was easy. The giblets were used to make gravy. When it was ready for cooking, Mother boiled the hen gently first, then roasted it slowly and the end product really was delicious. Naturally, the bones went towards making chicken soup.

Breakfasts were always rushed meals as far as I recall. However, I do remember a time when we sat down to porridge or Shredded Wheat or Force. This was probably before we started school. After that it was a rush to get to school before the bell stopped ringing, or a rush to catch the train, or a rush to get to work on time.

Teas were simple meals of bread, butter, jam and, usually, cake. We always had something cooked for supper and here, again, I was often in a minority. Favourite supper dishes for the rest of the family were boiled tripe and onions (which I couldn't stand), boiled onions with a cheese sauce (which I thoroughly disliked), cheese and sausage which I liked very much. After a disastrous evening when I really did attempt to eat tripe, the very sight and smell of which nauseated me, I was sick and, as a result, we never had tripe and onions again, which was a great pity. They all loved it. I would have been happy with bread and butter, but that, I feel would not have been the way to bring up a child correctly.

Men demanded good cooking i.e. food cooked the way they liked it or had got used to and they expected a meal to be ready when they came in. Indeed, children also expected there to be at least signs of a meal when they came in from school. Except when she was in hospital and there was somebody else there to look after us, I never remember coming home and not finding my mother in.

All boiled food was cooked over an open fire in iron pans well acquainted with soot. Where water had to be carried and heated over the fire one dish of water sufficed for the washing-up after a meal. By the time the last plate had been disposed of, the water was like dirty grey soup. It was in this that the pans were washed.

Quite apart from the day to day meals there was other work connected with food. We never had bought jam. The top shelf in the pantry contained a wealth of jars of jam, all made at home. Strawberry, gooseberry, blackcurrant, redcurrant, rhubarb, raspberry, marrow and plum jams were all made from produce grown in the garden.

Mum made blackberry jam from the fruit we picked in the hedgerows, and marmalade from Seville oranges. In addition to all this jam, Mother bottled fruit so that we had fruit tarts, of which we were all fond, throughout the year.

Mum also made cheese from sour milk. The milk was put into a gauzy container and hung up when it was allowed to drip for several days. When all the liquid had gone salt was added to the remaining soft cheese and very nice it was. She also tried making butter by shaking cream in a screw top jar. It took for ever and the small quantity of butter resulting wasn't worth the effort.

Other foods stored were eggs which were put down in large jars and covered with waterglass when they were at their cheapest and most plentiful. These eggs were used for cooking. Cooking apples were also stored, wrapped individually in newspaper.

All meals were eaten sitting up at table. Where there were large families, forms were used instead of chairs. In very large families meals were eaten in relays.

For most of my young life, not only were breakfasts hurried meals, dinners also had to be eaten as quickly as possible. While I was at Bothal school and during my time as a Store lass, I had over two miles to walk and have a meal, all within an hour.

Food also brought treats. Sunday tea was, in itself, a treat. At Grannie Summers' it always had the air of a party. In fact, nearly all treats were associated with tea-time, because this meal was synonymous with sweet things which in turn were synonymous with parties.

Hot toast and butter or dripping tasted wonderful, particularly on a cold day. Toast was made in front of a red fire. The bread was impaled on the end of a toasting fork. Rigid forks meant one had to sit near the fire, when it wasn't only the bread that was toasted. One changed from hand to hand and attempted to move out of the direct heat, so that the resultant delicacy had been achieved at some pleasurable discomfort. The best toasting forks could be extended so that one was able to sit further away from the fire. Really up-to-the-minute toasting forks could be placed on a rest so that they didn't have to be held by hand. To a generation used to some kind of discomfort as a necessary adjunct to living, this was rather like cheating.

Bread and butter sprinkled with sugar or spread with condensed milk, jam or syrup was also a treat as was new bread, teacake and scones on baking days.

Bought cakes were a treat for the simple reason we hardly ever had them. In fact I only remember being sent to buy cakes once and that was when we had unexpected company in the middle of the week. As far as bought cakes were concerned, the one that surpassed all others was Gardiner's custard tart, a deep-filled creamy custard held in delicious short-crust pastry. It cost twopence which was then the price of a cream cake. I have never since tasted its equal.

Just as we never had bought cakes, neither did we have bought fish and chips except very rarely. A piece of fish cost twopence, the chips to go with it a penny. This was called 'one of each' which entitled the buyer to ask for screnchems, the little bits of batter that had decided to leave the fish for an independent existence. Those who took newspapers to the shop could expect a few extra chips. Indeed, newspapers could be bartered for chips.

Most ice-cream shops made their own ices. During the summer this ice-cream was sold 'round the doors' from a cart. It was placed in a metal container, itself packed in ice. Some ice-cream was better than others so that, when the cart was in the vicinity one had first to find out whose it was. When we patronised the cart, I was given a basin and two pence. After my twopennyworth had been meted out the vendor put two wafers on the top. Before I handed over my twopence I asked for 'six more wafers, please'.

I cannot remember visiting an ice-cream parlour when I was a child but I did, on rare occasions, visit a café for tea and cakes when a selection was brought on a plate.

One of the drawbacks to summer weather was the tendency for milk to go sour, butter to melt and meat and fish to go off. Milk was usually boiled straight away; meat and fish cooked. Little could be done for butter except stand it on the pantry floor. Summer and autumn brought a bonus in that we could, when we got the opportunity, eat fresh peas, gooseberries and rhubarb from the garden, blackberries from the hedgerows and bagies (small turnips) from the fields. Also there was always the chance of a little apple-scrumping. If these were forbidden, then they tasted the sweeter. Hips and haws did not come into their own till during the Second World War.

When we had company the table displayed the best my mother could provide in the way of culinary art. What I learned from these occasions was a form of behaviour which I thought was part of company manners. Men were served first and they took the food they were given for granted. Women always said, 'There's too much meat there for me. Take some off and give it to the men. One small piece is enough for me.' When it came to the sweet things which followed, when men had finished, they were finished. With women it was different. When they said, 'No. No thank you. I've had sufficient,' they were never listened to.

'Go on,' the hostess would say, putting something else on her guest's plate, 'you can eat that. It'll not keep. Any way, there's nothing in it.' When she said this, she was probably referring to a sizeable piece of cake. We'd never heard of calories.

As food would not keep over the weekend, many people left their shopping till late on Saturday nights when food was usually sold off cheaply. This was particularly true of Paddy's Market which, to my great disappointment, I never visited. The only things I knew of in this respect were the cakes the Store bakery sold off cheaply on Monday mornings. When I was on holiday from school and I helped Mum with the washing on Monday mornings I was occasionally given twopence to go to the nearby bakery for twopennyworth of stale cakes. Over the weekend these rejected morsels must have clung to each other in sympathy for the cakes were all lumped together in the bag. It was a sort of lucky packet. The girl just picked up two lumps and put them in a bag. When I got home we separated them to see what we'd got. They were always good value.

We took to heart the saying, 'Waste not want not' in food as in everything else. The string round the parcels of groceries that came weekly from the Store was always carefully unpicked and put away to be used again and again, something that can't be done with sellotape. The brown paper was carefully smoothed out, folded and put away for re-use. Paper bags, too, were prized. So were newspapers. These were not just read minutely by every member of the family, they were saved. Like jam jars, they were currency. As I have already said, they could be exchanged for chips. Cut up into squares, they were a very necessary part of the necessary. They were also used as supplementary blazers for the fire. The blazer was propped up on the hob and a sheet of newspaper put over so that there was no draught from the sides or the top. This created a terrific draught at the bottom and one had a roaring fire in no time. The second before the paper would have burst into flames it was whipped off, faintly brown. It was then carefully folded ready for the next time.

All peelings and waste from vegetables went on the compost heap. Suitable scraps of food were added to the hens' feed. Scraps were given to dogs as well. Then, dog food and cat food was not sold in tins. Remaining waste (very little) went to someone who kept pigs. Tea leaves were used to clean the carpet. They were dampened and liberally sprinkled over the carpet, then brushed up. Ashes were used to clean the fender and fire irons and cinders to fill any holes in the road.

As I have already said, the food I liked wasn't good for me so that, by one means or another, I had to eat the things which, in the main, I did not like that I might grow into a healthy adult. Now that I am well advanced in adulthood little seems to have changed food-wise. Dieticians and healthy-eating authorities abound warning me that the food I like is fattening, unhealthy and likely to cause premature serious illnesses with their concomitant shrivelling of the quality of life, or even, the ending of life itself.

Chapter 11

Interim Report

I was born into a very close-knit community where everyone had a place and the place of a child was low indeed. We were by no means the centre of even our small universe. I accepted the conditions prevailing because there was no choice. It was as well to learn quickly that one had to take the rough with the smooth.

The overall feeling during my formative years was one of cosy warmth as far as Station Road was concerned. This might be because I spent a fair bit of time in bed recovering from one illness or another and because, at night, I was never really alone. The door of the room in which I slept was never closed. It opened straight onto the kitchen where the fire was never allowed to die out. There was always, at least, a friendly glow in the bedroom and, usually, I went to sleep to the sound of low voices.

In general, a little girl was expected to be good, obedient and pretty to look at.

'What are little girls made of?

Sugar and spice and all things nice.'

'All things nice' included the ability to please. Unfortunately, some people were very difficult to please.

The people who mattered were the adults in one's life of whom one's parents and family were at the forefront. We took them on trust as they were. We did not know they had thoughts or feelings because these were kept from us. We only knew they had duties. They were unpredictable sometimes, but that very unpredictability was also a stabilising factor. Today they were in a bad fettle. Tomorrow they might feel different.

There were occasional family rows. I hated these and hoped they would soon blow over as I knew they would. That my parents might part never entered my head. Divorce was something I knew nothing about. Like everyone else I knew in Ashington, I took for granted that most men worked in the pits and all women stayed at home and looked after the house.

Adults expected unquestioned obedience from children who, they considered, were too young to be reasoned with. Children expected adults to lecture them accepting that they had no right of reply. However reasonably it was put, to query what they said was 'cheek' or 'answering back' both of which were punishable offences.

Adults were also on their guard not to put ideas into children's heads nor did they give praise lest the child concerned got above himself or herself, or worse, became swollen headed. Generally speaking, adults were undemonstrative, feelings and sentiments were taken for granted. Except at New Year there was very little kissing, certainly none in public.

The rules for acceptable behaviour in children were handed down by word of mouth. When they are set out as under, the list is long.

At meal-times, sit up straight and keep your elbows off the table.

Close your lips while you are eating and do not take large bites.

Do not speak with your mouth full.

Ask to have food passed to you. Do not stretch across the table.

Hold your knife and fork correctly.

Do not make a noise when you are eating or drinking.

Eat all the food which is put before you. Chew your food thoroughly.

One piece of bread and butter, one piece of bread, butter and jam before asking for cake. Only one piece of cake.

Use a jam spoon when you take jam from the dish.

Ask if you wish to leave the table. (Permission to leave the table was rarely given if there were others still eating. Even if everyone had finished permission was not always given if the adults were talking in a general way. This was particularly the case if the child concerned was half way towards leaving when he or she asked.)

The general rules of good behaviour were,

Children should be seen and not heard.

Speak when you are spoken to and not until. Speak up.

Do not mumble. Do not tell lies. Do not interrupt.

Say please/thank you/sorry.

Put your hand over your mouth when you cough.

Sneeze into your handkerchief and say 'excuse me'.

Be respectful to your elders. Do not annoy them.

Do not meddle with things that do not belong to you.

Respect other people's property. If you do not, you cannot expect them to respect yours.

Put duty before pleasure. Speak the truth and shame the devil

Be obedient and grateful for what is being done for you.

Do not draw attention to yourself.

No matter how much you grumble, cry or whine, the answer is NO.

Do not fidget in church.

Thus did parents try, conscientiously, to bring their children up in the way they should go. Very often the standard of behaviour expected in one's own home was more relaxed than that expected of one on a visit. When visiting we were expected to behave well to show we had been well brought up. In this instance, it was really the parents who were on trial.

For those of us who went to church, the Catechism and the Commandments provided a cateract of do's and don'ts. We learned them all by rote. Much of what I learned has stayed with me although I did not understand much of what I was learning at the time.

Punishments when given were always carried out, usually immediately. Rewards, on the other hand, had to be earned first, then waited for. When one had done well, it was soon glossed over and forgotten, probably because of the danger of its producing a swollen head. On the other hand, when one had done badly, it was remembered for ages and sometimes punished. At school, the standard punishment was the strap. Sometimes it hurt, sometimes it was no more than a token recognition of the fact that one had misbehaved and, therefore, had to be punished. Sometimes, instead of the strap, one got a telling off. I preferred the strap. It was part of the day to day ups and downs and, at least, it was quickly over with. A telling off could go on for ever and the whole class listened. Punishments meted out at home were more varied. For corporal punishment a slipper, the back of a hair brush, the pit belt or one's mother's or father's hand was used in lieu of the school strap. As far as I was concerned, in this respect, I cannot ever remember being smacked by my father. Most often, it was Mother who administered corporal punishment, usually a quick stinging slap. Other punishments were, being sent out of the room, usually upstairs to a cheerless bedroom, being sent supperless to bed, not being allowed cake or jam at tea-time, having to go without the following Saturday's penny, not being allowed out to play for a specific length of time, being made to do a job in the house such as cleaning out a cupboard and being denied a treat such as going to the pictures.

The greatest punishment for me was that I had disappointed someone whom I admired, liked or loved. By far, the punishment I most disliked was the silent disapproval, so silent that I often did not really know why I was in disgrace. The knotted, shut-out feeling of being ignored was hurtful and distressing but, when I was eventually spoken to, the relief was so great I felt only gratitude that it was over and the overwhelming desire to try and see that I did not default in that way again.

The list of what one should and should not do appears formidable but it had, at its root, the desire to train children to have consideration for others and to respect other people's property. Unfortunately, the adult habit of not taking children into their confidence even when such a course would have been advisable, was often counter-effective. We did not realise that when we were told such and such a thing would happen, a long, exhaustive discussion had gone on between the adults beforehand.

For the child, too many and too rigid rules inhibited thought and retarded maturity. In my case, fearing that the truth might make me unacceptable, I took refuge in unconvincing, tongue-tied answers and I often pretended to understand things I didn't. Again, when one reached the age of revolt, of doing the opposite, not because one wanted to but *because* it was the opposite, there were so many rules and regulations it was easy to be defiant and break one or two without any serious damage to oneself or one's family. In my early and middle teens I had to be in by nine-thirty at the latest. All I had to do when I felt defiant was stand outside shivering in the cold and wet till the Council clock struck the half-hour and *then* go home. Today's youngsters have so much freedom and so many material possessions that, when it comes to revolt, they have to do something quite drastic.

As far as I knew, these rules and regulations applied to all children. They were a necessity of growing up just as earning a living and keeping a house clean were necessities of adulthood. I was never so repressed that I lost the ability to use my imagination or my initiative, nor did I lose interest in what was going on around me.

At 180 Station road, I got used to things being near at hand. The kitchen was the focus of activity. It contained nearly everything we needed. As the doors leading to the scullery and the other two rooms were never really shut, the flat was a unit with the kitchen its nerve centre. Letters, bills, reminders and important cuttings from newspapers were propped behind ornaments on the mantelpiece. Things in constant usage were near at hand in the cupboard.

At Ashbourne Crescent there were more rooms and more room generally. I had my own room which, at first, was a heady delight until I found out what sleeping alone meant. The fearfulness of it. The shadows. The sounds. How far away everyone was. How dark it was. Did the furniture move? Were there ghosties in the shadows? Were those knockings? And tappings? What did it mean? Did it mean death? My imagination ran riot and I quaked, powerless to do anything but lie there. If I pulled the blankets over my head I suffocated. I got no sympathy. To have listened to me or sympathised would have made me worse. I was terrified to go to bed alone but did not dare say so. I was a 'big girl' now. At six or seven years old I should know better.

By the time I was seven or so I had inherited a few chores which increased in number and range until, by the time I was ten I was able to clean boots and shoes, knives, silver and brassware, water the garden with a watering can, weed, help pick up potatoes, do errands, lay the table, wash and dry dishes, sweep and dust. At about twelve I could clean the kitchen range, empty the ash pan, clean out the

Linda outside   29 Ninth Row

fire and coax it back to life without actually allowing it to got out, brush the mats hanging out on the fence, scrub the steps and swill the yard. I was by this time, well used to the routine domestic chores necessary to good housekeeping, although what I did was in an auxiliary capacity only. Also, very important, one was expected to do all these things as soon as one was asked and do them without thought of reward. If, as sometimes happened, one was asked to go an errand for a relative or neighbour this also had to be done without thought of reward.

As I approached my ninth birthday the attacks of blood poisoning to which I was subject began to grow further apart and I took a more lively view of life in consequence. About this time one of the girls at school arrived with the news that she was going to have a birthday party. Five girls had been asked. I was not among the chosen few.

Birthday parties were a rarity. In fact, in our family we didn't celebrate birthdays at all except for the obligatory twenty-first. I was in my teens before I discovered the dates

173

of my parents' birthdays. Ages of adults were never mentioned. It was still considered bad manners to ask a woman her age or a man his salary. If I ever did ask the age of an adult the stock reply was, 'As old as my tongue and a little bit older than my teeth.'

This birthday party set the girl apart and she became the object of attention and even envy. Those lucky enough to be invited also basked in a state of glory.

My own birthday was growing near. I asked my mother if I could have a party and she replied with such firmness that it brooked no further argument.

'NO YOU CAN NOT. I never heard of such a thing! I don't care if every girl in the class is having a party, you're not. What other people do with their time and money is their affair, not ours.'

Now I had a problem on my hands because I'd already asked my guests, and as I was the centre of a fair amount of attention with many more friends than I realised I had, I didn't feel I could give up this novel and favoured position. After much thought I reasoned that another attack of blood poisoning couldn't be far off and when everybody was feeling sorry for me and the hot fomentations were being applied and the vile medicine administered I would endure it all and in my heated state ask them to tell a friend to tell the others the party was off. In my painful circumstances I couldn't possibly be told off or punished in any way.

However, as day succeeded day, my robust state of health continued and there were a scant five days to go before P. Day. As soon as I could get a bit of privacy I examined my body minutely for spots or blemishes. Nothing. Not even the palest flush to be fanned and irritated into something more aggressive. In desperation I went up to roughened wall and forced myself to drag my hand down. It smarted something awful and bits of the top skin had been reduced to little white curls but the pink under-skin remained intact. I went down to the station, keeping my distance till the train came in and, when the porter was busy taking tickets, I went up to the engine and, quickly before they shouted at me, gasped in great lungfuls of steam in the hope of developing bronchitis. I took off my hat and coat and walked slowly home to give the thing a chance to get a real hold. All in vain.

On the Friday night I decided the only thing I could do was run away and do a sort of 'Babes in the Wood' act. Wanting to leave as good an impression behind as possible on the Saturday morning I helped without having to be told, coerced or otherwise dealt with and my mother was able to say,

'You've been a real good help this morning. So good I've got nearly all my weekend baking finished,' and there, testimony to her words, on the scullery table, was a tray of scones, another of chocolate buns and two sandwich cakes. It made the going harder.

At half-past-two I left saying I was going out to play. When I considered the expanse of park I had to go through before I could even begin to run away I hesitated. Like a murderer, I was irresistably drawn back to the scene of my crime. I returned to the house and secreted myself at the bottom of the garden among the currant bushes and the gooseberry bushes at that time burgeoning into life. It was cramped and damp but I didn't have to wait very long. They came all dressed up in their best clothes and carrying little bags or parcels. Presents for me!

They knocked at the door and when my mother opened it they stood and she stood. After a bit, they went in and more came. And after another bit the door opened and out they all trooped still carrying their little parcels. (They'd each been given a chocolate bun and a drink of milk or tea in the house I learned later). They were quiet enough as they walked down the garden path and went through the gate, thinking no doubt (rightly) that they were being watched. But before long they burst into chatter loud enough for me to hear and what I heard gave me no incentive to leave my damp hide-out, ever.

The air got colder and I became increasingly cramped and hungry. The council clock struck again. How many more times, I wondered, would it strike while I sat there. Presently, my brother came down the path. He stopped half-way and shouted,

'You've got to come in now. The tea's ready.'

The epitome of misery I walked back to the house and Nemesis. My transgressions were enumerated and the punishment was no worse than I anticipated.

The next night the doctor had to be sent for and we were back to the hot fomentations, the salves and the vile medicine.

My mother and I were both such bad travellers that we never went anywhere by bus if it could be avoided. One day, in the early evening we, my mother, Billy and I, had been to Hirst on some business or other. To relieve the tedium of the walk back we played a game. Every third window we stopped and said,

'If I had all the money in the world I would buy that,' the 'that' referring to our choice of what was best in the window. In one shop window, Downie's, I think, my mother saw a coffee set made up of pot, cream-jug and sugar basin in a sort of earthenware in two shades of blue with a gilt trim. It was priced five and eleven pence. (29½p).

'I like that,' she said. 'Oh, I do like that. I would love that.'

'Would you really?' I asked. With all my heart I wished I could have bought it for her but it represented seventy-one weeks' pocket money, if, that is, I was given it regularly.

That autumn we had an exceptionally good year in the allotments.

'I don't know,' my father said when he came in one day, 'what we're going to do with all them cabbage. They're the best we've had but we'll never manage to eat them all and I don't see us being able to give any more away.'

Hardly had he spoken than I had an idea. To keep myself right I said very quietly,

'Could I have those cabbages?' and a lot louder, 'Please may I leave the table?'.

'Yes,' said my mother.

It was all I wanted.

The following Saturday morning I did the jobs I had to do lickety-spit and set off to do the messages (errands). But, I had another little job to do first. I went to the allotments. My father was right. We had cabbages galore. Big generous-hearted ones. Fortunately my brother's bogie was lying in front of the hut. Like other lads Billy had a bogie but he rarely used it. The wheels were of sluggish, heavy iron and the body of dull lethargic wood. I pulled fourteen cabbages from here and there without making any notice-able difference, put them in the bogie and with a great deal of effort pushed the lot over the clarty paths, out of the allotments and on to the road. Wansbeck Terrace was out of the question. We knew one or two people living there.

I settled on Park Villas. As far as I knew we had no relatives or friends there. I decided to look at the gardens and size each house up before I went to ply my trade. After fourteen calls I had two cabbages left and my confidence knew no bounds. As one woman said,

'They're good cabbages. Worth more than a penny really. Will you be round next week? Right. I'll have another if they're still the same price.'

I went up to the fifteenth door and knocked boldly, and then, completely discomfitted looked up at the woman who appeared before me. It was Mrs. X who came from the Wooler area.

'Er – please –' I managed to gasp out suddenly fearful. 'Do you want any cabbages? They're – they're – a penny each.'

She looked down at the two cabbages in the bogie then back at me.

'You're Margaret Gallon's lassie aren't you?'

I nodded unable to speak.

'Does she know you are going round the doors selling cabbages?'

I shook my head.

'Or your father?'

Again the shaken head.

'I should think not! Whatever next! What do you think they're going to say when they find out? Now take those back to wherever you got them from and go straight back home. Now.'

I nodded and seized the handles of the bogie. It was impossible to make a quick or dignified exit with that bogie. It just wasn't built for either. Contrarily, the near-side wheels went off course and veered over the edge of their garden and at the gate it ran into the near-side post. Red-faced and trembling I kept going till I was round the corner and out of sight when I stopped to take stock. I just didn't think I could manage to go up to another door but I wanted to sell my remaining stock. Two women were chatting at a nearby gate. I went up to them.

'Do you need any cabbages?' I asked. 'They're a penny each. They're all I have left.'

They looked at them, turned them over suspiciously, pressed their thumbs into the hearts – and bought them.

I returned the bogie, did my messages and got back in time for the mid-day meal. It was six o'clock before my father came in from the pit. As soon as he closed the back door I knew he knew.

He came into the kitchen and he was very angry.

'Is it true?' he asked looking at me and standing just inside the door.

I gulped.

'Is what true?' my mother asked.

'She's been selling cabbages.'

'WHAT!'

'I called in at my mother's after I left the pit and there was a message to say would I call in to see Mrs. X in Park Villas. When I got there she said Linda had been at the door looking like some back-street mugger (itinerant seller of mugs) selling cabbages.'

One look at me confirmed that what my father had been told was true.

'Where did they come from?' my mother asked.

'The lotment. You said I could have them. I asked.'

'I never said any such thing.'

'You did. Me dad said he didn't know what he was going to do with all the cabbages and I said "can I have them?" and you said "yes".'

'You did say that Archie,' said my Mother. 'But,' to me, 'I can't remember saying you could have them. How many did you take?'

'Fourteen. And I sold them all.'

'How much did you charge?'

'A penny. But one woman said they were worth more.'

'Where's the money now?'

'In Downie's shop.'

'What's it doing in Downie's shop?'

'Well. You know that coffee set....' and I went on to

178

explain.

'Can you remember who you sold the cabbages to?' asked my father, somewhat mollified, but still put out.

'I think so.'

'Very well. You'll go across to Downie's NOW. Get that money back and go and give it back to all the people you took it from.'

'And that she will not' interposed my Mother. 'She didn't take money from anybody. You said yourself we've got better stuff from the garden and the allotment this year than they have in the shops. I'm not saying she was right but I'm not saying she was wrong.'

In the end it was my father who had to give way. The following two Saturdays my mother went to the allotment with me to select the produce. The stock was extended to include beetroot, turnips and chrysanthemums, all done up in penny lots.

After three trading Saturdays I had enough to buy the coffee set but it was a pyrrhic victory and as far as I can recollect the set was never used. My father could not bear the thought that he might have made capital out of his neighbours. His feeling was the produce from the garden should be given away.

Every Saturday Billy and I were given a penny. This was the only money we were allowed to spend during the week. Anything else we happened to be given (a rare occurrence) had to be put in the thrifty from whence it found its way to the Penny Bank.

One day I went into a shop and there, ahead of me was Uncle Kit. There was a box of chocolate snowballs on the counter and as Uncle Kit paid for his purchase he said to me,

'Would you like one of those?' and when I said 'Yes please,' he told the shopkeeper to give me one.

It was the first I'd ever tasted and I thought it the most delicious thing known to man or woman. I was hooked and thereafter my Saturday largesse was laid out in half-penny chocolate snowballs.

One day as I was coming home I found a sixpence. I really only wanted to spend some of it, but this didn't seem possible. I couldn't say I'd found fivepence and I didn't see myself getting away with a lie if I said I'd found threepence. Hitherto, I hadn't had much success in getting away with a lie. There were, therefore, only two courses open to me. I could spend all of the sixpence and get rid of the evidence, or spend none of it and hand it over intact to the voracious thrifty – or, more likely, the house-keeping. We were hard-up at the time.

I went into Nixon's and bought twelve half-penny snowballs and slunk down the path that skirted the Methodist Church to the place behind the Church where the Store kept their heavy cars when they weren't in use. Standing among the carts, I started on the contents of the bag. Biting into that first crispy chocolate coating and filling my mouth with the delicious marshmallow, knowing there was more to follow was a rare treat. I ate with glorious abandon. By the time I came to the fourth one, the bites weren't so big and I didn't eat so quickly. After the sixth snowball I hesitated and looked around the 'shed' with its two walls, two open sides, corner post and rough, beamed roof. It occurred to me that it might be possible to secrete the number remaining and collect them at a later date. I soon realised this wasn't possible. The Council Clock, warned me that time was getting on and I gulped down two more snowballs. I had to force myself to swallow down the last three composed entirely of sickly, oily mush and reeled home, drunk on chocolate snowballs.

I managed to stagger into our outside lavatory before I was sick when, mercifully, I was able to flush away the evidence. Looking slightly green I wavered into the house.

The following Saturday when I went to inspect the stock in the various sweet shops before deciding whose takings were to receive a boost from my custom, I made a discovery. I had been liberated. I was free to choose between every kind of sweet that came within my price range. I never wanted to eat another snowball.

When it came to doing errands or odd jobs for other people, we were repeatedly told not to take money; even when it was offered. One day, I was returning home from a friend's house when a large car drew up to where I was. The driver wanted directions to one of the larger houses at the 'bottom end' of Ashington. He had obviously taken a wrong turning. I knew where he wanted to go but hadn't much confidence in my ability to give directions because of my not being able to distinguish between left and right. Besides, a car like this had not been seen in the Colliery Scheme before and I wanted to ride in it if I could.

'If you'll let me in,' I said, 'I'll take you there.'

There were four people in the car, two men and two women, all Americans. As this was their first visit to England, and thus to Ashington, I felt it incumbent upon me to point out the wonders of my home town...

'This is the Catholic cemetery. It's best not to walk past here at midnight but, if you have to, walk on the other side of the road and don't look over your shoulder.. This is the poliss station........Down there is the colliery yard. Would you like to see it? It won't take long....'

When we arrived at the house they wanted they had a discussion as to what they should give me and decided on half-a-crown (12½p), a mint of money as far as I was concerned.

'Oh no thank you,' I said to the man who offered it. They all said I must take it but I steadfastly refused. 'I think you are very silly not to,' said the first man. 'You've earned it.' But I wouldn't. I had enjoyed the ride and enjoyed talking to them. What I had done was nothing. It was wrong to take money for it, or so I had been taught to believe.

What, then, had I learned, if not by the time I was seven, at least by the time I was nine?

Generally speaking, I found it easier to do things as soon as I was told without grumbling. In this way the task did not interfere with my train of thought, especially if what I was asked to do was routine.

I got used to things that weren't quite right, clothes that didn't quite fit, fountain pens that didn't quite work, catches that didn't quite close and hand-me-downs that weren't what I wanted but had to accept because they were too good to throw away. Technically, the room was mine only because, having no sister, there was no need for me to share. In fact, it was only mine in that I slept there. To have allowed anything else would have been a terrible waste. The drawers were filled with other people's things and household articles, the wardrobe cluttered up with finery of a bygone age, too good, or too precious, to throw out. Any space left was filled with spare blankets and sheets. My favourite playthings were books, pencils and paper.

Probably because of the time I spent in bed, I could listen to the pulse of a room and determine from the way housework was being done, from footsteps, from the way adults spoke to each other – the tone of voice being used, whether the conversation was continuous or there were gaps broken only with essential words – the mood of the people concerned. Were they in a bad fettle, or a good fettle? Was it wise to speak, or wait for a more favourable opportunity?

I sometimes felt guilty at night when I said my prayers and had to be reminded to bless a member of the family I'd left off the list. Having regard for what I'd heard them say about that same member when they thought I wasn't listening, I had assumed they would not be anxious for God to bless them. And now I had to. As I'd been told that God saw and heard everything, I wondered what He made of that. This was a wicked thought and I felt guilty that I thought that way.

To be pleased with anything one had done meant one was guilty of the sin of pride. As a result being thanked or complimented made me very uneasy. To have been pleased meant that I was proud. I longed to please and to that end, I usually gave of my best.

Too often, I had not the courage of my convictions, especially when it came to putting my hand up in school for anything other than routine class questions. How I envied those who could actually stand up and say, 'I won't'. I never heard anyone say that at school, but I often did when I called on a friend and was invited into the house. My brother was much more forthright than I and I envied him his courage. In spite of these clouds, for they were no more than that, there were a great many jobs and delights to life at that time. I certainly did not feel myself badly done by, for I saw many who were worse off than we were.

It was about the time of my thirteenth birthday that I was confirmed. I would like to think that I approached Confirmation, with a deep understanding of its religious significance, but this was not so. I did that as I did all the other routine things that were an inevitable part of growing up. There was one exception.

There were parts of the Bible I was beginning to question, questions which I had not the courage to voice. Might not the Prodigal son have preferred a telling off? Did being forgiven like that make him feel worse for the awful things he had done to his father. I felt desperately sorry for the Queen of Sheba, getting herself all dolled up and taking all those jewels and gifts to Solomon only to be put in her place. And the Te Deum? I loved chanting this majestic piece (I still do) but it perturbed me. Surely if God was all they said, did He not cringe at this extravagant praise? And what of the man who kept his one talent intact and returned it to his master? Why was he wrong? Why was it taken from him?

One night, at Confirmation class, I was suddenly alerted to what the vicar was saying. He was explaining the parable of the Ten Talents. It made sense. I determined from then on that I would use what ability I had, to the best of my ability. The explanation did much to calm my troubled conscience, too. If I was wrong about the Ten Talents, then I could be wrong about the other things.

In fact, it was a timely lesson. I felt distaste for the thirteen-year old I was. I wasn't any of the things I wanted to be, things I thought would make me loved and respected. I wasn't good at any of the things I should have been good at. In a family of keen and productive gardeners I had mouldy fingers. The only things I attempted to knit were held up to a delighted class, thereby bringing a little light relief into the gloom of their grey concentrated efforts. As for sewing! All the hems were grey from having been taken out so often. The only bright spots were the spots of blood from an over-enthusiastic needle that would go where it was not wanted.

I wanted to be thought a nice girl. This was the pinnacle of attainment for girls, and for women, although growing up into a real nice woman wasn't something I looked foward to particularly. A real nice woman never thought of herself. She always did what others wanted without complaint, indeed, always with a smile. Privately, I thought that, as a goal to work for, this was cheerless in the extreme and I think it's true to say that, as I moved towards adulthood, I dragged my feet more than somewhat.

Fortunately, I enjoy work for its own sake. I found that it was far more difficult to pretend to do something than to actually do it. I took the Co-operative Movement's slogan, 'Learn to labour and to wait', to heart. I made a decision not to do anything of which, if it came to light, I would be ashamed. I learned to keep back tears and smile instead, however weakly. Where work was concerned, I was willing to volunteer for anything, to run and fetch things and to lend, even when the things I lent were not mine to dispose of. I learned to keep opinions (and jokes) to myself. I had my own opinions, but not the assurance I needed to voice them. I did not think I could possibly be right. When answers were wanted, I struggled to work out what was wanted in reply, rather than what I thought.

All these concentrated moral principles, ideals and ethics coupled with the desire not to be different from everyone else, left me with all the resilience of a piece of over-chewed elastic and I began to think about those who lived lives of abandoned wickedness. They never went to church. They played cards, bet on horses, drank, went to pubs, swore and generally misbehaved in every way open to them. That they were not destined for heaven didn't seem to worry them. I only thought about them. I had no real intention of joining their ranks. Indeed, I would have had no idea where to begin. I could not have cut loose from my circumstances and my home however much I might have wished to do so. In my case, I had no real wish to do so.

I can't ever remember being bored. Certainly, I'd never have admitted to being bored. Had I done that, someone would soon have found me a job to do.

I loved the sound of laughter and I was anxious that people should enjoy the things that had been arranged for their entertainment. I always enjoyed treats more if I could see my mother, father and Billy, or, in different circumstances, other members of my family or friends, enjoying them too. One of the things I enjoyed during these formative years was school.

Chapter 12
Almost the Happiest Days

There was no doubt at all but that, when we were five, we would go to school. Nor was there any doubt as to why we were going. We were going to learn our letters, our ABCs, to learn our numbers and to do what the teacher told us. If we didn't do these things we would get the belt. If we misbehaved we would get the belt. And it would be no good complaining at home. At best we would be told that's what teachers and schools were for – at worst we would be punished again (the very least of which was a telling off) because, obviously, we had not done as we'd been told and therefore the fault was ours. Indeed, the belt was almost synonymous with school and an adult, speaking to a child on his/her return from school, often said, as a matter of course, 'Well, did you get the belt the day?'

Linda at Bothal School. Linda (2nd left, 2nd front row) next to Joyce (3rd left).

Bothal was an Elementary, or Board, school in Ashington. It was also a Church school which meant that the vicar, the Revd. Samuel Davidson, visited regularly. Why he came or what he said on these occasions I do not know.

We sat up straight, hands behind back, while the teacher called the register after which the school day proper began when we were sharpened like pencils, briskly and to the point, prayers, scripture, mental arithmetic, arithmetic, English, history, geography, poetry, composition, spellings, dictation, parsing, analysis, drawing, singing, drill, needlework. We worked through all these lessons in a SILENCE broken only when the teacher explained something or asked a question. When this happened, hands had to shoot up vigorously, especially in the 'A' section.

Class discipline was good. Today we'd call it exemplary. Here, the teacher had one staunch ally already mentioned, the strap or belt, a thick piece of leather approximately eighteen inches long and four inches wide thonged or cut in strips for a third its length; the business end. Even if she rarely used it, we knew it was there, either in evidence hanging over the top of the blackboard or placed neatly folded on the top edge of the desk, or out of sight in the desk.

The strap felt worse on cold mornings when it stung something awful on chilled fingers. One could, of course, move one's hand, or actually pull it away as the strap descended, but it was best to stand firm and hold one's hand still. To move it or try to mitigate the punishment annoyed the teacher who usually doubled the punishment in number as well as ferocity.

Tests and examinations were part of school life even before we left the Infants'. There were the daily spelling tests, the weekly spelling Bee, the daily quota of arithmetic, the weekly composition, the monthly history and geography tests, the end of term examinations and the daily mental test which followed hard on the heels of scripture – 'three-pence halfpenny each, how much a dozen? One and six each, how much a gross? My bill comes to three and seven (17p) how much change from a pound? Come along. Some of you are too slow.'

Every teacher took home marking. They marked every

mistake in red pencil pointing out where the scholar (we were scholars then, not pupils) had gone wrong. Each child then had to do her corrections before she went on to new work.

Two lessons I abominated because I was so poor at them – singing and drill. In most classes, there being no piano, the teacher had to rely on the tonic solfa/modulator rolled down against the black-board and a tuning fork. She would sing a note then go round the class asking each girl to reproduce the note she had just sung. I never could. When learning a new song we dealt with a few bars at a time. Again we had to sing each bit individually when I was scarlet in embarrassed discomfort.

Drill was done in the mercilessly inflexible school yard except when blizzard conditions prevailed. Of course, we did not have anything remotely resembling gym kit. How hopeless I was! How much less agile than those tall, older girls who could leap frog over each other with such speed and grace, who could easily jump so much higher than I, their skirts tucked in the elastic of their knicker legs. Urging me to try hard was counter-effective. I do believe teachers and some adults were convinced children had no feelings. It was years before I realised I was a fairly good runner and that I could play a passable game of hockey. I loved drawing lessons. As I remember it, Drawing was done on squares of grey paper. We started the year with a snow scene, progressed to a snowdrop, a daffodil, an Easter egg, the bluebell woods, a vase with a flower in, an apple, a banana, the harvest moon with two trees, a rabbit and a hill in the distance, a Christmas card and we were back to the snow scene.

Teachers kept a permanently vigilant and thrifty eye on all school furnishings. School property was carefully looked after. Desks were in good shape considering they were probably put there more than half a century earlier. There was no wastage of pens, paper, exercise books, ink, pen nibs or blotting paper. We were forbidden to suck pens or pencils. Once I graduated to writing with ink, I always had inky fingers from both ordinary pens and fountain pens. Incidentally, the latter were banned from schools for some time because it was thought that they ruined handwriting.

To help her keep an eye on school property, the teacher

appointed monitors/monitresses. How privileged were these beings. How we sat up straight, our bodies straining to be noticed, our eye desperately trying to say what our tongues were denied, when a new monitor was to be appointed. There was the cupboard monitor. She kept the cupboards tidy and saw that each set of books, each box of pencils, each girl's piece of needlework, everything, in fact, to do with lessons, was in its correct place with no items missing. The book, pen, crayon and pencil monitors counted the items in their charge out and in and noted their condition. Pencil points that had been sharpened that play-time and were now broken (deliberately) were reported. Books that had marks on them not there when they had been given out were also reported. We were told that this property was only on loan to us as long as we were in that class. If we spoiled it, not only would we have to do without, those following would be similarly denied.

At Bothal, we had play-time. The girls' yard was adjacent that of the Infants'. Indeed, the girls had to cross the Infants' yard to get to the lavatories (not then toilets) as one set did for both schools. Both schools had a teacher on duty. They stood in their separate corners wrapped up in several layers of clothing in winter while in summer they walked around gingerly, trying to catch what sun they could.

Half-crazed with the idea of ten minutes' liberty after so much concentrated education all, except the few august beings in Standards 7 and X7 who made a more sedate exit, ran top speed into the yard. That is, the fearless ones did. Regardless of their persons, they expected the more timid to get out of their way or take the consequences.

The yard was a noisy place to be. Nearly all the games involved singing, especially those where skipping ropes were used. The ball games, when 'stotty' balls were used, also called for chanting. The great thing was to 'keep the pot boiling' – to get as much out of play-time as possible.

When the teacher on duty blew the whistle it was straight into lines, no dawdling, back into school and straight down to lessons. During play-time the monitors concerned with next lesson would have all the necessary equipment out on each girl's desk. The last part of the morning was given over to English grammar. The afternoon sessions were taken up with subjects which may have been considered not quite so important. It was then that the crayons, the large porridge coloured map on the wall with the British Empire coloured in pink, the Nature table, the sewing bags, the modulator, the silent readers and the poetry books came into their own.

By the time I left Bothal to go to the grammar school I had read a fair number of the books housed in the laundry basket in each successive class-room. Among them were, the Beatrix Potter books, *Little Black Sambo*, *The Secret Garden*, *Alice in Wonderland* and *Alice Through the Looking-Glass*, *Mr Midshipman Easy*, *Treasure Island*, *Winnie-the-Pooh*, *House at Pooh Corner*, many of the *William* books, *Tom Sawyer*, *Huckleberry Finn*, *Little Women*, *Good Wives*, *Jo's Boys*, *Gulliver's Travels*, *Pilgrim's Progress*, *Black Beauty*, *The Wind in the Willows*, *The Shepherd's Life*, *Tom Brown's Schooldays*, *The Fifth Form at St Dominic's* and, through the good offices of a friend, many of Marie Corelli's books over which my friend and I shed several tears, particularly over one named *Boy*. We also read the books of Ian Hay over which we laughed a great deal.

I learned and remembered many poems most of which I loved, though I did not always understand them at the time. Among those which stand out are, Wordsworth's and Herrick's *Daffodils*, Shakespeare's *When icicles hang by the wall*, Tennyson's *Morte D'Arthur* and his *Lady of Shallott*.

We also learned passages from the Bible in scripture. Among those I still remember are, David's lament over the death of Absalom, his lament over the death of Saul and Jonathan, the passages concerned with Naomi and her mother-in-law and the Queen of Sheba and the very beautiful, 'Rise up, my love, my fair one'.

Generally speaking, teachers were respected. More respected were His Majesty's Inspectors. Even teachers respected *them*, perhaps a great deal more than we children did. Another official who was universally respected, perhaps 'feared' would be a better word, was the School Board Man. He spent his days ceaselessly searching out truants and rounding up malingerers.

Of course, the reputations of the various teachers went before them. As my father, my uncles and aunts and their contemporaries had also been taught at Bothal in much the same way as I was, they knew the school and they knew the teachers. There was very little movement of teaching staff then. As far as we knew, there were only two sorts of teacher – ordinary teachers and Head teachers. There was nothing in between. Some were good, some were nice and hardly ever gave the strap, some were strict and some gave the strap for 'nowt'. Sometimes this made for confusion. As far as I was concerned, this was particularly true in Miss Dixon's case. She was never anything but pleasant to me, but she had a reputation, and it was her reputation I feared. For the rest, we were happy to laugh when the teacher did whether or not we understood why she was laughing. It meant she was in a good fettle and less likely to give the belt.

In fact, one couldn't get into any real trouble in the structured world of Bothal where there was always a hot line to parents, implied rather than evident. Parents rarely came up to school; it was an ordeal they'd rather forego. And there were no such things as Parent Teachers Associations.

Perhaps, however, children, especially girls, were able to work out any hostility they felt against teachers by playing 'Schools'. Several girls of my acquaintance possessed, as I did, a blackboard and easel. When one played 'Schools' one played in the yard of the girl who had the blackboard and she was teacher. When she turned her back to write on the board, usually 2+2, the 'scholars' broke into talk and laughter.

'Who's talking?' barked the 'teacher' turning round. Every 'scholar' sat up straight trying to keep her laugh in but making sure she did not succeed.

'I will not have talking in my class,' screeched the 'teacher' in a rising temper. 'Now. What do two and two make?'

'Five.'

'Come out here, girl. You have not been listening. Put your hand out.'

'Won't,' and the 'scholar' put her tongue out instead.

'You wicked girl,' and the 'teacher' came towards her using a pretend strap. The 'class' was then reduced to near anarchy, talking and giggling and making fun of the 'teacher' and refusing to put their hands out, possibly all the things they yearned to do in real life, but never did. 'Schools' could be played with a pretend blackboard, or even none at all with the 'teacher' just asking questions. Whichever method was used the format was the same.

A year or so after I left Bothal to go to the grammar school, the school system changed, at least at Ashington. The infants and under elevens went to a new, spacious school in Wansbeck Terrace and Bothal became a senior school.

In company with several of my contemporaries I went to Bedlington Grammar School then called Bedlington Secondary School. Each day I spent there from first to last was a joy. Not only did we have a uniform which marked us off from other schools in the area, we had a school song. It was a strange choice for a modern up-to-the-minute mixed grammar school – the Harrow Boating Song, 'Forty Years On', robustly masculine.

Here at Bedlington there was space to expand and grow. There were playing fields, lawns, flower beds and garden plots surrounding the school on all sides. There was a large hall wherein hung Honours Boards. There were labs for chemistry, physics and biology, a domestic science block, a woodwork department and a dining block.

The form rooms had parquet floors so that we had to change into indoor gym shoes or ward slippers when we came to school. Thus we had cloak-rooms with open lockers. We also had slipper bags to house our indoor shoes when they were not being worn.

At Bedlington, we each had a desk and a chair, both of which could be moved. Each desk had an inkwell but it wasn't long before it was understood that fountain pens were *de rigeur.* Shaking these pens continually to get a flow of ink meant that everything around one, including the parquet floor, became ink bespattered. The sort of fountain pen I had (Woolworth's $6d$ – $2\frac{1}{2}$p) depended on this treatment to function at all. We kept text books, exercise books, pens, pencils and mathematical equipment in our desks. Monitors were out. Instead we had a form representative whose duty it was to collect the homework in each morning and take it up to the staff-room to be placed in the locker of the teacher concerned.

We had longer holidays at Bedlington than we had at Bothal. We also had a mid-term holiday new to us, called half-term. We were given to understand that these longer holidays existed to compensate us for the extra work we did nightly at home.

In each subject, the first homework we were given was to back all our text and exercise books. We had first been given a little homily on the responsibility entailed in looking after all school books and apparatus. Any damage we inflicted on the latter had to be paid for. In addition to school text books, we had a wealth of property for which our parents paid, pens, blotters, compasses, dividers, protractors, set squares, rubbers, drawing pencils, mapping pens, rulers, hockey boots, hockey stick, gym shoes, tennis raquet, Bible, hymn book and etymological dictionary.

The staff at Bedlington had an added personal barometer – each wore a gown and there were as many methods of wearing those gowns as there were members of staff.

Mr Sykes (music and geography) had a tattered robe anchored on his right shoulder and from there it dripped down his back, till it reached the floor where it did its little bit to keep the parquet floors clean. He had large, alert eyes that seemed to work independently and when he thumped the piano for the hymn at Morning Assembly, his hands rising from the keys that they might come down with greater force, he kept one eye on the music while the other roamed the hall picking out all those who were pretending to sing but from whose lips no sound came. It was a job for which that eye was highly trained.

'Wilson, I noticed you were not singing this morning.'

'Sir, I have a bit of a sore throat and –'

'Ah. See me after school and we'll see if we cannot teach you to sing in a way which will improve your throat.'

Miss Skinner (biology and deputy head) wore her gown as an absent minded afterthought which turned out to be useful. The sleeves were somewhere to put the handkerchiefs she used to mop up the various chemicals that had been spilt on the benches where her beloved bisected frogs and live worms lived, the latter eternally churning up the soil in their big, glass dish.

On the rare occasions when he put in an appearance, Mr Williams wore his gown with all the dignity of a Roman Senator as became his position of headmaster.

Mr Greenhow (head of maths) was another who must have helped to keep the floors bright. At the back, his gown was draped from somewhere round his middle so that it floated behind him like a bride's train when he walked.

Most of the women had neat, tidy gowns as became their personalities. Generally speaking, it was the men who were the most colourful teachers.

Discipline was less rigid and the attitude of teachers to what I had looked upon as cheek amazed me at first.

Boys were called by their surnames. In my form there were two boys, cousins, their mothers were sisters who had married a Mr Wilson and a Mr Douglas respectively. The cousins were called Wilson Douglas and Douglas Wilson. It was perhaps inevitable that, in the lessons where they thought they would get away with it, the following took place,

"Wilson, translate from '*Je m'appelle Jean*'."

'Yes Miss. Certainly.' This with the utmost politeness from Wilson Douglas. 'I am called –'

'No. I didn't say Douglas, I said Wilson.'

'Yes, Miss. I heard you. Naturally I thought you –'

'Douglas you thought no such thing. Now, Wilson. Will you stand up and translate.'

'Oh, Miss, I *AM* sorry. Now I see what you mean. You said Wilson meaning Douglas Wilson and I thought you –'. And so it went on. It was a situation the two cousins could carry on in one, form or another, endlessly with straight faces and the utmost courtesy.

Another boy who early earned a reputation as a wit and a rebel was a lad called Sutherland. For some reason, very early in our career, the Head talked to us collectively and he had cause to correct someone who had replied to a question.

'It is not "*beeen*",' he said. 'You do not make such hard

work of the "*ee*". It is "*bin*". You use a light neutral vowel. I have "*bin*", not I have "*beeen*".'

Next morning, at the beginning of first lesson, Sutherland produced a bag of jelly beans.

'Sir,' he said to the maths master, 'may I offer you a jelly bin. You can choose any colour bin you like. Jelly bins are made in all colours.'

'All right. All right, Sutherland. Put them away and get your books out.'

'Don't you like jelly bins, Sir? Before I came to the grammar school, Sir, I thought –'. Men teachers could bring these little diversions to a speedy end.

From the beginning, physics and geometry were an open book to me. Rarely, if ever, did I get less than an A in these subjects. However, because I was a girl, I had to drop physics once I got into the third form. This left me with biology which I disliked and chemistry with which I fought a losing battle.

There was no corporal punishment for girls, only lines or detention. The ultimate punishment for both boys and girls was expulsion.

I travelled to Bedlington by train. The carriages were dusty and, most often, there were no straps on the window part of the door. In addition, many of the strings on the luggage rack were broken. Very often, these two acts of vandalism, particularly the latter, had been perpetrated by some young lad who wished to demonstrate his strength. He hooked a finger over part of the mesh that formed the rack and, pulling, broke it. The walls of the carriages were adorned by indistinct sepia pictures of people allegedly having a good time at Whitley Bay or some other favoured North Eastern resort having been carried there by courtesy of the London and North Eastern Railway. Every morning I joined Hannah Robinson, Helen Graham and Ruby Lowry (till she left) at Ashington station. When the train huffed its way in with a great deal of hissing and squealing of brakes, we made for the last carriage which had already been commandeered for us by Ivy Whitelaw and Topsy Siggins both of whom had travelled from the terminus at Newbiggin. The joy of meeting! The chatter. The friendship.

Throughout my stay at Bedlington, Hannah, Topsy, Helen and Ivy were my main friends and the last carriage was deemed to be 'ours'.

Linda, Topsy Siggins, Hannah Robinson and Helen Graham

Together with others we did the obligatory things. We formed a secret society and started a magazine, price one half-penny. It ran to two editions. Each edition covered the four sides of a double sheet of paper torn from our rough note books. As editor I was responsible for the serial which, very properly, began 'It was a dark, gloomy night....'. I was also responsible for the jokes.

At Bedlington I belonged to a particular year. At Bothal I had belonged nowhere. In common with one or two others, I was moved up as soon as I had mastered the work laid down for that class.

At this time, I was also a Girl Guide, a very enthusiastic member of the fifth Ashington which met weekly in the Parish Hall. I learned the Promise, the Law, First Aid, Morse Code, Semaphore and Knots.

As soon as I had been properly enrolled I began working towards my badges, intent on covering my sleeve with these emblems of specialist knowledge. I began with the easiest, the readers' badge. I also collected, pressed and named a wealth of wild flowers. My firelighter's badge entailed going to Sheepwash and there lighting a fire with twigs and

no more than two matches. Finally I set my sights on cook's badge. That I'd never had a cookery lesson did not deter me. (I was one of those who elected to do extra languages in lieu of art, geography and domestic science.) The test consisted of taking a freshly-baked loaf and a recently cooked stew to the South School, Ashington, at six o'clock on a Wednesday evening where the efforts of those whose aspirations were the same as mine were to be assessed.

I had almost finished my homework on the previous evening when I remembered my commitment for the following day, by which time I was too late to do anything about it.

'Couldn't you just sort of put a stew together for me?' I pleaded with my mother. 'After all, I've scraped carrots and peeled onions and turnips many a time for you and that's all stew is. And I've seen you make bread often and often. There's really nothing to it so, if you could just let me have a loaf....'

My pleading fell on deaf ears. I should have remembered the test earlier. It was I who was having the test, not my mother.

The following day I'd have had my work cut out to get to the South School by six even if everything had been ready.

When I got home the raw meat and vegetables were lying on the kitchen table. Feeling aggrieved at my mother's limited co-operation, I prepared the vegetables, cut up the meat, seasoned the lot, added water and put the pan on the fire. I changed into my guide uniform, rubbed my face and hands, gulped down some tea and transferred the stew which had only just come to the boil, into a basin with a lid and put it in a basket. My mother was adamant about the bread.

I ran out of the house and on to Grannie Summers'. She was preparing tea.

'Grannie,' I panted, 'can you lend me a loaf, please? I have to take a loaf and some stew to the South School. I have the stew but my mother couldn't let me have a loaf.'

'If you'd said yesterday,' she replied, 'I'd have baked an extra one for you.'

'I couldn't. Grannie, I'm in a tearing hurry. I'll bring the loaf back, honest. I've to be there by six.'

'You'll never get there on time.'

'I know. But I've got to try. Please, Grannie.'

She wrapped the loaf up in a clean towel and off I flew.

I was late, but so was the examiner who, for some reason, was in a bad mood. We had to line up behind two long tables, each girl's loaf and stew in front of her. I was at the end of the line, still struggling to recover from the rush. The examiner was definitely not pleased with what she saw as she interviewed each guide and looked at her specimens. When I had recovered sufficiently, I looked at my next door neighbour's offerings. Like me, I don't think she'd ever had a school cookery lesson. The loaf was decidedly grey and doughy-looking and the stew, now congealed, also had an unappetising greyish pallor. The girl herself was rapidly approaching a state of nervous imbecility. I was in slightly better shape because I had been spared the long dentist's-waiting-room interim beforehand. Presently, it was my neighbour's turn. The examiner gave her bread a pro-longed, hostile scrutiny.

'Did you wash your hands first?' she asked.

'I – I gave them a good rub on the towel, Miss.' The examiner sniffed. There was a four page adverse criticism in that sniff. Steadying the loaf with delicate fingers, the

197

examiner cut it in two with a bread knife. As far as I could see the loaf was generously supplied with little pockets of air.

'How did you make it?'

'I – I put some flour in the bread dish –'

'How much flour?'

'What me mam said.'

'How much?'

'Well er – well' – sniff – (indicative of utter hopelessness) 'about half a dishful –' and, haltingly, the poor girl went on with her recital till, thankfully, she got the dough into the tin, 'an' then I put a cross on it.'

'A WHAT!'

'A cross.'

'Why?'

'Me mam said. She always puts a cross on.'

'Why?' repeated the exasperated examiner, but the girl couldn't tell her. (Actually, this was an age-old practice to let the devil out, to ensure the bread was well baked). The examiner turned her attention to the stew, churned it up a bit with a fork, shrugged and turned to my specimens.

'Ah,' she said, as she picked up Grannie's loaf with its pale, gold crust. It still had the delicious smell of freshly baked bread.

'Now this,' she said showing the loaf to the rest, 'is what your loaves should have looked like. Just look at the even colour of the crust.' She turned the loaf over and tapped the bottom with her knuckles.

'Hear that?' she said. 'That's what a well baked loaf should sound like. Now let us see if the inside is as good as the outside.' and she cut the loaf in two. 'Isn't that beautiful,' she said, holding half of the loaf up, her anger gone. 'Just look at the texture. I really don't think I have ever seen a better loaf. Now gather round and I'll point out what I was looking for and what you should strive towards.' I listened, bathed in a warm, pink glow. This was my grannie's loaf she was talking about.

When the examiner had finished, she turned her attention to my stew.

'It's not cooked', she observed.

'No,'. I hung my head. 'I didn't leave enough time to do

it properly. I'm sorry.'

'I really oughtn't to pass your stew, but, because of your bread, you'll get your badge.'

I think I'm right in saying we all passed.

Flushed with success, eager to tell Grannie what the examiner had said, I ran homewards even quicker than I'd come.

'Grannie,' I burst into their kitchen, 'Grannie I've brought back your loaf and I passed.'

My grandfather was sitting at the top of the table reading a paper spread out before him. Uncle Lance was sitting on the long settle, his feet on the fender, reading a book. Grannie had been darning when I rushed in. She looked up and smiled.

'And, Grannie, do you know what the examiner said,' I went on, the words tumbling out, 'she said your loaf was the best she'd ever seen.'

'She didn't!' Grannie's eyes shone, her face alight with disbelief.

'She DID. She held it up for everybody to see and she said, 'This is the best loaf I have ever seen in the whole of my life".'

'Bill,' said Grannie, turning to Grandad, 'Bill, did you hear that?'

My grandfather looked at me over the top of his Woolworth's spectacles.

'What I heard,' he said severely, 'was you coming in here with a lot of noise and clatter. You would think that going to that school you would at least have learned to come in quietly without all that row. I can hardly hear myself think,' and he went back to his paper.

It was no use Grannie's appealing to Uncle Lance. Absorbed in his book he was totally oblivious to everything going on around him. Once he sat down to his supper while still reading. Some two hours later, he looked up in bewilderment to find Grannie ready for bed and Grandad winding up the clock preparatory to his going to bed.

'Mother,' he said gently, 'is there to be no supper tonight?'

'Supper!' she replied. 'You've eaten it. I cleared the table and washed up an hour ago.'

Grannie took hold of my hand after Grandad had finished censoring my behaviour and, like two naughty children, we tip-toed into the front room where, over and over again, I told her what had been said about her bread. Seeing her happiness, I gave the examiner credit for saying every word of praise I had in my vocabulary. Grannie gave me a piece of pushy-up cake, thick with butter and I walked home on air, sobering up as I came to our house. I decided to say as little as possible about the loaf and the test. My father was writing at the table, my mother busy in the walk-in pantry. I did not expect my father to take much more interest than Uncle Lance had in what I'd done other than a modified 'Well done'.

'Here's the stew back,' I said as Mother came in from the pantry. 'Would you like me to put it in a pan and finish cooking it?' I added helpfully.

'How did you come on?'

'I passed.'

'On a raw stew! It couldn't have been much of an examination. What did they say about the loaf?'

'I – er – I borrowed one from Grannie.'

My father put his pen down.

'You did WHAT?' he asked. (He knew more about the test than I thought.)

'I asked her if she'd lend me one and she did,' I said.

'Did you tell her what it was for?'

'She didn't ask and I was in a hurry.'

'Then you passed the loaf off as yours.'

'No. Not really.'

'What do you mean, not really? You did or you didn't.'

'The examiner never asked.'

'Of course she didn't ask. She assumed it was yours because you were there. You are a Guide, remember. What about the Law you promised to obey? A Guide's honour is to be trusted. She trusted you.'

I was beginning to feel sorry for myself.

'You should have seen the others,' I said in defence. 'I could have made a far better loaf if I'd had the time. And the examiner was in a right bad fettle when we started. At least the loaf put her in a good fettle. She said it was the best she's ever seen'.

'When she said that,' said my mother and father in near unison, 'she was talking about loaves made by children. It should have been the best. Your grannie's made bread twice a week for nearly forty years. The fact is,' finished my father quietly, 'you cheated and you lied. You didn't actually tell a lie, but you lied just the same. And for what? So that you can put another bit of material on your sleeve, for that's all it is now. You have no right to it. More than that. It makes all the other badges, those you have worked for, of no value. All the badges, all the work you do now, and you do work hard, will be suspect. What matters most is that you must know within yourself when you act honestly or dishonestly. You MUST NOT pull the wool over your own eyes. It's what you know inside yourself that matters.'

I was definitely very sorry for myself now.

'Well,' I said. 'I'll not wear the badge. Does that satisfy you?'

'No,' he replied, 'You still don't understand. It's not because you're a Guide that you have to behave honestly and with integrity. It's because of yourself. What you do about the badge must be what you think is right. Not because of what I say or your mother says but because in your heart you know it's the right thing to do.'

'I've said I'll not wear it.'

'And what will you say when the Guider asks you why?'

'I'll think of something.'

'Another lie? Don't you see? Once you start there's no end.'

'You don't mean to say I've got tell her what I did? I can't do that. Think of what she'll say. I might even be put out.'

'If you'd thought beforehand of what the Guider would think of your behaviour if she knew, it might have stopped you from doing what you did. I'm not going to tell you what you've got to do. It's something you will have to work out for yourself.'

'Well,' I said, crestfallen, and after a little time, 'I'll tell the Guide Captain, but will you not tell me Grannie. You should have seen her face when I told her what the examiner said.'

In the end, the air was fragrant with the perfume of forgiveness.

Almost incoherent with shame at what I had to admit to, I told the Guide Captain who said, with as much severity as she could muster,

'I hope this has been a lesson to you. Now run along and let's forget all about it, shall we?

But I did not forget. What my father had said was true. My behaviour had been unworthy and I had thought myself so smart at the time. Nevertheless, I did not suffer the remorse I should have done. My grannie had cooked meals at all hours of the day and night (with up to six workers on different shifts she had no option) for upwards of thirty years. In all that time no-one had ever thought of complimenting her on her cooking. She was very proud of her sons and her grandsons and was delighted with their every achievement, however slight, but having this compliment paid to her was totally unexpected and so very pleasant that she radiated the joy she felt.

As I approached my thirteenth birthday I was beginning to take a more mature view of life. Without my being aware of it, the ethos of Bedlington allowed me to begin to see I had to accept responsibility for myself. More lax regarding punishment, easy going when accepting excuses for homework either not done or not finished, Bedlington had allowed me greater freedom than I'd ever known at Bothal where, quite apart from anything else, I'd been under the weather for a lot of the time. The freedom I had at Bedlington was heady and, for nearly three years, I gave myself up to the 'good time'. Now I was beginning to count the cost. My work had suffered.

Most of us knew we were at school to work. We did not in the least despise the brainy ones; rather did we look up to them. We might call them swots but, in reality, we envied their ability. All around us was the implication that school was there for a dual purpose. We had to learn and we had to work hard.

However, the feeling was still widely prevalent that girls should not be forced. Book-learning wasn't for girls. The principal goal for them was still marriage and looking after a home and family and, perhaps, ageing parents. To educate a girl beyond the age of eighteen was likely to lessen her chances in the marriage stakes. No-one would be good enough for her. Men did not like women who knew too much. And, if a girl did get married after she'd been to college or university, then the parents would not be 'paid back' for the money they'd spent on her education, for there was an unwritten law that one paid back one's parents the money spent on education.

As far as I was concerned I was beginning to look at life more soberly. We had, by this time, moved into the Eleventh Row. Till then, we'd had a bathroom. Now, water had to be carried from a stand tap and heated on the fire. We bought a bath which resembled a zinc coffin in appearance. It took a lot of filling and at least two people to manoeuvre it outside, carefully so that it did not slop over, to be emptied. Weekly baths became the norm and I did not like it. Most of the time I didn't feel clean.

One evening, at a Guide meeting, a senior officer paid us a visit when she gave us a talk. We were now old enough, she said, to look after our own persons. Everyone ought to bath every day, just as everyone ought to change underwear worn next to the skin every day. It was no excuse to say we had no bathroom and no running hot water and no excuse to say we did not have a drawer full of underwear. Two enamel dishes and change of underwear was all that was needed and she went on to amplify her words.

She had, at least, one rapt listener. As soon as I got home I determined to put her suggestions into practice.

In the Rows, several people covered in their yards to make an extra room. This was called the back-end and usually it was furnished with a small rectangular stove standing on a concrete slab. This stove burned feverishly generating a terrific amount of heat. For the rest, there was usually a table, a form and mats on the floor. Here I determined to make my own portable bathroom, and a very agreeable method of bathing it became. In the interest of privacy, I draped the big clothes-horse with an assortment of old sheets and blankets. I filled one dish with warm water and stood it on the cracket (stool) together with soap and sponge. Below, on the floor, I placed a second dish of warm water and in this I stood. Beside me was a container with clean water. I had a sort of stand up bath and, when I'd finished, I poured the clean water over my person. The towel and the clothes I was about to wear hung on a line suspended over the stove. They were beautifully warm. After the 'bath', I washed the underwear I'd worn and hung them on the line to dry. Of course, it was more than likely that, while I was bathing, someone would jingle the sneck indicating they were about to open the door and come in. In spite of this and other little drawbacks, bathing and washing my smalls became my daily practice.

Although neither my father nor my mother ever suggested I left school before I had completed the course, I did, in fact, leave at fourteen. On my final day at school, I felt I had to take in every detail because it had to last me for ever. The teachers themselves appeared heart-breakingly kind and encouraging. Watching them walking round the quad to the staff-room, their gowns floating behind them was emotionally upsetting and the thought that I had denied myself the privilege of ever wearing a gown was almost unbearable. The parquet floor, the black-boards, the walls, my own desk, the cloak-room, the barely warm radiators would know me no more. I looked and looked, wanting to etch them into my memory for ever. This had been a Garden of Eden which I now had to leave, and I was fearful of the morrow.

Chapter 13

World of Work

In the beginning the word I heard was work. To live, it was necessary to work. It also seemed to be necessary to work till one was exhausted. Around me I saw women to whom work seemed endless. Women who got up early and went to bed late with no prospect that life would be any different on the morrow. At the end of their day's toil they had to draw attention to their weariness saying, 'I'm fair done', or, 'I can hardly put one foot in front of another', for no-one appeared to notice their tired condition.

One could not avoid seeing that men returning from the pit at the end of a shift had worked hard. Their blackened faces, soiled clothes and measured gait bore witness to their efforts. Even after they'd bathed, evidence of the hazards they ran were manifest in the blue marks and small scars to be seen on their bodies, the result of falls of stone and knocks that went with their jobs.

For women, the basic necessary domestic work was hard enough of itself. Added to this was extra work in abundance. Whatever the weather, the door steps had to be scrubbed clean every day and then decorated in fancy patterns with donkey stone. Any brass door furnishings had also to be cleaned daily.

For the housewife, the idiosyncrasies of the kitchen fire had to be thoroughly understood and pandered to. First of all, she had to contend with the load of coal sent to her. Different kinds of coal required different usage as far as the fire was concerned. In addition, she had to know about the direction of the wind, how the flue could be used to best advantage, whether or not the chimney was ready for cleaning and how to prevent billowing smoke suddenly belching down the chimney leaving smutty deposits on a newly cleaned kitchen or newly laundered clothes. On baking days, without benefit of thermometers or thermostats, she had to heat the oven to just the right temperature and keep it that way till she had finished her considerable family baking while, at the same time, coping with the demands of that same family and the shift pattern of the bread-winner.

For those who possessed front rooms, hours of the housewife's time was spent in scrubbing, cleaning and burnishing that apartment so that it took on the appearance of a shrine ever waiting for a critical inspection from some high-ranking official of an exalted order.

On the rare occasion when a married woman had to go on an outing she did her housework before she set out, got back as soon as possible and made up for lost time domestically speaking. Most women were not supposed to be idle even in leisure. Few women were nor could they be when one considers the endless darning, mending, knitting and sewing required by a family.

It came as a surprise to learn that there had been vacuum cleaners and electric kettles available during my childhood. In Ashbourne Crescent we had a Triplex Grate that only needed a wipe over to clean, unlike the huge black fireplaces still prevalent in other houses.

Apart from the man's job and his wife's household tasks there were other things to do which, whether those concerned wanted to or not, involved the whole family. We kept hens. They had to be properly housed, fed, cleaned out and their eggs collected. In addition, they all had to be shooed into their coop before night-fall. The broody hens had to be specially looked after. Her chicks, when they came, had to be carefully tended and nurtured. The call could come at any time, while I was reading, doing school work, or later, work for a night class or just ready to go out.

'Linda, just make the bran mash and take it to the hens. Put in them few potatoes in the dish under the apple tart behind the milk jug./Just run out and give the hens their corn. Mind and see you close the gate./Go to the hen cree and see if that dark one has laid yet./Just pop out and have a look at that clocker for me. See that the catch is fast. I don't want anything getting in./Keep your eye on these chicks and see they don't wander off the blanket or get too near the fire./Before you go out just bar the hens up for me.'

The hen coop was raised on bricks to discourage rats. The thought of this discouraged me a great deal more – but I did as I was asked (told) in spite of the rats and the fact that this was a job I did not really like. The smell in the hen-house was suffocating.

Thank goodness we didn't keep pigs! I was only ever at one pig killing. Once was more than enough. I was out playing when word went round there was to be a pig killing in the Eighth and I was among those who flocked there. In preparation the pig had been starved for the previous twenty-four hours and the family had filled the copper in the wash-house and boiled the water. This would be needed to scald and scrape the skin after the bristles had been burned off in the fire alight in the garden. The pig, already squealing, was tied by three legs, the fourth being free. I didn't want to see any more. I've no great fondness for pigs but I felt sorry for it and could not bear to hear it squealing. I ran off but could not shut my ears to the animal's frenzied cries as the knife was used and it worked its free leg frantically to get away. Underneath his leg was a large dish which caught the blood being shed. This would be made into black puddings. White puddings were made with lard from the pig, onions, oatmeal, pepper and salt. The intestines were washed and used as cases for puddings and sausages. Not all pigs were killed by this method. Some were stunned by a mell before the knife was used.

When the animal was dead everyone had to clean the carcase after which the pig was disembowelled and hung. In the end, every bit of the pig was used.

For those who had productive gardens and allotments there was, naturally, much work to be done and help was expected. There was a great deal of friendly rivalry about who would be the first to dig up new potatoes, who would have the best leeks, onions etc. even among those who did not enter the local leek shows and agricultural shows. Both my parents had green fingers.

Then there was the tedious time when it was decided that new ticking was needed for pillows and/or mattresses. Ticking itself was very hard to sew. Taking the feathers out of a pillow or mattress, cleaning them and putting them into their new cases was patience-trying in the extreme. Feathers are restless things at the best of times. They get agitated and develop itchy feet at the thought of the slightest breeze and, once they've got the wanderlust, they are almost impossible to catch. Also, it is essential that this kind of job is done in a closed room. In these circumstances it can get very, very stuffy and dusty and feathery.

As a member of a family, one can't sit outside all this activity – at least, I couldn't. I thought that to be enjoying myself when other people were working was sinful and I felt guilty. However, there are those who will not tolerate idlers, even when these same idlers are merely paying a visit.

'Did you hear owld Tom has been sent for? Just reach across and get that towel. You might as well dry these few dishes while you're standing there doing nothing. Aye, he's getten his time in. Not that he was that old. Not that much more than sixty. Hand me that spoon over. Last Thursday. No. I tell a lie. It was Wednesday, the day after the fish man. When you've finished you might as well wash these few things up. We'll be needing them. Aye. Wednesday it was. Somebody's spilt something on this grate and never let on. He never ailed a thing. One o' them. Didn't know what pain was. Many a time I've thought of him when I could hardly put one foot in front of another. But I've just had to get on with it. But his time was up. The Lord must have had need of him for something. Just put that on the pantry shelf. Not that one. The one above. Not there. Behind the butter. He was getting into his pit clothes when he took this bad turn. [BANG! BANG! BANG!] Get off that garden! Eh? Well get your ball and get out. DON'T STAND ON THEM PEAS! By but he's a cheeky laddy that. It's a good job for him I wasn't in the garden......'

Few children got paid part-time work before they left school. With the exception of delivering newspapers there were practically no jobs for pre-school leavers available.

Newspapers were not only delivered, they were sold in the streets and 'round the doors' till quite late at night. This was nearly always done by young lads, most not yet left school. Remuneration was one penny (or the cost of one paper) for every twelve sold.

At fourteen one was old enough to join the world's workers. The aim was to get a secure job because once one had a job that was it. One stayed in it for life, except for girls who got married. There was little freedom of choice.

The pit was by far the greatest employer of men and boys in the area. For girls there was service, shops, offices and nursing. For those who went on to higher education, there was teaching. Some girls weren't allowed to get a job. They were 'kept' at home.

For those who wanted a job at fourteen (the majority) very often the choice was between any job and no job. Adolescents had no clout till they started work. They had no money so that no-one in the business world catered for them especially. Certainly, no adult asked their opinion on anything. They were not old enough or experienced enough to have an opinion, nor had they a voice in the assembly.

For those who wanted a job with prospects, training was necessary. Girls who wanted to work in an office (they did not assume they would be called secretaries immediately) went to shorthand and typing lessons. For most, this meant private lessons in the home of the teacher. These lessons cost either a shilling (5p) or one and six (7½p) an hour. However well the student did, it was considered wise to have someone to 'speak for you', or at least, have someone in the know, when it came to actually getting the job. Offices were quiet places with clerks bent over their desks writing. The offices smelt of ink and leather, this last from the huge leather bound ledgers which, it seemed, was their *raison d'etre.*

Girls who wished to become hairdressers had to pay a premium. They got no wage for the first year and a nominal wage the second year.

My mother was apprenticed to a dressmaker for which position her mother had to pay a premium. She got no wages for the first two years the first of which was spent picking up pins, threading needles, taking out tacking threads, delivering finished garments to clients and being at the beck and call of everyone else in the establishment. During the second year she was allowed to tack, sew on hooks and eyes, plackett fasteners and buttons and make belts. In this occupation little had changed for the apprentices of my generation.

The great goal for boys was to become apprenticed to a trade. To have any chance of this they had to be 'taken on' by the time they were sixteen when they were bound for a full five years apprenticeship during which time their pay was small indeed.

A number of shops, particularly grocery shops, offered employment to boys before they were sixteen. Their job was to deliver goods on a bicycle with a huge basket in front. Those who possessed telephones and who wanted some commodity, however small, had no hesitation in ringing a shop to have it sent round. For this the errand boy was never tipped. It was his job. That was what he was paid for – usually five shillings per week. Sometimes women came into the shop and bought a few things, then asked to have them sent. A cousin who was a supervisor in Woolworth's tells a story of an autocratic lady who arrived outside the shop in a pony and trap. She parked her equipage, walked into Woolworth's and asked to see a supervisor to whom she gave sixpence for an article she wanted adding, 'And send it round immediately'. When errand boys reached the age of sixteen their services were usually dispensed with and they were replaced by a willing fourteen-year old. There was no dearth of replacements.

The Store (Co-op) did not do this. The errand boy was kept on and officially started his apprenticeship at sixteen. He remained a delivery boy, however, going out on the

Hallowells built the first motorised ambulance for Ashington Hospital. From left to right, Wilf Hallowell, Leslie Hallowell, Jack Hallowell and T.W. Hall.

shop bike at the drop of a hat.

Most firms, the Co-op apart, were family owned and those at the bottom actually knew and worked with those at the top. The workforce was not part of some large, unknown combine with head offices in some distant area and directors of whom they knew nothing. Loyalty and affection were given to employers such as Cook's, Snow's, Donkin's, Wheatley's, Hallowell's, Paddy Mullen's and Arrowsmith's. They were known to their employees and they lived in the area. True, they lived in bigger houses, but not that much bigger. Incidentally, Donkin's is the only long established family firm still operating in Ashington.

To be employed by the Store (Co-op) meant that one was an instant part of a community within a community, part of a fraternity in fact – one which contained not only employees and bosses but customers as well.

The coal owners, the Priestmans and the Pumphreys, visited their mines regularly, talked with their miners and had their welfare at heart. They, too, provided venues for holidays, leisure time pursuits and education.

In addition, a job was a job and most had that particular job for the whole of their working lives, if they were lucky. Thus, like the errand boy, most had a sense of duty and pride in work and stayed to finish a particular job without thought of over-time.

A great many children who left school took jobs that were well below their standard of ability and potential. There was so little choice. I often found the job I did monotonous and I was sometimes unhappy, but it never occurred to me to give it up. I had to earn my own living as had others and, like them, I just got on with it.

Whatever job we got, we began as a gofers – go fer this, go fer that and be quick about it. Everyone was disciplined. The newly appointed member of staff had much to learn and those who were older and more experienced saw it as their duty and responsibility to teach and guide the young. As for the young, they did as they were told. The sack was an ever-present spectre and there were always others to fill their shoes.

Like many others, I took the job available and gratefully made the best of it. Given a choice, I would not have opted for working in a grocery department, but I got to enjoy it very much. Getting a job certainly brought status, instant status. The applicants for the post I got must have numbered at least two hundred. It brought a good wage, and, security. From having no money I brought home either ten shillings (50p) or twelve and six (62½p) – but I think, the latter – a week in a pay packet. This I gave, with how much pride I can scarcely measure, intact to my mother. From this I was given one shilling a week pocket money.

At that time all young people 'tipped up' their wages intact. Those who went away into service or who worked elsewhere were expected to send money home. Some, especially those who were considering getting married, asked to go on to their board when they were twenty-one, that is, they paid a sum for board and lodging and kept the rest. From ten shillings (or twelve and six) my wages went up annually on a fixed rate, two and six a week, I think. The top wage was not reached till one was twenty-four or five, a rate which few girls actually achieved, mostly because they married and had to leave. When one considers the wages of miners at that time, ten shillings a week, plus the knowledge that this would rise at a fixed rate, was a very welcome addition to the family exchequer.

Also, after I started work, I visited a hairdresser for the first time. Till that date my hair had been cut at home, my mother being the family barber. It was not uncommon for the same thing to apply to young boys. Boys went to barbers where they had to sit and wait, quietly listening to the non-stop flow of talk that surrounded them, till the barber thought they had waited long enough. As they paid half the adult rate they did not necessarily get their turn. Hair cuts were meant to last. They got a 'short back and sides' after which a strong smelling pomade, one of the ingredients of which was the gummy tragacanth, was liberally and forcefully rubbed onto the recently shorn heads and the lot combed. Before long the pomade had set to the consistency of a stiff board.

Bosses were bosses. Their word was law. Very few places, if any, had the career structure prevalent today. There was the boss or the head and there might be a foreman or deputy and that was it, so that there was really only one person of whom one had to be continually aware, the Boss.

We neither stayed off work nor took to our beds for heavy colds, bilious attacks, toothache or aches and pains of a general character. Nor did we complain or expect work circumstances to be conditioned to, or for, our benefit.

The office-under-the-stairs, in which I was destined to spend a fair bit of my time while I was employed by the Store, could not have been less conducive to work or comfort of any description. It was small; it was airless; the lighting was poor. There were two places at which I could work, the side of a tall Victorian desk or a bench. To work at the desk meant standing at the side where the lid sloped down and where it was impossible to sit because there was nowhere for one's knees to go, the side being one unrelenting piece of wood.

On Thursday afternoons and on part of Friday mornings, three of us worked in this office totalling books. The bench was just long enough for two people to work at, if one was prepared to squash up in the corner. There were two seats; the very limited space could not accommodate more. One was a padded Victorian office stool, too high for the bench. The chair was too low. In any case, there was only room for one to sit at the bench. Nevertheless, there was a choice. One could sit sideways on the stool at the sloping desk. One could, but one didn't. At least, not for very long. The human frame and the organs it so efficiently keeps together are not really suited to this type of seating accommodation. The chair at the bench was the only real option, a choice made when the discomfort in one's ankles was greater than the discomfort of writing at a breast-high (when seated) bench. In the end, especially as, towards the end of my service with the Store, I spent the greater part of my time working alone in this office, I learned to stand throughout my working day.

All of this, I'm sure, was designed to improve the character of the British worker. It produced stoicism and endurance at its best. The highest accolade that could be bestowed on a man or woman was that he or she was a real, good hard worker.

Chapter 14

The Life and Times of a Bradford Barn Dancer

A Bradford Barn dancer was one notch above a Wallflower. The latter occupied the very bottom place on the continuum. It was she who, at a dance, sat on a chair against the wall smiling, trying frantically to look as though she were not desperate to be asked up for a dance. Still smiling, she appeared to be looking everywhere but at the corner where the young men congregated watching them out of the corner of her eye, hoping against hope that at least one of them would walk over to her and claim her. And, when all hope was lost for that dance, clearly she wasn't going to be asked up, it was she who tried to signal to all who might be interested (pitifully few) that she hadn't wanted to dance after all, but had intended to go to the cloakroom. And, trying to look as if she were enjoying herself, to the cloakroom – that chill, spartan chamber – she went forcing back the tears that would come to her eyes.

In that refuge she stood in front of the big mirror (already going spotty at the edges) combing and patting her hair, scrutinising her face, dabbing on a little more powder, putting on another layer of lipstick, smoothing down her dress, checking her stocking seams, looking down at her slippers and going through the routine again.

Towards the end of the dance proper, the complete Wallflower managed to disregard the rising lump in her throat and her impending tears because she hadn't been asked up all night even when the M.C. had drawn the attention of the lads not dancing to the young ladies still partnerless. She could still smile at the cloakroom attendant and say she would have to go now and, yes, she had enjoyed herself and, yes, she'd be back next time.

It was possible, of course, that two girls could dance together but this was a tacit admission of failure. However much they laughed and giggled together, ('Laugh as if you were enjoying yourself') determined to let the world know

214

they were having a good time, appearances were against them.

The only way out of the impasse on one's own initiative was to become a Bradford Barn Dancer – henceforth BBD.

The Bradford Barn Dance (of which there were usually two – one to start the evening off and one after the interval) was a fairly simple progressive dance executed in one big circle. It consisted mostly of gliding steps forward, gliding steps backward, a waltz turn, gliding sideways and releasing one's partner when the girl moved on to the next man.

Usually the intending BBD signalled her intention of breaking-in to the dance by standing up, at the ready, so to speak. She took her stand at the edge of the dance floor to one side or other of the entrance. Here there was the greatest collection of dancers because it was here that those who'd just arrived or those who had belatedly bethought themselves of getting up, joined the circle. The BBD's tactic was to slip into the circle casually, as though she were part of the dance, at the change of partners. She then laid claim to a man who had just been released before his rightful partner got to him. Of course, this left one girl out, but this was an every-woman-for-herself situation. If the girl was pretty it was likely that some gallant young man who had elected not to join the dance, seeing her partnerless, would oblige. If this did not happen, a girl with spirit just stood there and waited till the next change to regain a partner. If, however, she felt that she could not do unto others as they had done unto her, she took refuge in the cloakroom.

Again, two girls could have got up together, but this would have meant one girl taking the man's part and a lot of girls did not like dancing with their own sex. In this event, the girl taking the man's part might, if she were clever enough, reverse her role as soon as the opportunity offered.

The committed BBD soon learned that not all men were good dancers and not all men had taken the trouble to learn. Among the latter group were those who stumbled happily on and among the feet of their partners, often with no apology thinking, perhaps, this was the way to dance. A few cheerfully admitted they'd never got the hang of it, but, obviously, they didn't look upon this as a drawback. Those girls who were not good dancers paid the penalty by having to sit out. Not so the men. One had to pretend they were all good dancers, even those who seemed possessed of ten big toes and two left feet. There were others who ignored the music entirely and went round at their own pace and those who perfected an all-purpose (for them) step which they used for every dance regardless of tempo. Some took giant strides so that their two steps took them to the centre of the hall and beyond. Unless their partners were trained athletes the best they could do was to allow themselves to be dragged along. Some took their partners delicately as though they were soiled, smelly rags to be held at the greatest possible distance with the tips of the fingers on one hand and a limp wrist on the other, a wrist which did not make contact with their partners' backs. Others grabbed their partners with such strength that the breath was squeezed from their bodies and there was no room for refills.

Of course, having got into the dance, the BBD had to make the most of the opportunity and sparkle in the hope that she might thereby be claimed for the next, or a later, dance. She looked up and laughed and appeared excessively interested in the merest grunt of a reply in the hope that her partner would find her worthy of at least one dance even though he had the agility of a lead weight. To the Wallflower and the BBD any partner was better than none.

Sometimes, however, the BBD was partnered by a good dancer (and they were the majority) whose person was more than pleasing to the eye. How desperately eager she was to talk and please – and how abysmally she failed. Nothing would come. Rack her brains as she might, she was quite unable to say one word.

Having broken the ice and gate-crashed the Bradford, the young lady in question could now look forward to at least three other dances, even if she had not, as yet, found a partner. She could get up in the Ladies' Excuse Me, that is, she could go up to a dancing couple and, tapping the girl on the shoulder and saying the words 'Excuse me', she could take over her partner. This was not for the faint-hearted

Jack Summers' band. Jack on accordion and M.C. Tommy Brooks (left).

because the young men most often excused were the popular ones. This meant that the girl who had done the excusing was often, herself, left stranded on the middle of the dance floor.

In each programme there was a Ladies' Choice. Timing was important here. If she dashed up too soon to claim a partner, she was being too obvious. If she lingered too long, somebody else got him. No wonder girls thought lads were lucky! It never occurred to us that they, too, might have problems.

The third dance was the Paul Jones. Here, after a brief waltz, the music changed to a march when the couples broke up, the women forming a circle in the centre while the men formed a circle on the outside. The circles walked in opposite directions. When the music stopped men and women took the partners nearest to them and together did the dance the music dictated till, once again, the tune changed to a march. There should, of course, have been as many of one sex as the other, but, alas, after the first break there were more women than men. The ranks of the former had been augmented by the BBDs. Thus, when the music stopped after a march, there were several partnerless females. The choice before them was either to partner another female and make a resolve not to be left next time, or to walk off the floor aggrieved because they had obeyed the rules while others hadn't.

Two of the important rules of etiquette in dancing were, one, the man came up to the woman and said, 'May I have the pleasure of this dance, please?' Many did but some just walked in the direction of the partners they had in mind and, individually, having caught her eye, he jerked his head in the direction of the floor. Some positioned themselves in readiness and simply looked in the direction of their chosen partner and said, 'Haway then'. Most gave a less cissified form of the format.

The second rule was that if a young man asked a young woman to dance and she declined then she had to sit all that dance out no matter how much she might want to dance with a subsequent would-be partner. The only way she could refuse and still dance was if she had already been asked and her partner had merely absented himself for a few minutes.

The candles for these social moths were, in the main, the Arcade Ballroom, the Princess Ballroom (more often called the Rink because it doubled as a roller-skating rink on Monday evenings) and the Harmonic Hall. In addition, there were numerous others from the Parish Hall to the smallest wooden hut belonging to some organisation religious or otherwise.

Loyalty demanded that I mention the Arcade first because I was a Store Lass and the Arcade belonged to the Store (Co-op) but, in fact, the most plush and ornate of these halls was the Princess with its shaded alcoves, its superior cloak-rooms and its band which boasted a resident singer, Ronnie Hope. Moreover, the band wore a sort of simulated evening dress uniform.

For sixpence (2½p) at the twice weekly dances (or hops) at both the Arcade and the Princess one got a band – piano, drums, saxophone, clarinet, piano-accordion, violin and, at the Princess, a vocalist. In addition there was an M.C. who kept law and order, who saw to it that young lads got up to dance and didn't stay larking about in groups. He also saw to it that young lads NEVER danced together. It was the M.C. who announced the next number.

There was a wide variety – Foxtrot, Slow Foxtrot, Quick

Step, One Step, Two Step, Three Step, Military Two-step, Eva Three-step, Dashing White Sergeant, Veleta, Gay Gordons, Samba, Strip the Willow, Tango, Circassion Circle, Rumba, Waltz, Modern Waltz, the Lambeth Walk, Paul Jones and the Bradford Barn Dance. The Charleston was no longer popular, nor was the Black Bottom. The Grand March, the Lancers and the Eightsome Reel were usually reserved for the big, Annual dances or Balls held during the winter months when there would be twelve musicians in the 'Princess' band. On these occasions, when the Lancers was announced, the M.C. always added, 'Gentlemen, Do NOT SWING YOUR PARTNERS, please.' In spite of that, it was a rare Lancers that did not see young women swung completely off their feet, screaming with excitement as they were whirled around.

All dances ended with the Last Waltz. There were markedly fewer couples on the floor for this dance because it was obligatory that the young man who asked a young lady up for the Last Waltz also took her home. Thus, asking a girl up for this dance was fraught. If the girl had clicked and her suitor was really keen, then where she lived was of secondary importance. But, if he had no more than the faint stirrings of a 'bit fancy' then the girl's address *was* of importance. Not only might she come from the furthest corner of Ashington when he came from the opposing furthest corner of Hirst, she might have come from as far afield as Ellington, Lynemouth, Newbiggin or Seaton Hirst. As both were going to walk to their respective homes, distance was important. Thus the young man concerned might have a walk of at least six miles before him till he finally got home; no small consideration if he was 'in first' next day. The reward for all this effort was no more than a 'Goodnight'. We girls had to be very careful not to throw ourselves away.

The churches and chapels gravitated towards socials rather than dances. Those attending the social were required to bring some item of festive fare which was handed in at the door and passed to the helpers who were setting out the meal. As these experienced ladies opened each bag they were able to assess accurately from whom each contribution had come.

These socials were not for the avante-garde. Most attracted no more than their fraternity. Among them were married couples still young enough to shake off the staid concomitant of wedlock, steadies who had committed themselves to matrimony and would find nothing in the socials to incite them to change their minds and the young and unattached. As far as this latter group was concerned socials were not for wild-oat sowing. Definitely not. True, technically a hundred percent paid-up Wallflower didn't exist at socials. The most gauche young maiden could expect, after several couples had taken the floor and rejection was beginning to set in, an older relative (married), a brother (duty), an ageing superintendant or other factotum (large-frog-in-small-pond *bonhomie* 'We can't have pretty girls like you sitting out, can we?' providing an instant clumsiness-maker, a duller of eyes, an I-wish-I-were-dead sensitivity that suffused even the stoutest heart) or reluctant friend of her father's pushed by an insistant wife, to come and claim her for a dance.

Nor did the committed BBD fare any better. She needed none of her hard-earned guile. At these Bradfords there was usually sufficient room for couples to be seen as entities so that gate-crashing was out of the question and the BBD was forced to move down one and accept the fate of the erstwhile Wallflower.

The constitution governing dances of this kind was unwritten, but it was there. 'You give my wife a dance and I'll give your wife a dance and we'll split the duty dances between us.' The monthly Toc H dances held on Friday nights in the Harmonic Hall were of this nature as were some Masonic dances. Splendid affairs for the initiated but not quite so good for those on the fringe, if not the outside. (Of course, one would never admit to this. However much teeth-gritting it took, one had always had a good time.)

At the invitation of two very kind older relatives who wanted to 'bring me out' I attended these dances through-out the winter I was sixteen. The trouble was, I was the only uncommitted person there and, too often, what was intended for my enjoyment turned out to be heart-sinking despondency which added to an already developed in-feriority complex. On the other hand, I have been to some very pleasant Harvest Socials, Scout Socials and YMCA dances.

As far as a girl was concerned, when she was preparing to go to a dance or social it was incumbent upon her to do far more for herself than Nature had bargained. For those who could afford neither a permanent wave (seventeen and six – 87½p) nor a fortnightly set (one and six – 7½p) curlers and/or tongs were a must because curls and waves were *de rigeur.*

Getting one's hair permed was probably as painful and uncomfortable as going to the dentist but one was happy to go for the former and apprehensive, if not downright cowardly, when visiting the latter. Perming involved the hairdresser seizing one's hair in little clumps, clapping a rubber pad to the roots so that heat from the machine did not penetrate to the scalp (it always did) then firmly winding the hair on some sort of roller. This was wound as tightly as possible and as near the scalp as possible to ensure a curlier perm that lasted longer. As the hairdresser progressed one's head got heavier and heavier and one's scalp more and more stretched with the weight of these rollers and the dedication of the hairdresser. The remaining perm fluid was generously applied over the rollers with stinging results to those who had sensitive eyes. Next, the hairdresser brought forward a fearsome stand hung around with flex tentacles at the ends of which were clamps resembling the more determined kind of bull-dog clip. These remorseless clips were clamped in position, one to each roller and the heat was turned on, literally, as one's hair cooked and, thereafter one's head and face. When the heat was such that the most stoic person could stand it no longer, a wad of cotton wool was wedged in among the ironmongery on the affected part.

For those who wanted a set but could not afford (or were not allowed to have) a perm there were two alternatives both almost obsolete, the Marcelle wave (done with hot tongs) and the Water wave. This last was induced by curved clamps with vicious interlocking teeth.

The home hairdresser used curlers which were kept in till the last possible minute, or curling tongs heated in the fire and tested out first on newspaper. The tongs were apt to

Linda's first perm.

singe the hair and burn the ears of the inept or nervous user.

There were still those who called make-up 'paint and powder'. The beauty preparations then available to the girl preparing for the dance were mostly Pond's cold cream and vanishing cream, Sno(w)fire vanishing cream and powder, Velouty powder cream, Phul-nana, mascara, nail polish, rouge and lip-stick. With these products we tried to make ourselves look like film stars, finishing off with a dab of Evening in Paris, Californian Poppy or June perfume behind the ears.

According to the makers of Bile Beans (little black coated workers), one Bile Bean a night before retiring would have obviated the necessity of so much titivating before the mirror. That nightly Bile Bean would assure a soft complexion, sweet breath and sparkling health. 'The kind of girl men wanted to marry.'

Young people of both sexes just starting to attend hops wore their Sunday clothes to begin with. A girl, if she was lucky, got a dress to go to the dance in. One dress. It needed all her ingenuity and the help of a magazine fashion editor to ring the changes. A belt, an artificial flower and artificial jewellery were her most important accessories. The latter most often consisted of a string of beads that would go with anything and at least one pair of earrings.

Most girls had their ears pierced at home. A threaded needle was sterilised in the flame of a match, a cork placed behind the ear and the needle passed through the lobe. The thread stayed in the ear and was moved a little each day to keep the hole open.

Generally speaking, both young men and young women wore dancing shoes as soon as they could afford them. When carrying them to the dance, young men probably just put one shoe in each pocket, but young women had to put theirs in a bag or proper shoe case. They also needed evening bags into which they could put the obligatory powder compact and powder puff.

The first dance I attended was held in the Arcade. I was fifteen and, with two friends Joyce and Margaret, I was still attending the Store Classes. This particular class was held on a Wednesday night. Numbers were dwindling. We had as our teacher a handsome young man from the Drapery with whom we were something of a favourite by virtue of the fact that we had now attended his classes faithfully for a year or two and he felt confident that, not only would we stay the course, we would acquit ourselves reasonably well in the examinations at the end.

One Wednesday, at the start of the Spring term he told us that the class due to be held a fortnight hence would be cancelled.

'It's the Store's Annual dance,' he said, 'and I'm going so I'm afraid I'll not be seeing any of you that night, unless, of course, ha ha, some of you are going. If you are, I have tickets for sale, price two and six (12½p) including Whist Drive, Supper and Spot Prizes.'

The three of us looked at each other.

'Fancy going?'

'Wouldn't mind.'

'Me too. It'll make a change.'

'Shall we order the tickets?'

'Yes. But next week will be soon enough.'

This conversation was, of course, brinkmanship, although the word had not then been coined. We were simply showing off. It was a conversation I could take part in as if our going was a probability because I knew that there was no possibility of my mother's allowing me to go.

'Yes,' Mother said. 'Yes. You can go. But you'll have to buy your own ticket and you're getting no new clothes till Easter so don't go thinking about a dance dress.'

'But I can't go to a big dance in my Sunday jumper and skirt!'

'You should have thought of that. I'm not forcing you to go. If you want a dance dress you must buy it yourself.'

I was flabbergasted. My only hope now was that Joyce had been told she couldn't go, but in fact, both she and Margaret had been given permission. Margaret was having her dress made. Joyce had managed to get a reasonably priced blue silky dress in Snow's sale.

Bewildered at the way things had turned out, devastated at this blow to my carefully hoarded small savings, I went up to the Arcade dress department. I confined my search to their sale stock finally choosing a dress whose only merit was that, at four and eleven (nearly 25p) having been twice reduced, it was the cheapest there. In fact, it was probably the most expensive dress I've ever bought.

The dress had never been designed as a dance dress. True, it reached my ankles but that was because it had been made originally for a much taller woman whose vital statistics were considerably greater than mine. The material of which it was made, elephant crêpe, was well named. It did, indeed, resemble the hide of an elephant in colour and in texture. In fact, to the casual observer, there was no difference. The dress had been cut on the cross to emphasise the curves of the wearer. Unfortunately, at that time I had no curves to speak of. The top of the sagging puffed sleeves began well below my shoulder, the Vee neck would have shown a fair bit of cleavage if I'd had one and the waist hugged what bottom I had. My mother insisted I wore a long white petticoat underneath and a modesty vest to modify the worst excesses of the Vee neck.

I had no suitable shoes but my mother came to the rescue. She bought me a pair of flat-heeled black sateen court shoes. They were cut rather low at the front and I had difficulty keeping them on so Mother sewed on pieces of white elastic in lieu of straps.

I think we were the first to arrive at the dance. The Whist Drive was already under way but that was being held in another part of the building. As we walked into the hall the members of the band – Joe, Harry, Roland and Billy Gray together with three others whose names I have forgotten – were setting up their instruments. We returned to the cloakroom and spent as long as we could shivering therein. Joyce looked very nice indeed in her blue and Margaret, too, looked most attractive in a pretty pink dress. As I still wasn't allowed to wear make-up I could do little but stand. When we considered the band was well into its stride, we went back into the hall.

We stood together in a group on the left hand side of the room and smiled at each other and watched the dancers and went to the cloakroom and came out and stood at the right hand side of the room and smiled to each other and watched the dancing and went to the cloakroom but couldn't get near the mirror because people were beginning to arrive in numbers and we went back to the hall and told each other that things were beginning to warm up and smiled at each other and watched the dancers. After a century and a half our aching facial muscles did actually register pleasure when the M.C. announced that those who wanted supper now could go to the Supper Room where it was ready for the first sitting.

Not being sure where the Supper Room was we had to wait and see what others were doing. Nor had we taken into account that the Whist Drive was over and the players thereof had made a bee-line for the Supper Room. When we got there, the fairly small Store Café, redesignated Supper Room, was already full to overflowing and we had to wait in the queue for the next sitting (or possibly the one after that). It was the first break we'd had since we got there.

Finally, we were allowed in. The trestle tables were closely packed. There was just enough room to squeeze into the places allotted to us. To save time, the coffee had already been poured out. The person following me was pushed against the table. As he fell forward, he knocked over a cup of coffee the contents of which poured down the skirt of my dress. Fortunately, the coffee wasn't all that hot. Everyone was very sorry about it, but, as I sat there, damp and uncomfortable I felt sorriest of all. When we were finally released I found that the part of my dress that had been soaked had shrivelled to a tight little black ball. This left a fair expanse of white petticoat on view. Joyce and Margaret shielded me as best they could and we returned to keep our determined vigil. We had been told to leave the dance no later than half-past-eleven. It never occurred to us to go one second before that time, nor did it occur to us to say anything other than that we'd had a good time.

As I was paying for the dress no-one could comment on its condition. In fact, I never wore it again. When I thought things over I had the feeling that, somewhere along the line, I'd been taught a lesson, especially as, the following year, my mother bought me a very beautiful pink dance dress.

After the session at the Store class ended I attended the Learners' Dancing Class at the Arcade where we danced to records. Looking at us all and seeing our reluctance (especially that of the lads) to get up on the floor no-one would have guessed we'd gone of our own free will and that we actually wanted to learn to dance.

When the Learners' Class was over the girls went back to their seats along one side of the hall and the boys rushed back to their corner and there they stayed. A trickle of custom filtered through the double doors and the band came in somewhat despondently. The M.C. shot his cuffs, straightened his tie and took charge. A minion had finished laying French chalk on the already waxed floor. The M.C. tested the floor, sliding a foot along the surface here and there before he pronounced himself satisfied. The board on the easel said, 'Bradford Barn Dance'. A mutual nod between Joe Gray, the leader of the band, and the M.C. and the dance had started.

'Gentlemen,' bawled the M.C., 'take your partners for

the Bradford Barn Dance.'

The newly elevated lads tried to behave like connoisseurs and, from the security of their corner, looked along the row of seated females. We were there for a pleasant evening. I believe we are supposed to take our pleasures sadly. In this case 'fortitude' was the operative word. Just sitting there and smiling called for a great deal of self-discipline and the ability to dissemble. I, in common with many others, stuck it out and climbed the ranks from Wallflower to having a reasonable number of partners.

Quite apart from the exercise and the pleasure of dancing on a well-sprung floor to a decent band, the dance halls provided an acceptable meeting place for young men and women. The dances were well conducted. The M.C. would not allow any unruly behaviour. The man who took the money at the door would not allow any drunk, or even tipsy, persons in and, usually, after ten o'clock when the pubs came out young men were not allowed in at all unless they were bona fide *habitués* of the dance hall.

Chapter 15

Courting

To each new generation Love comes as though it were newly minted for their benefit. Today's young find it difficult to accept that sex, love, passion and desire were alive and kicking years and years ago. As long ago, indeed, as when I was young. It was just that, in my youth, we treated sex differently. For one thing, we did not find it necessary to talk about it quite so much. In fact, in one way, we couldn't. It was a subject that had no name. Generally speaking, love and the desire that goes with love were considered to be very private matters. What went on behind the bedroom door was also considered private. One did not kiss and tell about the people for whom one cared. The only people whose names were bandied around were those women who were considered 'fast' and who distributed their favours too quickly and too generously. Those who talked the most were the men who had benefited from these favours, or said they had. The overworked (heavily over-worked) adjective 'sexy' had not then been coined. People and clothes looked good/handsome/pretty etc., etc.

Adolescent girls and boys were kept chaste because of the inhibitions of the day. Unwanted pregnancies were so called because of the stigma attached to an unmarried mother and because it was recognised that looking after a baby was a great responsibility. It had to be provided with food, clothes and shelter all of which had to be paid for and there was no such thing as a Welfare State.

Girls suffered acute misery and great anxiety when they had 'gone too far'. These were the girls who looked at the calendar with apprehension. The plight of the girl whose period hadn't arrived was great indeed, especially when she didn't have a lad i.e. was not officially courting. She was the one who had to face up to telling her family. The natural result of this was a visit from the girl's father to the putative father of the unborn child. If he admitted to being the cause of the girl's being pregnant, then there was only one course open to him – he would have to marry the girl whether he wanted to or not, or whether he could afford to or not.

Marriages under these circumstances were hurried and ill-prepared for. If the couple could not get, or could not afford, rented accommodation for themselves, the only answer was to 'live in', that is, live with either set of parents, neither of whom would really have room. This was usually the worst possible start to married life. Thus, a lad, if he thought anything of the girl, did not 'try anything on'. If he did become too passionate in his caresses, it was up to the girl to stop him. Engaged couples were looked upon with greater indulgence. They had merely 'jumped the gun'.

The alternatives before an unmarried girl with no prospects was an illegal back-street abortion, having the baby 'away from the place' and having it adopted or suffering the disgrace of being an unmarried mother.

However, once a boy had 'got a girl into trouble' it wasn't so easy for him to evade his responsibilities in an enclosed community. Even his parents endorsed the un-written rule that 'he'd had his fun and now he had to pay for it'. So that he, too, had to be careful. It was by no means unknown for a girl to coerce a young man into marriage by this method. I remember when the contraceptive pill was first used a woman being really concerned about it.

'If everybody takes those things', she said to me, 'how will girls get themselves married?'

She had five sisters. Every one of them got married because they had to. She thought it was normal procedure. No lad would get married unless he had to.

After a certain age it was almost a disgrace not to be seen out with a companion of the opposite sex. 'What! Have you not got yourself a lad yet? What's the matter? Is there nobody good enough for you?'

Young people were nudged into marriage. What parents wanted for their daughters was 'a good sit down', husbands who would be good to them and give them a good home. Girls were not thought capable of doing this for themselves. All they could do was fill in time till Mr Right came along. Any girl who had high flown ideas about what she was going to do and talked of them was soon quietened.

'Just wait till Mr Right comes along. He'll soon change your ideas.' When she finally met him, it would be Mr Right's ideas that would occupy her mind. Her own had no validity. She was not expected to stand on her own two feet or think for herself. Her father would hand her over to her husband.

There were ground rules and anxieties. First parents worried in case their daughters started going out with lads too soon and then they worried in case they weren't going to get a lad. Generally speaking, up to the age of sixteen (sometimes later) one wasn't allowed to talk to lads or be seen with them. This, of course, added to their interest.

Often the greatest excitement about meeting lads in the street, going for walks with them or meeting them at the pictures was in the thought that one might be seen. The very fact that it was forbidden added to the romance of the situation. Indeed, it often WAS the romance. Spies, it seemed, were everywhere.

One hot Sunday afternoon when we were fifteen, as we walked round the Dene, Joyce and I met two boys we knew and with great daring they walked back home with us. We stopped at the bottom of our garden behind the hen crees which were well away from the house. A laburnum hedge ran along the side of the garden that bordered the road. As we chatted I was aware of two hats, a bowler and a navy summer straw, bobbing along the top of the hedge. There was something vaguely familiar about the straw. Then I knew. The owners of those hats would pass the end of our garden and see us.

'Joyce,' I said in alarm, 'your mother and father have been out. They're coming along the road now. Nearly here.'

'What'll I do?' she asked.

'The hen crees,' I said. She did just that. Darted into the hen crees. Those hens did not take kindly to having their privacy invaded one bit. In a second the air was full of squawking and feathers. The noise must have wakened all those within a half mile radius who were sleeping off their Sunday dinners. Joyce came out a lot quicker that she went in. She dusted herself down and, very apprehensively, went home to tea.

When I went to seek her for church, as I neared the

house I saw the curtains of an upstairs window being vigorously shaken and somebody waving at me. It was Joyce telling me to go away.

Next morning I waited for her at their corner end to catch her before she went to work to find out what had happened.

Of course, her parents had seen everything, lads, hens, the lot. When she got home her bicycle had been taken upstairs and shrouded in the mangle cover the latter now naked in the back-end. Metaphorically speaking, Joyce was put on bread and water and, literally, sent to her room where she had to stay for the rest of the day. Also, she was not allowed to go out, except to go to work, for a fortnight. The risks we ran just to be able to talk to a lad.

Then there were the guidelines – for girls. How girls should behave and look. This last meant spending some time in front of the looking glass so that one looked as attractive as possible. This was important because looks mattered to a girl. She was expected to make the best of herself. There was a great deal of difference between being dressed for work and dressing to go out. Nor was it just the immediate preparation. There was the ground work. The idea still lingered that hair should be given a hundred strokes of brushing before one went to bed. I don't suppose many did, but what most did do was put in curlers which were covered in a thick net to keep them in place during sleep. One got used to sleeping on the tight little bumps curlers produced. During the day, many wore an invisible net to keep the resultant set in place.

In one thing girls had it easier than their mothers had. During menstruation it was usual for womem and girls to use special cloths, such as torn up sheeting, which were washed and kept for that purpose. Now sanitary towels and even tampons were common. Sanitary towels originated in America in World War One when the nurses used surgical material which they disposed of after wearing.

When it came to behaviour with boys, although it was the mother who gave the advice, I think this advice must have originated with men. One had to listen to what young men said, and, in listening, appear interested. One had to ask them questions so that they could talk about themselves. What sort of job did they do? Which football team did they support? Did they play tennis or cricket? The end product of all this was often a monologue on pit work or football. At least one learned to keep at bay the glassy eyes and the desire to interrupt.

One of the dangers a girl had to beware of when talking to a lad was not to appear too eager in which case she could be accused of throwing herself at him.

For those who wanted to make a definite date, the choice was between going to the pictures, going for a walk or going for a bicycle ride. These last two involved no money at all so that an impecunious young man was not embarrassed by the fact that he had little to spend. Young men asking a girl out were expected to pay for both. They were reminded that, once they started courting, a twopenny pie cost fourpence. The one place they most certainly would not have gone to was a public house. Young girls, or women either for the most part, just did not 'go out drinking'.

After a few dates, when the couple had been seen together several times, the question then was, were they going steady? There was one way to find out. The girl asked the young man to tea on Sunday. If he accepted it was tantamount to his saying he was serious, or, in the old phrase, his intentions were honourable. Thereafter, the girl was courting. She had a lad. She could work towards getting her bottom drawer together. From then on, they spent almost all of their available time together. Most evenings would find the young man going home after work, changing and going round to the tart's (short for sweetheart) where he would go into the house without knocking, a sure sign that he was accepted. After two years' steady courting, the engagement would be announced and, about a year after that, the marriage.

Physically, courting proceeded at a much slower rate than relationships do today. When they went out on their preliminary walks, would he, or would he not, hold her hand? For two people to hold hands in the early stages of their love is, in itself, thrilling. Thereafter it was a kiss and then, after he'd been to their house for tea, snogging, mostly kissing and cuddling, in sheltered doorways, country lanes and shadowy bin corners, the murmurs, the little scuffles, the silences. Girls had to be careful. Boys did not respect girls who 'gave in' to them and soon tired of them. Sometimes this created a 'no win' situation. If the girl did not relax her rules the young man would leave for someone a little more amenable; if she did, she lost him anyway. The only answer was, 'All right. Get someone else,' whether she meant that or not.

There is no courtship now, no slow build up of a relationship. All the trembling excitement seems to have gone, all the saving together for a home, for couples (unless they had to) didn't get married till they could afford to.

In my own case, early on, I got my ideas of love and courtship from an old girls' Annual written circa 1924. I was possibly nine at the time it fell into my hands. I read the book over and over again, one story in particular holding my interest. It depicted a young man and young woman who met occasionally in the presence of others and, when he finally got her alone for a few minutes (having sought permission from her father) he, with great daring, took both her hands in his and intimated his wish (which had her father's approval) to spend the rest of his life making her happy. Actually, I did not see the connection between this and marriage. It had to be pointed out to me. Other stories I read concerning love were of the worthy Sunday Stories' type until I gravitated to the (forbidden) 'Red Letter'.

My first flesh and blood encounter happened when I was fourteen and I met a young man of similar age at a Co-op Summer School. The just being there without the restraint of parents or relatives being round the corner when we walked in the park at Southport or sat together when we went by train to Manchester, was, in itself, wonderful. We held hands, kissed briefly when we parted company and vowed to write every day. I never saw him again.

The following year, again at Summer School, I met a young man from Altrincham in Cheshire. Like me, he worked in the local Co-op. Unlike me, he still had more holiday available to him. He said he would like to spend this coming up to Ashington to visit me and wrote to my parents for permission. He would come with a friend. If he was allowed to come, could we make arrangements for the two of them to board somewhere. No doubt my parents had a discussion on the matter, but I did not take part in it, nor did I hear of it. I was only told that, yes, he could come. The two young men were cycling up, a distance of some one hundred and sixty miles. They could not leave till Monday morning and they hoped to be in Ashington by Wednesday.

The plan was that we, Joyce and I, would go to their digs on Wednesday to meet them at whatever time they arrived, Joyce having got permission. On Thursday we had to work but, in the evening, the four of us would go to the first house pictures and return to our house for supper. On Friday morning they would leave to be back home on Sunday night, in time for work on Monday.

My parents wanted to know what film we intended seeing and I mentioned the one currently supposed to be the best. On the Monday evening they went to see it and gave it the thumbs down. I have no doubt, its being a love story concerning a chorus girl (I think) high kicking her way into a man's heart, they thought it might prove unsettling and it might even inflame the passions of a youthful quartet unchaperoned in the cinema. We were allowed to go to some perfectly innocuous film about an Irish priest showing at the Buff. I hardly saw anything of it. I was far more interested in Harold (yes, that was his name) who held my hand and kept looking at me and sighing while I kept looking at him, sighing and thinking, fancy, he came all the way from Altrincham on a bike to see ME.

But, as Aunt Bella used to say, 'I'm getting before me story', as she took us back to page one, chapter one. We dashed home from work on Wednesday, (half-day holiday) changed and made our way hot-foot to the digs. No young men there. We waited, walked along the road to see if we could meet them, then panicked in case they'd come in a different way, and finally, went home to tea and then back to the vigil. The two young men did not arrive till ten o'clock. It had taken longer than they thought. Harold had brought me a box of chocolates. Boxes of chocolates then were large and ornate. There was usually a picture on the lid and a piece of wide ribbon tied with a huge bow round the box itself. Inside the chocolates were surrounded in white paper lace.

The following morning, when I left home for work, there he was waiting for me, just as he said he would be. Mere words are inadequate to describe my feelings as I walked to work that morning, anxious that I should be seen. Emotions tumbled, euphoria, satisfaction, inner excitement, disbelief, exhilaration. I couldn't keep from smiling. I was in a state of complete felicity. Here was a young man who had travelled miles to see me, who had got up early that he might walk to work with me, who would be waiting for me at dinner time, walk me home and back again to work and would be there again when the shop closed, his idle day spent in doing nothing other than waiting for the time that I should be free. And it was all open and above board.

On the Thursday night we left the pictures early that we might walk the long way home. It was a heavenly moonlight night, as soft and sweet and gentle as the brief meeting we were having. We held hands as we walked. On Friday morning he walked with me to work before he set off for home. We corresponded feverishly for some time, but other things took precedence and I never saw him again. By modern standards it wasn't much of an encounter, but I wouldn't have had it any other way.

There were dead-lines for girls that didn't exist for young men. A girl was expected to be married, or at least, engaged by the time she was twenty-one. A great aunt of mine told me that when the young man next door had his twenty-first birthday party, the house being full, they had the doors wide open. As the party progressed the noise level rose till the young man felt he had to say something about it.

'Make a bit less noise, everybody,' he implored. 'We have an Old Maid living next door.' My aunt was twenty-two! She did not marry till she was twenty-six and referred to herself as having married 'late in life'.

Thus, often girls in their late teens who were not courting began to make excuses and look around that little bit more diligently, often trying to think themselves in love. Perhaps they were really in love with the idea of being in love and almost any personable young lad could have worn the mantle. Subconsciously, they might have been trying to measure up to what was expected of them. There was also the feeling that the sands of Time were running out. It was only when one was young that it was possible to fall in love. After a certain age (which might be as young as twenty five) one was on the shelf after which spinsterhood loomed ahead and to be an Old Maid was almost criminal.

Then the miracle happens. One does fall in love. There is no other love like that first love, especially if it has been waited for. One wants to give everything to the beloved, one's thoughts, one's time. Friends and family take a back seat. Possibly friends disappear altogether. The slight blush when his name is mentioned, the inward trembling at the sight of him, the body that turns to water at the thought of him, the dizzy effect of 'our tune' which cannot be heard often enough, the drooling over letters stamped on the back with SWALK (sent with a loving kiss) or ITALY (I'll truly always love you) the contents of which are mediocre and repetitive but HE has written them, nothing and no-one else matters. The ecstacy.

Sometimes one had to pay a high price for this. Jealousy, that corroding state of mind, makes its presence felt when one senses a slight slackening in the beloved one's ardour. The misery of waiting. The greater misery of knowing. The hell of it. The pain of it. The advice of those to whom one has opened one's heart. Make him jealous. Go out with someone else. Get yourself all dressed up and go out and have a good time. Enjoy yourself. There are bigger shipwrecks at sea. He's not the only pebble on the beach. It's not the end of the world. All such useless advice because it is impossible to put into practice. The habit of being in love with him is already firmly established. It persists. 'Our tune' raises all the old desire, the trembling feeling. It is over. One has been ditched. Life will never be the same again.

When the couple had been engaged at the time of the break-up it was customary for them to return the presents they had given each other. When it was the man who caused the break, he asked for his ring back. If she felt strongly enough about it, the girl could sue for breach of promise. She had given him the best years of her life. (An indication, surely, that women were not expected to have many 'best years'. She would soon be 'past it', whatever that meant.)

Obsessional infatuation is a different matter. When one falls in love it is probably because, at the very least, some part of the beloved is lovable. This is not necessarily so in infatuation. An infatuated person can admit in his or her own heart that he or she is being treated with disdain, used as a doormat or considered merely as an outlet for sexual tension. It makes no difference. The one with whom one is infatuated exerts a hypnotic influence. There is absolutely no getting away from him or her, no matter how hard one tries, no matter how badly one has been treated. One lives only to be with, to be near, the object of one's infatuation even when the being there brings no real joy. How one suffers at the missed dates, the late arrival for a carefully prepared meal, the jealous wondering where he (or she) is and with whom. Is it the blonde he chatted up at the party while you stood on your own feeling absolutely awful? Perhaps he just isn't coming back. But he is not as kind as that. He knows how far to go, how to dismantle the defences one has so resolutely set up. He is confident that he has the upper hand. It is you, not he, who will apologise. It is you who will come crawling, hating what you are doing and helpless to do otherwise.

One's esteem in oneself, never high, drops to zero. He occupies so much of one's time, time used up in thinking about him, wondering if he'll come tonight, finding excuses for his negligent behaviour, waiting for him, hoping, spending money one can ill afford on clothes or make up that will, hopefully, make one more attractive, only to find the results are not even noticed. With all this, not only has one no time for others, one is not really fit company.

When release does come, when the scales finally fall from one's eyes, the memories are shame-making. How could one have done it? How could one have been so blind, so stupid? How could one possibly have put up with so much? For, assuredly, this was not love, although one thought it was at the time.

Lip service, at least, was paid to the understanding that a girl was a virgin when she went to the altar. Her white wedding dress was an outward sign of her virginity.

Virginity was not expected of a bride-groom. Who gave him his experience was a closely guarded secret and, to the enquiring mind of a young girl, an enigma. Men were men with innate animal passions that somehow had to be satisfied. How this was done was not for the sensibilities of a nicely brought up girl. It (sex) was a forbidden subject. Outside marriage it was a sin. Parents were much too embarrassed to discuss the subject with their children, while most children were too embarrassed to ask anyway, all of which made for widespread ignorance among young girls, and even, brides.

Chapter 16

One Sunday

I loved Sundays. If I did happen to be out of sorts it was because of circumstances that had nothing to do with the day itself. On this particular Sunday in January I was a peace with all the world. I had been to church, come home and had a pleasant dinner with my family, helped with the clearing up and got ready to go out. The others were going to tea at Grannie Summers'. I had been asked out to something a little more than tea, but not quite a party. A friend had invited a small group of boys (young men) and girls to tea and supper and I was one of the number.

I hadn't gone far after leaving home when I discovered I didn't have a handkerchief. I decided to call in at Grannie Summers' to borrow one. Knowing her routine, I expected her to be on her own, just clearing up after dinner and putting any necessary finishing touches to the food for tea. She was, in fact, just wiping the table down as I breezed in sure of my welcome, as always.

She looked up and smiled.

'What happened, you didn't call in yesterday or the day before?' she asked. 'I felt right off the crooks and I looked forward to you popping in and you didn't.'

'You're not ill, are you?'

'No. Not what you would call bad. Just as I said off the crooks.'

'Well, you know I work late on Fridays and Saturdays. I would have come, honest, if I'd known you were feeling bad. Are you all right now?'

'Canny. Canny. I'm not grumbling. Are you stopping for your tea?'

'I can't. That's why I've called in. I've been asked out and I've forgotten a handkerchief, so I've come to borrow one.'

'I'll get you one in a minute. Will you come for your supper?'

'Grannie, I'm sorry. I really am. But I've been asked to stay for supper as well. But I'll call in on my way home.

239

Promise.'

'Don't forget. I'll bring in the handkerchief drawer and you can pick one.'

'Any one'll do. But a plain one in case I lose it.'

She went into the front room where my grandfather was sleeping soundly, and returned with a box of handkerchiefs all neatly folded.

'Here,' she said. 'Take your pick, but if you're bent on losing it, I should have thought a bit of rag would do.'

'Of course I'm not going to lose it,' I replied, 'I was just afraid you were going to give me some expensive lace-edged piece of silk, some treasured heirloom. I couldn't have borne the responsibility. As it is, I'll take this one, attractive but serviceable. And,' I went on, dramatising as I spoke, 'if a highwayman should accost me when I leave here and say, "Your handkerchief or your life" I shall say, "Take my life. It is worthless when compared with the handkerchief which was given into my charge."'

She laughed. 'Go on with you,' she said. 'You want hitting on the head with a flannel hammer.'

We laughed together. Had we been a 'kissing' family, used to little outbursts of spontaneous affection, I might have hugged her and kissed her briefly, but, to have done that would have embarrassed us both. As it was, I went out smiling about her little age-old joke of the flannel hammer, saying as I crossed the threshold,

'I won't forget to call in on my way home.'

But I did forget.

I had a very pleasant afternoon and evening at my friend's house. The deadline for my being in at night was still nine-thirty, but there were often reasons for its being extended so that the edges were a little blurred. Today, my mother had said as I left the house,

'Be sure and be back before half-past-ten. Remember your father's in first.' This meant he would have to get up at five and he never went to bed till everyone was in and on their way to bed at least.

At ten o'clock I said I would have to be going. I got home about twenty-past-ten. The kitchen was warm and cosy. My mother, father and Billy were sitting round the fire reading. It was a very welcome scene to come home to.

240

'Did you call round at your Grannie's?' asked my mother as soon as I came in.

'Oh, no!' I said, dismayed. 'I forgot.'

'That's a pity,' Mother went on. 'She looked for you all night. She kept saying, "Linda should be here soon. She promised to come".'

I looked at the clock. 'I'll pop round now,' I said.

'I wouldn't, if I were you,' Mother replied.

'No,' said my father. 'Leave it till tomorrow. She had a busy day. She'll be tired.'

I hesitated. 'All right,' I said. 'I'll go round on my way to work tomorrow. Were there many there?'

'Everybody was there. Even your Uncle George and Aunt Lizzie looked in. They didn't stay for their teas. They were on their way to the Hardys'. But Jack and Jean and Billy were there and Anna of course with Kit and Harry and Lance and Marie and the bairn, Ian, and Arthur. It was a houseful. We all stayed for our suppers. Your grannie will be sixty on Tuesday.'

This was the very first time Grannie's age had been mentioned. As far as the family was concerned, the only age I knew was Arthur's and that was only because he had celebrated his twenty-first birthday some three years earlier. Other than that, we did not celebrate birthdays at all so that I didn't think the fact that Grannie was sixty was at all noteworthy.

We had a little more pleasant chit-chat and I made my way to bed in a very agreeable frame of mind. Tired, I fell asleep the moment my head hit the pillow.

Startled, I sat up in bed. There was a loud banging on the front door. My grandfather was shouting for my father. 'Archie! Archie!' It was like a nightmare except that it wasn't. I joined my mother standing at the top of the stairs while my father made his way down as quickly as he could, calling, 'I'm coming. I'm coming.'

He opened the door and my grandfather almost fell over the threshold, greatly distressed.

'Oh Archie,' he said. 'Come quick. It's your mother. Archie. I think she's dead,' and he turned and rushed away. Stunned, we went back upstairs without speaking, frantically pulling on what clothes came to hand. After a

241

few minutes, when we came downstairs still fumbling with buttons, my mother said she thought Billy ought to stay at home, he was too young, and the poor lad was left in the house on his own wondering what had happened and what was going on.

Without any further talking, the three of us went out into the night air, a shaken little group. I did not, as was my custom, walk ahead to get my circulation going, but stayed behind my parents, the three of us walking at my father's pace. When we passed the end of the Tenth Row houses, Grannie's house came into view, a gash of light in the sleeping Rows. The back door stood wide open. We went straight into the kitchen. My grandfather was sitting in his carver chair at the end of the table, his head in his hands. A woman stood before the fire, a neighbour. As we came in, she shook her head and nodded towards the room. My father went straight there and turned towards the bed. We heard his cry as he knelt down by the bed and said, 'Oh, Mother. Mother.' After a few moments the neighbour said, 'Arthur's gone for the doctor. He should be here soon.' Apart from that, there was no other movement and no sound as we just stood there. Presently Arthur came in looking pale and shaken. 'He's here,' he said and Mother and I shuffled away from the door lest we impeded the doctor's progress.

'Father,' said Arthur gently, 'the doctor's here.' My grandfather looked up and began to get to his feet. The doctor patted his hand.

'Where?' he asked. The neighbour told him and the doctor went into the room. My father, still very upset, came out.

'What happened?' he asked. My grandfather's voice quavered as he spoke.

'It was just gone midnight. We were sitting in front of the fire reading the papers before making ready for bed when Lizzie – when – when she says "I feel dizzy". "Bed's the place for that" I says and she just got up and fell on the mat. I tried to get her to come round but she just lay and I ran outside to get somebody. There were no lights except Mrs Thompson's in the next block so I ran there but it was too late,' and he buried his head in his hands again.

'I come straight along,' said Mrs Thompson, 'but there was nothing I could do. Eh, dear.'

The doctor came to the door and motioned my grandfather to go into the room. My father went with him. We waited. Finally, they came out, my father holding a piece of paper in his hand. The doctor nodded to us all and left. Then, and for some days later, I continued stunned. I was aware that something catastrophic had happened but I couldn't take it in. I needed everything to stop for a minute that I could right myself, but the world kept turning and I could only stand there till I was told what to do.

My grandfather went back to his carver chair.

'The others will have to be told,' said my father.

'Get Anna,' said my grandfather.

The neighbour, a Mrs Thompson who lived several doors away and whom we rarely saw, realised her job was finished. There was now another woman there who could take charge, my mother.

'If there's nothing else I can do,' she said, 'I'll just away back home. Ee I'm sorry I couldn't have done more.'

'You did your best,' said Grandfather, adding, 'and thanks for coming. I hardly know where I am. I didn't know where to go or who to get.'

She nodded sympathetically. 'I know,' she said. 'It was an awful shock,' and, with that, nodding to everyone, she left.

'I'll see to these,' said my father, indicating the list in his hand. 'I'll go and seek Mary Ann Thompson and Mrs Algar first. Then there's George and them.' The 'them' referred to Auntie Anna, my father's sister and his brothers George, Lance and Jack, Grannie's mother and her (Grannie's) sister, Lena, and their brothers Strickland, Fenwick and Jasper together with Uncle Tommy, Aunt Bella and Uncle George, Grandfather's siblings. With the exception of Lance who lived at Morpeth and Jasper who lived at Fernybeds they all lived within a two mile radius.

'I'll see if I can get the police to get in touch with Lance and Uncle Jasper,' said Dad.

'I'll go and tell the others,' said Arthur.

'And I'll go with you,' I put in. At least it was something I could do.

243

We went out into the dark, sleeping street. I felt so chilled inside that I hardly noticed the cold of the winter night. As we walked we heard the loud knocking at Mary Ann Thompson's door.

We went first to Auntie Anna's. This was right and proper. Auntie Anna would take over, saying what was needed and what should be done. My father, as eldest son, would see to the paperwork, but, from then on, Auntie Anna would see to everything that went on in the house. My mother was only a stand-in till she arrived. I was there to do any messages, any fetching and carrying that might be needed.

The street was deserted except for two policemen patrolling with measured tread. They said 'Good morning,' as we passed and the best we could manage was 'Aye'. We didn't feel disposed to talk any more than was necessary.

At Auntie Anna's in Park Road, sorry for those we were going to wake up unnecessarily, we banged on the door and waited. The curtains parted in the bedroom window of the house next door and someone looked out. We banged again and a light appeared in their bedroom and we could hear footsteps on the stairs. Uncle Kit opened the door.

'What is it?' he asked as we went in.

'Bad news,' said Arthur, and, putting his arm across his forehead, he started to cry.

'Sit down, lad,' said Uncle Kit. 'Take your time. I'll stir up the fire.'

Auntie Anna had appeared by this time.

'What?' she asked.

'Me mother,' said Arthur. 'Oh, Anna, she's gone.'

'Gone? How –? She can't have –?'

By this time Harry was wakened and he was standing behind his mother.

'Come on, lad,' said Uncle Kit. 'It's all right. I'll take you back to bed.'

Arthur told the brief story of the night's happenings and, naturally distressed, Auntie Anna went upstairs to dress. Uncle Kit came down and said,

'The bairn's gone back to sleep. Eh, lad, I'm sorry. She'll be an awful miss,' then, to me, 'I'll walk Anna down and come straight back. Do you think you could stay and look after Harry till I come back.'

'I'll go and tell Jack and me Uncle Fenwick in the meantime,' said Arthur, 'and then I'll come back and we'll go to me Aunt Lena's at the Hirst.'

I saw them go with some apprehension. I didn't like being left on my own; fertile ground for my over-active imagination. I wandered round, trying to straighten things out in my mind but I couldn't help looking over my shoulder. Finally, I felt better sitting at the top of the stairs where I could hear Harry's gentle breathing and get the first intimation that someone was coming back.

At Aunt Lena's no sooner had we banged on the door once than a quavering voice said, 'Who is it? There's somebody at the door. Who is it?' In the darkness, and bearing in mind our message, it was eerie. The voice was that of my great-grandmother, she of the clay pipe. She was now bed-fast and had gone to live with Aunt Lena as she could no longer look after herself. She had been lying awake when we knocked.

Aunt Lena answered the door and we tried to whisper our news in the passage so as not to upset the old lady more than we had to, but as we talked she quavered,

'What is it? What's up? Nobody tells me?'

Finally, Aunt Lena went to tell her, but I don't think she took it in.

And so on, till, as we walked back, lights were appearing in windows as miners who were 'in first' prepared to go to work.

'Be careful,' said Arthur. 'If you hear anything keep out of sight.' (It was thought to be very unlucky for a miner to see a woman on his way to work. Some men turned back in spite of the fact they couldn't afford to lose a shift.) This was the only conversation we had as we walked through Ashington and Hirst that night.

When we got back to the Ninth Row my uncles Jack and George were already there as was Aunt Bella. The neighbours had been to lay Grannie out and the undertaker had been to do what he considered necessary. The neighbours had also arranged to do Grannie's washing between them. It was time for my father to change to go to work. Before we left Mother said,

245

'Linda will go across to the store as soon as it opens in the morning to get black ties and stuff for the black arm bands. If you tell her how many you want she can get yours at the same time.'

Arrangements had been made that, as soon as Mother had finished her washing, she would go across to let Auntie Anna go home and do her weekly wash. Mary Ann was going to help her.

When my father had left for work, Mother decided to start the washing straight away. No-one mentioned my going to work. Together, Mum and I did the washing. At a quarter-to-nine, I went across to the store for the black ties and black ribbon. Almost everyone I met stopped me and asked if what they'd heard was true, namely that my grandmother had died in the night. When I went into the drapery department, the young man behind the counter said,

'It is true, then. I heard your grandmother had died and I just couldn't believe it.'

Both Aunt Bella and Aunt Martha found time on a busy wash-day to come and tell Mother she was to leave the ironing; they would come along and do it. Aunt Martha also offered to make extra bread for us so that Mum wouldn't have to bake that week.

Back at the 'Ninth' Grannie was already 'coffined'. She lay in the front room. All day, but more especially at night, callers came to offer their condolences. They shook hands and spoke to Grandfather first, then Auntie Anna and then the rest of the family in order of age. After that, they were taken into the room to see Grannie. This was Auntie Anna's job. When she went home to do her own chores and make arrangements to move into the 'Ninth' for at least a week, my mother deputised for her.

By early evening I was so chilled and tired I could scarcely stand up but I couldn't bring myself to go home and go to bed alone in the house. Joyce came. There were so many people in the house, I could only speak to her in the passage.

'Did you hear the news?' she asked. I shook my head. The outside world was of little interest.

'They said, "The king's life is drawing peacefully to its

close". It's terribly sad.'

It was, but I had exhausted my capacity to feel.

The following day we bought our black. Fortunately for me, they thought I was too young to go into black; I got navy blue instead.

During these days, my father, his sister and brothers, had several meetings in the room to discuss what was to happen. For the funeral it was decided to dispense entirely with mourning coaches. Everyone would walk behind the hearse except the two who carried the main wreath and Mr Mallaby, the undertaker. They led the cortége. Custom ordained that two men should carry the wreath, but again, they dispensed with tradition and had Grannie's two life-long friends carry it instead.

From experience the adults in the family estimated there might be as many as six or seven sittings at the funeral tea even though they were using two rooms. To accommodate the food required for this number every available space in the pantry had been cleared. On the day of the funeral, wreaths arrived in abundance so that the air in the front room was heavy with their perfume. It was also dark. No curtains had been drawn since the Sunday.

The bakery van drew up at the door and the van man began to bring in the food for the tea. It was then that it hit me. All my life Grannie had made magnificent Sunday teas and Christmas Day meals. Tray upon tray of special food, the sort only eaten at Christmas and parties, was being brought into the house, all ready prepared, and she wasn't going to be there. She was never going to be there again. I went out and leaned against the high railing at the side of the house and sobbed as though my heart would break.

Uncle George came out and put his hand on my shoulder.

'Yes,' he said. 'You're going to miss her. You and Billy. She thought the world of you both.'

Billy, Jack and I, the only grandchildren there, took our places in the cortége behind Grandfather, my parents, my uncles and aunt, my great-aunts and great-uncles and their spouses. Groups of people stood waiting at the ends of the Rows to join the cortége as it passed. When the minute bell began to toll we moved forward. Every shop between the

Portland Hotel and the church had its blinds down while the shop-keepers stood on the pavement outside. All men stood bareheaded as the cortége passed and the route was lined with women from the organistions in which my grandmother had been involved. The service itself was fully choral which meant that some men had had to get time off work. This was a mining village's tribute to one of its number.

When Grannie died, the house died with her. Within a fortnight it was being prepared for other tenants. Grandfather went to live with Auntie Anna, Uncle Kit and Harry. Arthur went to live with Uncle George, Aunt Lizzie and Jack and the family became fragmented. We no longer knew of the day to day happenings of every member.

Except in memory and in dreams I would never again run into Grannie Summers', sure of my welcome, of laughter and of warmth. When Grannie died she took with her my Ashington childhood.